PENGUIN BOOKS

THE BOOK OF DEMONS

The Book of Demons

Including a Dictionary of Demons in Sanskrit Literature

NANDITHA KRISHNA

PENGUIN BOOKS

An imprint of Penguin Random House

PENGUIN BOOKS

·USA | Canada | UK | Ireland | Australia
New Zealand | India | South Africa | China | Singapore

Penguin Books is part of the Penguin Random House group of companies
whose addresses can be found at global.penguinrandomhouse.com

Published by Penguin Random House India Pvt. Ltd
4th Floor, Capital Tower 1, MG Road,
Gurugram 122 002, Haryana, India

Penguin
Random House
India

First published by Penguin Books India 2007

ISBN 9780143102021

Typeset in Sabon MT by Eleven Arts, New Delhi

Printed at Repro India Limited

www.penguin.co.in

MIX
Paper from
responsible sources
FSC® C047271

This is a legitimate digitally printed version of the book and therefore might not
have certain extra finishing on the cover.

Contents

Acknowledgements

The Book of Demons was the brainchild of Ravi Singh of Penguin India. He has been extremely encouraging and very patient, in spite of the fact that the book was terribly delayed. The problem is best described by Ravana's ten heads. Each time one was cut a new one or new information would surface, which could not be left out. My special thanks to Ravi, Paromita Mohanchandra and all the others at Penguin India who were involved in the publication of this book.

The C.P. Ramaswami Aiyar Foundation and its staff have always supported me enthusiastically in all my writing endeavours. I must particularly mention the librarians K. Sujatha, S.P. Vijayakumari and V. Kameshraj; G. Balaji and M. Amrithalingam who sourced images to photograph; Prema Srinivasan and Y. Venkatesh who did the sketches; and others like P. Sudhakar, Malathy Narasimhan, P. Sumabala, and S.M. Sujatha who helped me find some rare books. Michel Danino gave me material about the Indus culture and T. Gopalakrishnan the book *Scenes from Ramayana*, which had fascinating early British drawings. Most importantly, my secretary, H. Manikiandan, performed the very difficult task of keeping track of the text, photos, sketches and the various papers that I accumulated as I was writing this book. My sincere thanks to all of them.

Every book is a burden on the family of the writer and my husband, Dr S. Chinny Krishna, and my sons Prashanth and Rudra, were particularly accommodating and encouraging, in spite of long nights with the lights on all over the house and books and papers strewn everywhere, besides long monologues about demons which they were forced to hear.

The demons of Hinduism are as colourful as the gods, and I enjoyed researching and writing about them. I hope this is merely a beginning and more people will search for the demons that haunt the folk literature of every Indian language.

Note for the Reader

This book has so many Indian words that the entire book would have been full of diacritical marks, making reading difficult. To avoid that, a general rule has been followed regarding spelling:

❖ Popular spellings have been used for all proper nouns— names of people, places and books. For example, although the sound 'sh' is written differently in Devanagari in the names of Shiva and Vishnu, I have followed the popular spellings. However, I have retained Brahmana (instead of Brahmin or Brahman) as my preferred spelling.

❖ Where the sound may change the meaning, either a double vowel or a diacritical mark has been used. For example, Maya was the demon architect, while māyā (pronounced maayaa) means illusion.

❖ The following words appear very frequently, so putting diacritical marks or double vowels throughout the book would make it difficult reading. I have therefore listed the words below:

- Rakshasa is pronounced as Raakshasa (to be distinguished from rakshas).
- Yatu and Yatudhana are pronounced Yaatu and Yaatudhaana.
- Danava is pronounced Daanava.
- Pishacha is pronounced Pishaacha.
- Rama and Ravana are pronounced Raama and Raavana respectively.
- To distinguish between the male and female, the double

vowel has been used, as in the male Hidamba and his sister Hidambaa. Similarly, Naraka means hell and Naaraka means an inhabitant of hell.

- Dasa, Dasyu, Naga and Nishada are pronounced Daasa, Daasyu, Naaga and Nishaada respectively.
- Pragjyotisha and Patala are pronounced Praagjyotisha and Paataala respectively.
- Rambha and Rambhā are distinct entities: a demon and an apsaras respectively.
- Apsaras is the singular form of the word, the plural being apsarases.

PART I

*Of vain hopes, of vain actions, of vain knowledge and
    senseless,*
*They verily are possessed of the delusive nature of
    Rakshasas and Asuras.*

Bhagavad Gita, 9. 12

The World of Demons

> *'Without Contraries is no Progression. Attraction and*
> *Repulsion, Reason and Energy, Love and Hate, are*
> *necessary to Human Existence . . .'*
> William Blake[1]

Demons are found everywhere, in every culture and society. From the *Rig Veda* to local folk literature, the belief in demons is found all over India. Demons represent everything evil: malice, mischief, iniquity, vice, immorality, malevolence and every form of wickedness. They have inordinate powers. Many were originally human and even heavenly beings. Those who met unnatural or violent deaths, those who were terrifying in their lifetime, and those who had inadequate death rites and so are frustrated become demons. Many were fallen divinities. They may be male or female, native or outsider, Indian or foreign and of any caste, religion or lineage. They have one thing in common: after their deaths, they are figures of malice, figures to be feared and figures to be propitiated. In short, they are demons.

Demons mean different things to different people. A strict teacher, a harsh boss or an autocratic ruler is a demon to those who fear him. A cyclone, drought or flood that destroys is a demon to the affected population. An enemy who is hard to defeat, whose ways are different, unpleasant and threatening, is yet another form of demon. People are said to battle with demons in their mind when they are confronted with problems. An abandoned, lonely or ill-kept place or building is called the haunt of demons. Saddam Hussein became a living demon for George Bush Sr. and Jr.—it would not be surprising if, in a few years, children's stories were to treat him as a demon. A demon is feared because it is beyond human comprehension and control. In the Indian context, the forces of night, darkness and death, menacing and uncontrollable, were demonized.

Demon, devil, fiend, imp, sprite and evil spirit—the words mean different things in different cultures, yet they are similar in that they describe something evil and beyond human understanding. Demon is an ambiguous term applied to almost anything perceived to be beyond human control, and therefore, evil. A demon is generally an anthropomorphic form of a person or place or object or a negative natural phenomenon. Demons are powerful beings challenging human existence and even the existence of the gods themselves. Human inability to control these forces creates myths of supernatural power, trickery and magic, which enhances the reputations of the demons and makes them into supernatural beings or spirits.

Many castes and tribes are distinguished by their worship and propitiation of demons, which may even exceed their reverence for the gods. Often, the demons gain the upper hand, although a combination of divine power and human prayers ensures their final defeat. They demand horrendous blood sacrifices and varied rituals, from devil dancing to human sacrifice. They are defeated, but never totally so. As long as there is evil on earth and within human beings, the demons return to trouble us.

Sanskrit texts often represent the demons as the primitive inhabitants of the subcontinent, ruling the jungles and disturbing the expanding influence of Vedic religion by throwing flesh into the sacred fire and disturbing the sacred yajña. Thus their defeat and destruction was imperative.

Most Indian myths are based on the conflict between good and evil: Indra versus Vritra, Rama versus Ravana, Krishna versus Kamsa, Buddha versus Mara and so on. Barely is one demon defeated and either killed or relegated to hell than another pops up, often a new incarnation of the previous one. Vishnu incarnates himself to defeat the demons and save mankind, but does not always kill them. Krishna does not kill Kaliya; he merely banishes him. Thus the forces of good and evil are maintained in a state of equilibrium. 'The contrast here stated in moral terms—that goodness within an individual becomes valuable only when it is pitted against evil—is recognised by the Hindus in cosmological terms: that the good in the universe is valuable only because it exists together with evil . . . Goodness cannot, by definition exist without evil.'[2] The demons often become negative role models, to teach the consequences of evil actions and of neglect or repudiation of rituals. The world becomes a battleground between good and evil, and it is the duty of everybody to prefer good and fight evil.

There is consanguinity between the gods and the demons, for both are the sons of Prajapati. The Vedic Asuras are not merely brothers but elder brothers of the Devas or gods. In the *Mahabharata*, Arjuna asks, 'Do the gods prosper without killing their kinsmen the demons? The gods won their places in heaven by fighting. Such are the ways of the gods and the eternal dictates of the Vedas'.[3]

Gods and demons are in conflict over several issues: acquisition of power, control of people and minds, control of land and so on. They are born equal and alike. The demons finally fail because of their demonic nature: delusion, untruth, desire and anger. Thus, the battle between the two becomes the opposition between dharma and adharma. Heretics and materialists are defined as given to adharma.

Demons are easily corrupted: Indra deludes the Jaina Raji and his sons, placing them beyond the Vedas and dharma. Then he kills them. Shiva corrupts the three sons of Taraka who had built the triple city of Tripura, for they offended dharma and became greedy for immortality. Shiva destroys all the inhabitants of Tripura with a single arrow. Again, as the Buddha, Vishnu corrupts the demons by making them preach against the Vedic sacrifice and dharma. In the next stage, they will be destroyed by Vishnu as Kalki. By identifying Buddhists (not the Buddha) with demons, the defeat of their heresies is justified, and Vedic religion reigns supreme again. However, the Buddha incarnation is regarded as a positive one, even if the Buddhists themselves are not, and his identification with Vishnu total. In fact, many of the demons are from heretical sects inimical to the Vedic religion, who are destroyed by the gods themselves. However, the acknowledgement that demons like Prahlada and Bali were 'good', the identification of the Buddha with Vishnu and even the worship of Shiva by several demons like Ravana all indicate that the definition of evil itself is nebulous, and that demonization is a matter of necessity rather than conviction.

The history and spiritual heritage of ancient peoples survive in myths and legends. Animals that people fought in their struggle for survival, tyrants of another age, natural phenomena that are beyond human control and people's hopes and fears have come down in time as myths. If a story needs a hero, a villain is equally essential to enable the hero to act heroically. The repetitive, regenerative and renewable villains became the demons of myths and legends.

Mythology is an essential medium for transmission of information about heroes and demons. Mythology becomes a study of society, where natural phenomena are explained and classified according to the principles that prevail in the social organization. The individual and society are merged in a 'natural-divine cosmos', and traditional social structures and practices are grounded in a divinely instituted cosmic order.[4] As practitioners of magic, demons bring into focus an important tool of ancient people who, preoccupied with economic survival and food security, resorted to magic, 'the expression of a wishful thought or ritual'.[5] To quote Frazer, 'Religion consists of two elements: a theoretical and a practical, namely, a belief in powers higher than man and an attempt to propitiate them.'[6] Religious ideas are transmitted through myths and legends, most of which are allegorical. 'All the doctrines of the philosophers are hidden within fables.'[7]

The role of mythology has to be understood to apply it to a complex phenomenon such as the clash between gods and demons or between people and demons. Mythology has been described as the science of primitive man, his manner of explaining the universe.[8] As a symbol-using animal, man appears not only to act but also to give reasons for his actions.[9] The chief concern of primitive religion is to maintain cosmic, social and personal harmony. Natural phenomena are explained as the actions of mythical beings and express the hopes and fears of people who had not yet understood the natural order of the universe. Invasions, migrations, dynastic changes, foreign and new cults and social reforms are recorded in the mythologies of the ancient world. With the advance of civilization, myths tend to get altered, even acquiring sophistication. However, whatever the alteration, they tend to retain the basic elements of the original composition. Myths are not history, yet they contain kernels of historical events.

Although the historical content of Hindu mythology has, over the ages, become very involved in the two extremes of legend and philosophical speculation, it is still possible to study a myth to speculate why and how a deity was conceived by his earliest worshippers. The demon becomes a necessary foil to project the goodness of the deity or hero.

Mythology gives life to unknown and incomprehensible forces and mythical traditions guide us to explore and ascertain the contents of our own inner selves. Myth is often more than mere story—it is the reliving of past reality cloaked in a tale to be used as a lesson for future generations.

The gods and demons are sometimes physically indistinguishable, a fact that is often the basis for their strife. They share the power of illusion or māyā, whereby they can change form at will. They are distinguished only through battle.

According to Heinrich Zimmer, 'The secret of māyā—the apparition of living forms out of formal primal substance . . . the phenomenal mirage-like character of all existence, earthly and divine—is the identity of opposites . . . energies that are at variance with each other, processes contradicting and annihilating each other: creation and destruction, evolution and dissolution, the dream-idyll of the inward vision of the god and the desolate nought, the terror of the void, the dread infinite . . . Opposites are fundamentally of the one essence, two aspects of the one Vishnu.'[10]

Demons are present in every ancient culture and religion. While there is no independent evil force in Judaism, Satan or Shaitan dominates both Christianity and Islam. Christians interpret the temptation of Eve by the serpent as the work of Satan. Jesus Christ and Mohammed wrestle with demons within and outside themselves. Medieval Christianity is replete with tales of the Devil who appears from time to time, only to be conquered by the faithful, many of whom were canonized as saints. Eastern religions were no less concerned with devils and demons. Hinduism has a pantheon of demons, while the Buddha is tempted by and defeats several demons. The demon is essential to contrast the superiority of goodness versus the inferiority of evil. In other words, if there is no evil, how can there be anything called good?

Often, demons are the negative thoughts and temptations within the minds and hearts of people, and the individual's choice between good and evil is described as the temptation of the devil.

HEROES VERSUS VILLAINS

Gods and demons, heroes and villains are two sides of a coin, like the *yin* and the *yang*.

'The Great One separated and became Heaven and Earth. It revolved and became the dual forces . . .' (Li Chi).

'The circle divided into the light and the dark . . . An above and below, a right and left . . . the world of the opposites . . . These opposites became known under the names *yin* and *yang* and created a great stir . . .

'The dark begets the light and the light begets the dark in ceaseless alternation . . .

'When *yang* has reached its greatest strength, the dark

power of yin is born within its depths; night begins at midday when *yang* breaks up . . . to change into *yin* . . .' (I Ching).[11]

In every battle, there is invariably a hero, who takes on the villain single-handed. Thus, even as Hanuman devastates the demon army and burns Lanka, and the Vanara army fights the Rakshasas, the final battle is between Rama and Ravana. This is not unique to India: Hercules kills each of his contestants single-handed, thereby taking all the credit. The single greatest villain of World War II was Adolf Hitler. The hero is either Winston Churchill or Franklin Roosevelt or Josef Stalin or Charles de Gaulle, depending on whether the writer is British, American, Russian or French respectively. The final hero and enemy are always single individuals. This is rooted in our primordial memory of hand-to-hand battle where two individuals fought for individual supremacy, when only one could win and the other had to lose. Heroes fight in solitude against those who halt their progress.

In human conscience, the eternal conflict between good and evil, heaven and hell is a permanent search which has haunted individuals and societies the world over. It is an age-old quest to resolve the tension of opposing forces, with opposing claims and interests and, above all, the struggle for survival. Anything that made survival difficult was the enemy, even while it was affirmed and accepted as integral to life itself. There is a necessary interdependence of creation and destruction, light and darkness, life and death, spirit and matter, all involved in an eternal struggle, the struggle between 'us' and the 'the other', representing the forces of brutality and evil. The effort to achieve an ideal order—described variously as rita or dharma—necessitates the destruction of those forces arraigned against the order.

The hero faces and experiences the mystery and irrationality of life itself, and our own demons—violence and anxiety, the isolation of the self or ego, pride, and a sense of being threatened, alienated and betrayed. By overcoming these demons, we become more fully in harmony with the universe and ourselves. Thus, even as most encounters take place between peoples, societies, traditions and value systems, they take place even within each category and within the human mind. Sometimes a historical figure or saint-prophet takes on legendary and divine proportions, as did Rama or the Buddha. Often, the hero is a pathfinder, a mediator between gods and people.

The deep connotations of a category of images relating to the mythological heroes and villains of the past speak with unsuspected power. These are lived out anew in each age. There can be no single or exclusive meaning to any of the hero–villain encounters, not even from religious or aesthetic points of view. At best, interpretations can challenge, not prove, what the most enduring myths have to communicate.

Nature is made of forces and events that are opposed to each other, and may be favourable or unfavourable to the human world. Heat and cold, rain and drought are a part of nature. Gain and loss, success and failure, praise and censure originate from man. Those that favour him are good and pleasing. Those that do not are bad and dissatisfying. The latter become the demons. The hero is one who is neither elated at achieving the agreeable nor dejected over the disagreeable. He chooses good over evil, and views both with equanimity.

Symbolically, the hero attains dominion over the various natural elements and seasons. Life energy is created through the interplay and resistance of opposites, essential for the eternal struggle. At a certain point, the hero makes sacrifices, renounces the world, descends into a cavern or under the ground to transcend and outgrow his past in the process of renewal and rebirth. The hero makes the effort to fight evil, to undergo sacrifices and inner discipline and encounter the darkest depths within and around, shunning fear. He thus symbolizes control over the negative aspects of both material and spiritual power.

The sources of fear in the ancient world were many. If the sun, moon, day and night were fixed, predictable and orderly, the waxing and waning of the moon, eclipses, droughts and floods, famine, hunger, abundance and survival were frightening, as were death and life itself. There were also impenetrable forests ruled by lions, tigers, snakes and other ferocious animals, apart from unknown people.

Event and symbolism, outer phenomena and inner vision merged. People's struggle with the mysteries and hazards of the external world tended to overwhelm the inner aspect of the hero–villain encounter. The hidden meanings of symbols emerge as we re-experience them. Understanding symbolism, therefore, requires experiencing the event itself.

The hero is generally young and lightly constructed, in contrast to the massive, enormous and strong demon. In Balinese tradition, the hero is not conceived as a big strong man but as a symbol of reason, intelligence and refinement of spirit. A small David fights and defeats a huge Goliath. A young, lithe, forest-dwelling Rama fights the ten-headed demon king of Lanka, Ravana. Krishna was first a baby, later a young boy playing a flute, fond of dancing and playing tricks on the cowherdesses, with even a vague hint of femininity. Yet he kills the most villainous demons. By exaggerating the physical strength of the demon and understating the physical stature of the hero, a case is made for the spiritual superiority of the hero,

HERO AND DEMON

which defeats the stronger but evil villain. Thus, the destruction
of the enemy is enhanced and justified.

Allegory, derived from symbolism, is used to describe the
actions and experiences of the hero. Symbolism relates to the
unconscious imagination, and particularly to that of the
people. It is found in a more developed condition in folklore,
myths, and legends. Mythology is not static, it constantly
renews and regenerates, just as heroes and demons reinvent
themselves. 'The primal powers never come to a standstill; the
cycle of becoming continues uninterruptedly . . . Between the

two primal powers there arises again and again a state of tension, a potential that keeps the powers in motion and causes them to unite, whereby they are constantly regenerated . . .' (I Ching).[12]

Interestingly, the heroes represent change, while the demons represent the status quo. Heracles and Perseus of ancient Greece kill the dragon, which represented the status quo. With the rise of Christianity, saints like St George took over the killing of the dragon. The monster represents power and tyranny, pride and physical strength. He thinks of his physical strength as his own, as do tyrants like Hiranyaksha, Hiranyakashipu and many others. The hero, on the other hand, comprehends that he derives his power from a higher source and is appropriately humble, acknowledging the superiority of the victorious gods.

People with different beliefs and behaviour patterns were condemned as barbarians in the West. In India they became demons.

INDIAN DEMONS

Generally, demons are of two types: malignant supernatural beings and evil spirits—not ghosts but beings of an order higher than human beings, yet lesser than the gods. But there is a third type in India: demonized enemies. India is a happy hunting ground for demons, with every village, state, caste, community and tribe having its own myths and legends to account for a vast range of demons to whom every illness and ill luck is attributed. The demons are then propitiated out of fear, a fear of the unknown and the possible consequences of their wrath.

Demons are present throughout Indian tradition, in the Vedas, Epics and Puranas, as well as in the folk traditions of every state. They are the remnants of human memory, representing forces that were antagonistic to the people as they pushed forward in their quest for land and their struggle to survive in inhospitable conditions. Even tribals, in their mythology, have demons that are defeated. Sanskrit literature is full of powerful demons and demonesses who play an important role in shaping events. Some, like Ravana of the Ramayana and Kamsa of the Mahabharata, are essential to the story. Without them, there would be no hero. Others, like Vritra, the demon of drought, represent destructive powers of nature, which are constantly threatening the gods and the survival of man. Demons like Mahisha narrate an ancient tale of warring tribes. Even Kama, worshipped as Kamadeva, the god of love and desire, is sometimes demonized to represent an evil within that must be conquered by the worthy individual.

Evil spirits were common among both Aryans and non-Aryans, and were not borrowed by one from the other. However, they were certainly coloured by their association with each other.

Most of Indian mythology consists of orally transmitted tales. It was used to teach good values, whether by a parent to a child, a teacher to a student or a ruler to his subjects. The demon became an important part of this oral transmission. Figures of evil had to be constructed to prove that evil would fail and good alone could prevail. To build up local acceptance, defeated rulers were associated with demons of mythology and their end justified to their people by the conquerors. Thus, demonization had several uses.

The sources of information about demons are endless, particularly in regional literature where local demons play an important role. However, this study is restricted to demons in Sanskrit literature and popular Hindu tradition. Who were they? Why did they fall from grace? Why were they feared so much?

Demons play an extremely important role in Hindu mythology. They may be male or female, depending on their role and the location. They may be human, animal, plant, or even a concept, but they invariably have supernatural qualities that give them an advantage over their unfortunate victims. There are buffalo-headed, horse-headed and multi-headed demons, while demonesses are generally wild and unkempt. Most have the ability to change their appearance and even disappear. Many are spirits, reflecting the absorption of primitive beliefs into the Hindu religion. However, demons finally lose the battle, reaffirming the triumph of good over evil.

Some demons are great scholars or rulers who derive their powers from the gods themselves after years of penance. Inevitably, the acquisition of power makes them proud and haughty, thereby re-emphasizing value systems such as the importance of humility and the old adage that pride comes before a fall. They terrorize the earth and even turn on their lord and mentor. Finally, either a divine incarnation or even the god himself has to destroy the demon. The demons have assistants and engage in secondary battles until their final defeat. Some demons are killed outright; others are kept in subterranean homes protecting the nether world. Some may return when natural events are propitious, but the gods finally always control them.

Saddam Hussein was said to own weapons of mass destruction and nuclear powers he never possessed, attributes that were used to justify the conquest of Iraq. It is essential to build up a larger-than-life role to justify the destruction of another, particular a ruler of a country. Thus Bali, a much loved king of Indian mythology, had to be destroyed 'to prevent him from taking over the world'. However, a closer look at the story will indicate that he was a much loved figure ruling his people peacefully, who was demonized to justify his destruction.

Demons obstruct the sacrifice, hovering around the altars where the rites are performed. If they are not performed properly, the sacrifice is rendered useless, as the demons devour it. If a person neglects even a part of a ritual or does not perform a ceremony in the correct prescribed fashion, the demon could take possession of and ruin him. Thus vague, formless figures were created to frighten the people. In time, they became creatures of substance.

Demons are dangerous, but always defeated. After all, the victors wrote the myths: the losers became demons. Some demons are members of opposing tribes who were earlier settlers in the region and were supplanted by new arrivals. They were either annihilated or chased away into the forests and hills, where many still live as tribes. Some were absorbed in a process of acculturation. Many god–demon battles recreate the conflicts between food gatherers and food producers, which is as old as the history of humankind. However, most demons are representations of natural phenomena that are beyond human control and require to be controlled by the gods.

Vedic gods were dynamic and moving, as befitted a pastoral people. Non-Vedic gods were static and born of the earth, hence the term bhuta (for spirit), which means born of the earth. The various streams were united in the epic story of the Mahabharata and in the philosophy enunciated in the *Bhagavad Gita*, which included current beliefs, and froze them in the all-encompassing Vishvaroopa.

One man's god is another man's demon, and vice versa. The Vedic Asura became a demon while the Avestan equivalent Ahura was the supreme god. The Vedic Deva was a god while the Avestan Daeva became a demon. The word demon itself comes from the Latin *daemon* and Greek *daimon* meaning deity. Thus the confusion between the demon and deity was not unique to the Indian and Iranian traditions. The meaning of *daemon* changed with the advent of Christianity, when the ancient gods were relegated to a netherworld of pagan devils. The horned god of pagan pre-Christian Europe became the horned Satan.

India was far more accommodating and absorbing, yet the non-Vedic Bhutas lived on the fringes of the heavenly host, as demonic spirits. The *bhutagavana* of Udupi in Karnataka and *theyyam* of Kerala are Bhuta rituals that continue to be popular. Their leader, Shiva, became Bhutanatha, one of the primary deities of composite Hinduism. Rudra-Shiva combined the opposing forces of nature, of violence and tranquillity, of Vedic and non-Vedic traditions. Many of these were imprisoned in his persona: the flowing tresses were the forests trapping within them the mighty river Ganga. His vibhuti or sacred ash was the symbol of fertility. But he was also the ascetic rishi of Vedic tradition meditating on the mountains. Similarly, Vishnu-Narayana was the dynamic Vedic sun traversing the sky, as well as the non-Vedic Narayana, god of the waters, resting deep beneath the ocean on the serpent Adi Shesha. If there was opposition between Vedic gods and non-Vedic demons, there was also unity between Vedic and non-Vedic deities, who became the main gods of Sanatana Dharma or composite orthodox Hinduism.

While some demons have extra-terrestrial or phantasmal origins, many are demonized enemies. Many non-Vedic tribes beyond the pale of the Aryan dharma, speaking strange languages and observing strange customs, would undoubtedly have been demonized. A question often asked is whether there is a racial bias. If Dasyus and Gandharvas are prototypes of non-Aryans, who are the prototypes of the giants 'big as mountains', demons like 'walking trees', with 'one wing, one eye, one leg'? If red-haired and bearded Rakshasas have a racial significance, what of the blue and green Rakshasas? Giants and fairies are creatures of fancy. Primitive people crouched in a cave or spending sleepless nights in a stormy forest conceived, with childlike minds, of demons thirsting for their blood and giants of wind and fire determined to destroy the universe. Trees and animals were deified: the pipal and neem were sacred, so they kept away evil forces, but spirits were believed to live on other trees like the tamarind. Many animals were deified out of fear, like the cobra which lived in anthills or the tiger god Hulideva and bull god Basava of Karnataka. Both Vedic and non-Vedic religions shared an affinity with nature. Temple-centred worship originated much later, with the chaityas and stupas of Buddhism that were far more structured, thanks to royal patronage.

Life is not perfect, so creation is obviously imperfect. The gods fight against demons and demonic forces who try to destabilize the divine order. How do the demons get their power? Will there ever be a final victory over wickedness and anarchy?

Demons are born from the same progenitor as the gods: Prajapati or Kashyapa. Many of them are elder brothers of the gods and therefore the rightful rulers. Yet they lose their right to rule. During the Vedic and Brahmanic period, when sacrifices sustained the gods, those who rejected the sacrifice or tried to steal it were demons to be destroyed. Later, the power of penance was available to gods, men and demons, and many demons developed supernatural powers, including the ability to be invisible and invincible. Gods like Indra had to fight and defeat demons like the serpent Vritra. But there had to be fairness in battle, and therefore mortal Rakshasas could not be destroyed directly by a god. So they were given boons which gave them power and Shiva and Vishnu had to incarnate themselves on earth several times to kill every new demon that rose from the ashes of the old. Ascetic practice or tapas could bestow power to equal that of the gods; sometimes tapasvis would invoke a god (like Brahma) who granted these powers as a boon. Finally, another god had to take an earthly incarnation to destroy the demon. A sectarian element crept in and the demon created by the reigning deity of one sect would be killed by the god of another.

Much of this is caused by karma. The good deeds of one lifetime ensure a good birth. An evil demon would be reborn as another demon. Thus the wicked Kalanemi, brother of Bali, was reborn several times as several demons and finally, as the wicked Kamsa, uncle of Krishna. He is killed and his karma burns out in the presence of the Lord.

Often, the demons knew magic. While it could control and frighten, there has been a consistent dislike of magic and the occult. This dislike of magic prevented Tantra from gaining a foothold and growing beyond a fringe cult. Magic could not be mistaken for siddha, superhuman powers derived by practising austerities. While the Asura Bala knew ninety-six kinds of magic to trouble the Devas, Hanuman knew the ashta (eight) siddhis which gave him superhuman strength and control over his faculties. The Asuras had a life-restoring magic that they used against the Devas. The gods and the demons churned the ocean for the nectar of immortality which, finally, the gods succeeded in obtaining.

But demons are many other things—physiological, emotional and social—and the Ramayana and Mahabharata are a mine of information about them. Indigestion, for example, is a demon. In families where marriage laws are violated or

children are born malformed, or a land is ruled by a wicked
king, evil Rakshasas are blamed. When a woman faints,
Rakshasa-slaying mantras are chanted over her. Her disease
is, itself, the demon. Pus coming out of a sore is a Rakshasa
head sticking to the sore. The Brahma-rakshasa, who is a
Brahmana reborn as a demon, sins involuntarily, his evil
coming from woman's evil and evil produced by the womb.
He drinks Sarasvati's blood and blames lack of religious
teaching, evil actions and sexual faults for his nature. The
caste system operates here also. Brahma-rakshasas do not hurt
the sacrifice. They are associated with Chitragupta and are
attendants of Shiva, who is Pramathanatha. They haunt those
who sleep at the foot of a tree, eat unholy food, lie in the
wrong direction, pollute water, or do not purify themselves
after sexual intercourse. Good people, and those who carry
about or keep at home any one of the following are protected
from demons: gorochana (orris root), the skin or claws of a
hyena or a hill tortoise or a cat or a black or tawny goat.
Those who keep the sacrificial fire burning will not be troubled
by demons as these are all pratighāta that counteract against
the demons.[13]

Demons are identified with natural phenomena, from which
they derive their names and with which they are compared.
They have roaring voices and physical monstrosities (such as
ten heads and faces like gargoyles or animals). They can change
shape, become invisible and disappear. They receive boons from
Brahma which make them strong and invincible. Their vices
include pride, anger and delusion, which are, themselves, demons.

There is a pattern to the creation of a demon and his
subsequent destruction:
(1) A king does great austerities and develops superhuman
    powers, making him nearly invincible. If he is not already
    a demon, he becomes one.

(2) But there is always an innocuous loophole which makes his future killing possible.
(3) The demon defeats the gods and takes over their space and lands.
(4) After creating the demon, the gods ask either Shiva or Vishnu to incarnate or create someone to kill the demon.
(5) The demon is defeated and either killed or banished to another world.
(6) The gods and rishis (and, consequently, the people) praise the demon killer.

There is also sectarian strife to be seen in the god–demon war. Often, demons killed by Vishnu, like Ravana, are worshippers of Shiva, and vice versa. But, in the end, Shiva and Vishnu combine to destroy the demon. In this we see the intrinsic unity of different cults within the Hindu ethos.

The demons return time and again. As long as there is human craving for the fulfilment of desires, demons keep on reappearing, coming as they do from the mind and actions of human beings. At times, there is not much difference between a Deva and an Asura: both are equal progenitors of mankind. When the character is good, he is a Deva. When he is bad, he is an Asura. Finally, the jivātma, or individual soul, merges with the paramātma, or Supreme Soul, and becomes part of the Oneness. At this point, demons cease to exist.

O'Flaherty sees the influence of Manicheanism[14] in the dualism of good and evil, light and darkness. Adi Shankara's definition that the gods and demons are opposed and that the battle takes place within the human senses is regarded as a Manichean influence.[15] But the god–demon opposition had been current for two millennia before Mani. Both the Vedic and Avestan religions are based on dualism, or the battle between the opposing forces of good and evil and the ultimate triumph of good over evil. It is a recurrent theme in both Hinduism and Zoroastrianism. Evil is never fully destroyed. It recurs again and again, and it is up to each individual to choose good over evil, both in thought and deed.

INDIAN DEMONOPHOBIA

Khanam's *Demonology* divides Indian demons into two categories: (1) Non-human spirits and (2) Human spirits of those who die an unnatural death. Asuras, Danavas, Daityas and Rakshasas are grouped together in the first category as 'free agents' who can 'choose between good and evil, but a disposition towards evil preponderates in their character'. They are described as personifications of 'the hostile powers of nature or mighty human foes, both of which have been eventually converted into superhuman beings'. This group derives its powers from pre-animistic beliefs, 'dread of powers' and vague impersonations of the terror of night, hill, cave or forest, the result of pre-animistic beliefs common to both Aryans and non-Aryans. It was coloured by the Aryan association with the indigenous races. There is similarity with the Arabian *jinn* as 'beings invented to explain what seems to fall outside the ordinary pale of Nature, the wonderful and unexpected, the superstitious imaginations of men who fear'. The second and more important class, according to the same book, is that of the ghosts of human beings, the Bhuta, who are malignant spirits of men who cherish hostile feelings towards the human race. Disease, death and calamities are regarded as the work of evil spirits acting either on their own initiative or incited by a sorcerer or witch. The terms Bhuta, Preta and Pishacha are synonyms to describe these spirits, further divided into (a) spirits of the murdered, with the special Brahmana demon

(Brahma Rakshasa, Brahma Daitya, Brahma Purusha) being the spirit of a murdered Brahmana whose ghost has the potential for good or evil; (b) spirits of dead people with unsatisfied desires like unhappy widows and widowers, childless women, pregnant women who die during childbirth and so on; unhappy children and the unmarried dead; (c) spirits of dead foreigners whose valour, cruelty or other qualities have impressed the minds of a subjected people.[16]

The forthcoming chapters suggest a different point of view. The origin of each demon is different. Asura, Rakshasa, Danava, Daitya, Pishacha, Bhuta and others have their own myths and legends, suggesting a varied and hoary past when tribes defeated each other and cruel men left memories of fear and tyranny. The gods and heroes of defeated tribes became demons. The fear of the dark, of death and the unknown also created a world of spirits, which combined with the fallen gods and enemies to become additional demons. The various demons finally converged in a subterranean world of evil spirits, but their origins were not always from that world.

The references to the gods as arya and demons as anarya (non-Aryan) must be treated with caution. Arya, in India, never had a racial connotation. The word meant 'gentleman' or 'sir'. In modern parlance, it is equivalent to the Hindi 'ji', Tamil 'ayyā' and Telugu 'gāru', a respectful suffix or form of address. The definition of an arya was also very subjective. If an individual or group was a part of or friendly with the establishment, it was arya, while an unfriendly individual of even Brahmanic or upper-caste origin (such as Ravana) was a demon. Nowhere is the term Dravidian used to describe a demon, as Sanskrit literature never uses the word. It is a myth that Dravidians were demonized. The so-called Dravidians of south India were as much a part of the Vedic establishment as north Indians, upholding the religion of the Vedas. Demon was always the enemy, and arya always the victor, even if neither had demonic or upper caste origins. As the Sanskrit texts uphold the Vedas, the gods, heroes and their practices are referred to as Vedic, while the enemies were Asuras, Rakshasas, Danavas, Daityas, Pishacha, Bhutas and so on. Rama, a Kshatriya, was an arya, while Ravana, a Brahmin, was a demon.

NOTES

1. Blake, William, *Book of Job*, William Blake, London, 1825.
2. O'Flaherty, W.D., *The Origins of Evil in Hindu Mythology*, p. 47
3. *Mahabharata*, 12.8.28.
4. Bellah, R.N., 'Religious Evolution', *Reader in Comparative Religion*, Harper & Row, New York, p. 79.
5. Read, *Icon and Idea*, Faber & Faber Ltd., London, 1955, p. 21.
6. Frazer, J.G., *The Golden Bough*, Macmillan & Co. Ltd., London, p. 50.
7. Norman, D., *The Heroic Encounter*, p. 9.
8. Spence, L. *An Introduction to Mythology*, George G. Harrap & Co. Ltd., London, 1921, p. 21.
9. Kluckhohn, G., 'Myths and Rituals: A General Theory', *Reader in Comparative Religion*, Harper & Row, New York, p. 148.
10. Zimmer, H., *Myths and Symbols in Indian Art and Civilization*, pp. 46, 54.
11. Norman, D., *op.cit.*, p. 37.
12. *Ibid.*
13. Hopkins, E.W., *Epic Mythology*, p. 44.
14. Manicheanism was founded by Mani in Iran in the third century AD.
15. O'Flaherty, W.D., *The Origins of Evil in Hindu Mythology*, pp. 70–76.
16. Khanam, *Demonology*, pp. 18–29.

2

Fallen Gods—Asuras

'It neither dies, nor is It born;
He who regardeth It as a slayer, he who thinketh It is
   slain,
Are equally unknowing'

Bhagavad Gita[1]

Sura comes from the word surati—to rule or to possess supreme or superhuman power, and means god, divinity or deity, a synonym for Deva, 'the shining ones' or the gods themselves. A-sura is the opposite, a non-god. Asura is also derived from asu meaning breath or life, which makes Asura the 'possessor of life-power', or immortal, or even healer, the last description an attribute of Varuna, greatest of the Vedic Asuras. Asura also means a spirit, incorporeal, divine. Later this was qualified to be an evil spirit, demon and opponent of the gods. Many Devas, such as Agni, Varuna and Mitra, were originally called Asura in the *Rig Veda*, but the term was applied to the enemies of the gods by the end of the book.

Sura is also the name of the plant *Sinapis Ramosa Roxb*, made into a drink.[2] According to the *Shatapatha Brahmana*,

ASURA

the sura was given to Indra by Namuchi during the shautramaṇi
sacrifice, also described as a laukika (folk tradition), not vaidika
(Vedic tradition) sacrifice.

Who or what was Asura—god or demon, good or evil?

ASURA IN EARLY SANSKRIT LITERATURE

Asura appears frequently in the *Rig Veda*, nearly as often as
Deva. Initially they are heroes and monarchs, great leaders
worthy of receiving the offerings of the Aryans.

In the oldest books of the *Rig Veda*, Books 2 to 7 (Family

Books) of the Veda, the term Asura appears twenty-nine times, while its derivatives asuryām (asuraship), asuryā (adjective: asura-like), asurahān (asura-killer), and asuratvā (asura qualities) appear in twenty-six verses. Agni—the god of fire—is most frequently called Asura. He is praised as:

'Lofty Asura . . . steer of eternal law, Agni . . . the Asura' (R.V., 5.12.1)

'Wise Ordainer, ancient and glorious . . . Enthroned in oil, the Asura, bliss-giver, is Agni' (R.V., 5.15.1)

'Agni, kindled by Manu . . . the Asura we will praise at sacrifice, very powerful, the messenger of true speech between the two worlds' (R.V., 7.2.3.)

'Praise the high imperial monarch, the Asura, the man of the people' (R.V., 7.6.1)

'Agni, the Asura, shall sit as high priest, calling here the gods' (R.V., 7.30.3)

Agni was 'brought to light from the Asura's body' (R.V., 3.30.14), where the Asura is, apparently, Dyaus.

Varuna was the great Asura of the *Rig Veda*, addressed as 'You, O Varuna, are king of all, be they gods or be they mortals, O Asura' (R.V., 2.27.10). He is the 'Wise Asura, king of wide dominion' (R.V., 1.24.14) and 'the Lord of all wealth, the Asura who propped the heavens and measured out the broad earth's wide expanses. He, king supreme, approached all living creatures. All these are Varuna's holy operations . . . Varuna the Mighty . . . The wise guard of the world immortal' (R.V., 8.42.1–2). Varuna is most frequently addressed as Asura. Thus one of the greatest gods of the Rig Veda was an Asura.

Mitra-Varuna form a powerful pair of Asuras, and are addressed as 'O Mitra-Varuna, O Asura, One powerful one of you is a strong unerring leader, and the one called Mitra stirs the people to work' (R.V., 7.36.2). 'Since these two are Asuras of the gods, these noble ones, may they make our lands very fertile. May we reach you, O Mitra-Varuna, where heaven and earth and the days may bless us' (R.V., 7.65.2).

The Asuras know magic, a pre-requisite to rule in the ancient world. Mitra-Varuna cause the sky to rain with the magic of the Asura (asurasya māyā) and protect the vows with the same asurasya māyā (R.V., 5.63.3).

Varuna is the 'great' and 'wise' Asura, the destroyer of enemies. Later, Varuna becomes the god of the starry night sky, associated with death. He is also a māyin. The *Taittiriya Samhita* calls Varuna 'O wise Asura, O king'. The term Asura is used for Varuna in the *Rig* and *Yajur* Vedas in the sense of 'spiritual, incorporeal, divine or supreme spirit', and this supernatural spiritual power is called māyā. According to the *Rig Veda*, he sends rain through asuramāyā. With Mitra, Varuna protects the earth through asuramāyā and envelops the night and creates the dawn with asuramāyā. Varuna is the famous Asura who, with his great magic, 'stood up in the middle realm of space and measured apart the earth with the sun as with a measuring stick'. According to O'Flaherty, the images of the two opposing armies of gods and demons 'combine in a metaphor suggesting that sky and earth themselves form a phalanx in the fight between gods and demons', while the Asuras are described as 'ancient dark divinities, at first the elder brothers and then the enemies of the gods (Devas)' (R.V., 5.85.5).[3]

Rudra is referred to as Deva and Asura simultaneously, suggesting that the two words were synonymous, and the Asura or ruler of the great heaven was a shining one (diva). Here again the word Asura means both god and king. In a highly adulatory hymn, the poet says 'never let the Asura power draw away from this vast world' (R.V., II, 33. 9). In this hymn Rudra is a leader of the gods.

Another verse to several gods (vishve devāh) specifically mentions the 'three heroes of the Asura rule' (R.V., 3.56.8). In fact there are several references to unnamed Asura heroes (R.V., 3.53.7). Other gods who are occasionally called Asura include Aryaman, Pushan and Parjanya (R.V., 5.42.1; 5.51.11; 5.83.6).

Asuryām is ascribed to Indra, the hero of the Rig Veda, for killing Vritra (R.V., 6.20.2). His asuraship is great (brihad) (R.V., 6.30.2) when he assumed the leadership of the gods (R.V., 6.36.1). He is the 'asuric one' (R.V., 4.16.2), providing 'asuric rulership' (R.V., 7.21.7), possessing 'asuric power' (R.V., 3.38.7). Indra is 'king' and 'Asura'(R.V., 1.174.1) and is addressed directly as Asura (R.V., 8.90.6; 10.96.11). Thus even the hero-god of the Rig Veda is addressed as Asura.

'Asuryām' or 'asuraship' is attributed to several gods: Agni, Vaishravana, Varuna, Mitra–Varuna, Rudra, Soma–Rudra, Indra, Adityas, Brihaspati, Apam Napat and Sarasvati. In the hymns cited, it is a reward for their 'insights' (kratum), establishment of order and attainment of dominion. Asuryām is maintained by the Adityas, who possess and maintain rita, the cosmic order. The word asuryā (Asura-like) is generally an adjective for various gods. On one occasion, Sarasvati is described as asuryā nadīnām or 'first (or lord) among rivers' (R.V., 7.96.1). 'Great,' says the Rig Veda, 'is the unique asuraship of the gods' (R.V., 3.55.1). In a hymn to Vishvakarman (R.V., 10.82.5), the poet speculates as to what is beyond the sky, earth, gods and Asuras, where the Asuras seem to be undoubtedly human. 'The gods created for themselves trust among the powerful Asuras' (R.V., 10.151.3), and are even described as godless and weaponless (R.V., 8.96.9).

Asura in the singular is invariably used in a good and positive connotation. Even in the later books of the *Rig Veda*—Books 1, 8, 9 and 10—Varuna is the 'wise Asura king', the 'all-knowing Asura'. Both Varuna and Indra are addressed as king and Asura, as are several others—Surya, Rodasi and Ushas, who are also addressed as Asura, for the first time.

The Devas qualified for asuradom by performing the mantras prescribed, when the team of Ushas settled in the land of the cows (*R.V., 3.55.1*) There is an Asura called Rama who attends a music performance (*R.V., 10.93.14*). The Devas and Asuras co-operate to build the first sacrificial altar, chanting the Vedas together. The Asuras readily pay their share of the expenses for the yagna. Āsurī duhitā means sister in the early Vedas. The Asuras were the elder brothers of the Devas.

Human beings, like gods, are also called Asuras. In the second book of the *Rig Veda* (2.30.4) Brihaspati is called upon to kill the 'heroes of the Asura Vrikadvaras', who is definitely not a god and is never mentioned elsewhere. First Indra, then Indra-Vishnu kill the 'ninety-nine firm castles of Shambara' and 'one thousand heroes (men) of the Asura Varchin one hundred times' (*R.V., 7.99.5*). In the fifth book of the *Rig Veda*, the Asura is addressed as satpati or 'leader of the raid' (*R.V., 5.27.1*), and 'more excellent than any other patron'. The Maruts are beseeched to provide 'a powerful hero who is an Asura of the people' (*R.V., 7.56.4*). Here the word undoubtedly means leader. Several Asuras are nameless, like the Asura king who gave 100 pieces of gold, 100 horses and 100 cattle to the poet Kakshivan, while others are named, like the Asuras Rama and Pipru.

In the *Rig Veda*, there are some references to Indra as asurahān (killer of Asuras). These are generally references to his ability to defeat kings, rather than to any specific instance of Asura-killing. Indra, 'the asuric one' is described as 'dasyu-killing', for dasyus were the enemies of Indra. There are also indications that the Asuras have become hostile enemies:

'The godless Asuras (asura adeva) are weaponless. Destroy them with the wheel . . .' (R.V., 8.96.9).

'O Indra, the pleasures which brilliantly you took from the Asuras . . .' (R.V., 8.97.1).

'The gods having slain the Asuras when coming . . .' (R.V., 10.157.4).

In the *Rig Veda*, we are told that 'Indra, working with Rijishvan shattered the fortresses of the māyā-possessing Asura Pipru (a dāsa)' (10.99.11). The battle between the two is mentioned in nine verses of the *Rig Veda*. Indra destroys Pipru's fortress and helps Rijishvan kill Pipru. Pipru has fifty thousand black followers, is avrata or vowless, has pura or fortresses and has ahimāyā or serpent-magic. Pipru is obviously an enemy leader—now called Asura—a human being who possessed magical power or māyā. He is listed with other Asuras like Vritra, Namuchi and Shushna in *Rig Veda* books 1, 6, 9, 10. Four distinct groups are identified in the *Rig Veda*: devān (gods), manushyām (men), asurān and rishīn (seers).

The tenth book of the *Rig Veda* is a later interpolation and it is apparent that, by this time, the Asuras had become the enemies of the Devas. *Rig Veda* 10.124 records the struggle between the Devas and the Asuras, where several deities, including Agni, Soma and Varuna say a kind word to the father Asura, but choose Indra and abandon the father. 'The Asuras have lost their powers of magic'. This is a later hymn, which seems to suggest that some of the gods abandoned their parent Asura and came over to Indra. However, Indra, Agni, Varuna and Soma were already allies. Agni's words 'I the god go from the ungodly (adevād) one' probably hold the key. This hymn is important in that it is an indication that the Vedic Devas were detaching themselves from the Asuras. In other words, heaven and earth were separating. Importantly, Asura is identified with the demon Vritra for the first time. Asura's fall is complete.

In *Rig Veda* Book 1, the sun-bird (suparna) is identified with the Asura and the sun. *Rig Veda* 10.177 conceives of Asura as the divine sunbird (suparna) or eagle, a solar deity and father of all creation. The sun-bird is anointed with creative power (māyā) of the Asura. Asura is addressed as the Bull, a

SUN-BIRD SUPARNA

Vedic symbol of power; dyaurosuro, divo asurasya (heaven of the Asura), and the asurasya vīrah (the brave men of the Asura) are the sons of heaven. The Asura's creative capacity earns him the name Vishvaroopa.

Several gods are addressed as Asura in the *Atharva Veda*. There are several references to the magical spells and charms of the Asura. In fact, the Asuras even make poison ineffective. There are several instances in this Veda where Asuras are described as the enemies of the Devas. Indra overcomes the Asuras, for which he uses charms and plants. This book treats the Asuras as enemies conquered by Indra. The Indra–Dasyu battles are frequently likened to the Indra–Asura battles (*A.V.*, 10.3.11). The *Atharva Veda* mentions the fortresses of the Asuras, and those of the Danavas (*A.V.*, 10.6.10), but there is no indication yet that Asura and Danava are synonymous. However, there are indications that the Asuras are enemies who were conquered by an alliance of the gods 'at the beginning' (*A.V.*, 11.10.15). There are four classes of beings: gods, men, Asuras and seers (*A.V.*, 8.9.24) and even one more, the ancestors (*A.V.*, 10.10.26). Whether the enmity is supernatural or not, the Asuras have started appearing as the enemies of the gods, a role that was to increase in later literature.

As the relationship between the Devas and Asuras turn sour, the latter hide a sorcerous doll (krityā) on the former's land, hoping to prevail over them. But the Devas dig out the doll and their magic renders ineffective the māyā of the Asuras (*Shatapatha Brahmana*, 3.5.4.2–3). The Devas attack the 'weaponless' Asuras with Indra's wheel (*R.V.*, 8.96.9). As the Asuras became enemies, even Dasas like Varchin, Namuchi, Pipru and Svarbhanu are addressed as Asura, a term of insult rather than identification.

The Asuras also lose their māyā through Varuna's power. Later, he becomes a punisher of transgressions with two nooses: one terrible and another beneficial (*Maitrayani Samhita*, 2, 9.6). The horse was Varuna's symbol (*Taittiriya Brahmana*, 2, 2.5.3; 3, 8.20.3), and he seizes those who take the horse, for he is a destroyer of foes (*Taittiriya Samhita*, 5, 6.20). He punishes those who offend by meting out diseases such as tuberculosis (*R.V.*, 1, 122, 9), and physical deformity (*R.V.*, 2, 28.5–8). The same verse implores him not to 'wound with your weapons that wound the man you seek when he has committed a sin.' The *Taittiriya Samhita* gives him the power to heal (6, 6.3), yet the Asuras also lose their māyā and powers because of Varuna's wiles (6, 210). By the epic age, he becomes the lord of waters and is associated with snakes, which adds to the darkening role of the Asura. S. Bhattacharji sees the gradual degradation of the Asura in Varuna's role as a threatening and punishment-meting figure.[4] However, whereas Varuna is at least made a dikpāla guarding the oceans, the Asuras become demons, and are divorced from Varuna. His early primacy as the lord of the skies ensures that he still receives respect.

When Varuna ceased to occupy a position of supremacy, Asura also came to mean an evil demon. Whereas māyā initially, in early Sanskrit, meant 'wisdom, extraordinary or supernatural power', it later came to mean 'illusion, unreality, deception, fraud, trickery, sorcery, witchcraft and magic'.[5]

The *Atharva Veda* provides the transitional phase between Asura as a human and divine ruler and Asura as demon or supernatural enemy of the gods. In several *Atharva Veda* verses, the meaning of Asura is identical to that of the Brahmanic period: 'supernatural beings opposed to the gods'. The descriptions of the Asura have become grotesque and highly exaggerated, which was a typical feature in the ancient world when the appearance and abilities of enemies were exaggerated. The magical practices of the Asuras were clearly disliked. If we juxtapose this with the growing popularity of the yajnas and Brahmanic rituals, we can see how the magic of shamans is giving way to elaborate rituals.

The other Vedic texts vacillate between identifying Deva with Asura and Asura with the enemy (Dasyu) or the supernatural magicians, the Rakshasas. In the *Rig Veda*, 'the merciful and helpful Asura, the good leader with golden hands . . . routs the Rakshasas (demons and sorcerers)'[6]. *Vajasaneyi Samhita* (2. 29) identifies the Asuras with the Rakshasas for the first time.

By the period of the *Brahmanas*, Asuras had become demons, and were constantly at war with the Devas. There are no more good or divine Asuras. Individual demon kings belong to a class of Asuras, just as individual gods belong to a group of Devas. According to the *Taittiriya Samhita*, both Devas and Asuras were born of or created by Prajapati, but he invariably helps the Devas win. Often, the Dasyus and Asuras are liberally interchanged in the conflicts, most of which owe their origin to the Aryan desire for something belonging to the Dasyus or Asuras, such as land ('these worlds'), which is a major bone of contention. What is important is that the Dasyus, or the defeated people, were identified with the Asuras in the post-Vedic period.

The *Taittiriya Samhita* goes on to list varied conflicts: the Asuras steal the wealth of the Devas (1.5.9.2), or the gods battle for the sacrifice (6.3.7.2). The gods always win, generally by performing special rituals. The message is that he who performs the sacrifice can defeat his enemies in the same way that the gods defeated their Asura enemies. These battles are very similar to those between the early Aryans and the Dasyus, except for the fact that the Devas and Asuras fight on a cosmic scale, traversing the skies and taking the help of the heavenly bodies. In most cases, Indra or Agni defeats the Asuras. Further, many of the solutions are to be found in the ritual—the yajna or sacrifice—which has the power to defeat human and extra-terrestrial demons: in the *Yajur Veda*, it is a rite, in the *Sama Veda*, it is a sāmam. The *Aitareya Brahmana* frequently says that just as the Asuras are in conflict with and defeated by the Devas, so too can a sacrificer 'prosper and defeat his rivals'. The *Shatapatha Brahmana* is full of stories of battles between the Asuras and Devas for superiority, for the sacrifice (1.5.3.2), and for land (9.2.3.8), with the rider that the sacrificer will be equally prosperous. According to the *Kaushitaki Brahmana* (23.4), Indra uses certain verses to escape from the charms of an Asurī or female Asura (asuramāyā).

The *Aitareya Brahmana* uses the terms asuraviśam (Asura people) and asuryavarṇa, which sound like references to a separate tribe or caste. The *Brahmana* also combines the terms asura and raksha into asura-raksha (2.11; 2.36; 6.4). A verse in the *Kathaka Samhita* also suggests that one born in the Asuravarna was not fit to become a priest, so they were obviously an enemy race. The *Shatapatha Brahmana* says that they were different and had barbarian speech (3.2.1.24). The Asuras and easterners make round graves (13.8.1.5), and sepulchres (mounds) above the earth (13.8.2.1), suggesting an early and rudimentary form of the stupa. But these traits could also have entered the Asura identity through other tribes with whom they were now identified.

The Asuras are described as descendants of Prajapati (*Shatapatha Brahmana*, 3.5.4.2). The *Shatapatha* and *Taittiriya Brahmana* tell us that Prajapati created the Asuras out of his breath. The *Taittiriya Aranyaka* says that when Prajapati created the gods, people, ancestors, gandharvas and apsarases out of water, the few drops that were spilt became Asuras, Rakshasas and Pishachas, all demons. Manu says the Asuras were created by the Prajapatis. The term Asura is also interchangeable with the terms Daitya and Danava.

Christianity made the Greek god, *Daimōn*, into a malevolent being. Similarly, the Vedic Asura was made into a demon by the post-Vedic cults of Shiva and Vishnu. Many Asuras were destroyed by these two deities as they gradually supplanted the Vedic gods.

Interestingly, in early Christian interpretations, Satan or the devil of the Hebrew Bible is originally an angel who acts as a heavenly prosecutor (Zechariah 3:1–2), hence the name Satan meaning accuser or adversary in Latin, while devil comes from the Greek *diabolos* with the same meaning. In the Book of Job (1: 6–12; 2: 1–7) he is a functionary of God, his powers limited by God, and acts at the behest or concurrence of God. Satan as a force of evil with an agenda from hell is an image of the New Testament (cf. Books of Matthew, Mark, Luke, Romans, Corinthians, Ephesians, Thessalians, Timothy, Hebrews, James, Peter, John). Obviously the tradition of interchanging heavenly beings with the devil was a universal phenomenon in the ancient world.

DIVINE BEING?

Sanskrit scholar W. Norman Brown believed that Asuras were a class of divine beings, along with the Devas, with the good Asuras called Adityas led by Varuna, and the bad ones called Danavas led by Vritra. According to him, the basic meaning of the word Asura is 'lord', but adds that it came to mean 'powerful, a creature of power'. He points out that in the *Rig Veda*, only Varuna, Mitra-Varuna, Indra, Agni, Surya, Rudra, the Adityas, Devas and their enemies are called Asuras (they are also called Devas). The word is never used for the Ashvins or Ushas, and only twice for Dyaus, all of whom are definitely Devas.[7]

The major limitation to this theory is that some Devas are singled out as Asuras and therefore creatures of power, leaving out some others. There is no explanation for this selection. Further, the status of the Asuras deteriorated with time and did not grow as it should have, if they were truly divine beings. Again, no explanation is given. Asura starts off as powerful, and descends to demonism. And, most importantly, Vritra was never an Asura—or divine being—in the early books of the *Rig Veda*.

MAGICIAN?

A.A. MacDonnell suggests that the use of māyā or occult power discredited the Asuras. This would make the Asuras human beings, not gods.

The early meaning of the word māyā was supernatural power. Later, it came to mean magic or occult power. The *Rig Veda* mentions that the Asuras had māyā which was potentially applicable to hostile beings (R.V., 10.12.4). He also ascribes the origin of the word sura, which first appears in the Upanishads, to the opposite of the negative image of the a-sura.[8]

It is likely that the perceived supernatural power of the Asuras was described as occult power when they were discredited. However, it does not seem likely that they were discredited because of their māyā. After all, this was an age when magic would have been an inevitable part of the ritual.

FORCES OF DARKNESS?

J. Garrett suggests that as Suras were the personification of light, Asuras were those of darkness, and that the existence of these terrible and malignant beings may be traced to the fear that man experiences in the darkness, convinced that he is surrounded by invisible ghosts and goblins.[9]

However, Asuras as ghosts and goblins is a later idea, since they are equated with the gods in the early Vedas. Later, when they were demonized, they represented the forces of darkness.

SOVEREIGN LEADER?

W. E. Hale suggests that the word Asura obviously meant 'lord' or leader in the early or 'Family Books' of the *Rig Veda*, especially since the term was used both for gods and for human beings. This seems a very acceptable meaning, for all the descriptions given above suggest leadership. Asura was obviously a synonym for ruler or respected leader, a role shared equally by Devas and human beings. According to him, one could not be an Asura by birth or nature, but had to be made an Asura—a lord or leader—by his followers. Asura is not yet a grouping: it is only used in the individual context.

Hale goes on to say that from the occurrences of Asura in the early books of the *Rig Veda*, the word suggests a 'lord' (or ruler/master). The Asura is a leader who commands respect and is backed by an army. He may also have magical powers. The term refers to both gods and human beings, but since the hymns are addressed to the gods, Asura refers more to the gods, especially those who represent sovereignty.

When Asura appears as a derivative or compound (asuryām, asuryā, asurahān, asuratva), it refers to the qualities of the Asura, maintained by the gods. Hale concludes that one was not an Asura by birth but was chosen to be a lord or Asura by his people and maintained his authority with their continued support. Hale also points out that as Asura does not appear in the plural in the early books, it could not be a term for an 'organized group'. Asura appears in the singular in the early books, specifying individual gods or humans. Thus the Asura 'seems to have been a lord or leader chosen by his people, who maintains his authority by their continuing to support and follow him'. Asura appears forty-one times as an individual and thirteen times as a derivative in the later books of the *Rig Veda*. It is shortly after this period that the meaning changes from good to bad.

Based on examples in early Sanskrit, the above instances— and many more in the later books of the *Rig Veda*—one is inclined to agree with Hale's description of Asura as 'lord', a translation that appears from time to time. It is an epithet for several Devas, or gods, in the *Rig Veda*, making it impossible for the word to mean anything as negative as demon. He translates the word as 'lord', a respected leader of a fighting force, a sovereign. Several gods support or maintain asuryām, which means that one became an Asura by the consent and support of one's followers. The Asura's insight or planning ability (kratu) was an important quality. What is mentioned in connection with the gods would have been applied to people also.[10]

INDIAN ASURA = IRANIAN AHURA?

Ahura, in the Iranian *Avesta*, is addressed as 'lord' or 'ruling prince', with human and divine connotations. Like the kratu of the Vedic Asura, Ahura has xratu. It is also an epithet of Mazda, Apam Napat, Mithra and others. The usage is very similar to that of the Indian Asura, prompting Hale to describe both as 'powerful, respected lords with some kind of military force in their command' with one major difference: Asuras were selected and installed in their position, while Ahura lordship passed from father to son.

Sanskrit had three words for the gods—Asura ('lord'), Yagnata ('he to whom the sacrifice should be offered'), and Deva ('shining one'). In the Iranian equivalent, Ahura became the supreme god and Yazata covered those deities who were not Amesha Spentas, but Daeva came to mean demon. The term Ahura was applied to the six Amesha Spentas, associates of Ahura Mazda, whereas the Vedic Varuna ('supreme, sovereign') was the foremost of the Asuras. In the Iranian *Avesta*, Varuna's equivalent is Varana the sky, another name for Ahura Mazda, which means 'lord of high knowledge'. Later, Varana became the site for a mythical battle between the storm god and the storm demon. Darmesteter points out that the changes in meaning, if any, probably occurred separately in the Iranian and Sanskrit languages.[11]

There is no doubt that the word Asura, which originally meant divine, corresponds to the Persian Ahura. Varuna is 'the wise Asura and king' and 'the all-knowing Asura who established the heavens and fixed the limits of the earth.' Later, Asura came to signify the opposite and became synonymous with demon in the latest parts of the *Rig* and *Atharva Veda*, while Ahura Mazda, in Persian tradition, became 'the wise god'.

The ancient Persian language interchanges the 's' in Sanskrit with 'h'. Thus the Sanskrit Asura was the Persian Ahura. On the other hand, the Vedic Deva or god is similar to the Persian Daeva with one important difference: Daeva came to mean demon in Persian. The root *asu* means 'the air of life' while Deva is derived from the root *div*, which means 'to shine', hence

Deva means 'the shining one'. The gods of one civilization became the demons of the other and vice versa.

The change in meaning of Asura is perplexing. One explanation is that the term Sura came to mean god with the growth of the Krishna cult: Sura was the grandfather of Krishna and a member of the Surasena tribe. Asura would then mean 'not a sura' or 'not a god', in other words, a demon. But this happened much later than the *Rig Veda*.

Hale has summarized and criticized the various theories for the fall of the Asuras. The first to suggest that the Indian Asura and Iranian Ahura developed differently in the two regions because of a religious split among the Indo-European people was Haug, a theory that continues to be the most popular. Rudolf Otto suggested the existence of an Asura religion common to the Indians and Iranians before their separation, which was absorbed by the Deva religion in India, but remained undiluted in Iran where it was the source of the religion and teachings of Zarathushtra. Varuna and his band of Asuras and Adityas were absorbed by the Vedic religion. He equates Varuna's title *medhira* or wise, with Ahura's appellation *mazda*. Emile Benveniste interpreted the name Ahura Mazda as 'a being of the family of Asuras', indicating that he was a known god who was exalted by Zarathushtra, and identified Ahura-Mithra with Mithra-Varuna, while V. K. Rajwade saw them as people originally belonging to one stock who quarrelled and parted ways. Konow saw a Babylonian influence in the Asuras, while U.V. Rao equated the Iranian Ahuro Mazda with the Sanskrit asuro mahā[12].

The Ahuras of Iran and Asuras of India are undoubtedly similar. They were powerful and respected, commanding armies of followers. If the Asura had kratu, the Ahura had xratu. But whereas Asuras were selected by the people and installed in their position in the democratic Rig Vedic society, Ahuras are described alongside sons of Ahura, born to rule.

There are two sacred days in the Shiite Islam of Iran: Noruz (Navroz), the ancient Zoroastrian New Year, and Ashura, the martyrdom day of Imam Hussein. Shias remember Ashura with self-flagellation and mourning. In Iran the day is celebrated with a ritual involving jumping over a fire. As the Shiites—Iranians and Iraqis—were originally Zoroastrians, it is likely that this ceremony goes back to a time when Asura/Ahura was the ruling deity.[13] The tenth day, in Aryan tradition, is the last and most important day of mourning (even in modern Hinduism). Ashura, in Shiite Islam, is marked by public displays of crying and sorrow. 'The depth of sorrow cannot be felt for a man of whose reality these people know nothing. Their heartbreak can only be over their own lives and their own losses . . . much of Zarathustra's theology has been transferred straight over to Iranian Islam.'[14]

As the Indo-Iranians developed separately and at a distance, their popular gods and religious traditions developed differently, for various local reasons. There is no archaeological or historical evidence to suggest a common people who had split. On the other hand, the similarities between Iranian and Aryan linguistic and cultural traditions are too strong to ignore.

INHABITANTS OF THE INDUS VALLEY?

A favourite theory of many twentieth-century Indologists was that the Asuras and Dasas were the inhabitants of the Indus Valley cities which were destroyed by the invading Aryans. This has reference to the puras or fortresses destroyed by Indra. The terms *arma* and *armaka* also refer to deserted ruins.

R.V., 1.133 says that the yātumatīs and amitras (friendless) lived in the armakas or city ruins. But archaeological data indicates that 'the city was already slowly dying before its ultimate end. Houses (were) mounting gradually upon the ruins of their predecessors or on artificial platforms in the endeavour to out-top the floods . . .'[15] Shendge even tries to read a religion from the Indus artefacts, and creates an elaborate myth to establish that the people of this area were the Asuras and Dasas, the latter described as lake dwellers, who shared a single system of agriculture, technology, engineering, seafaring, trade, irrigation and river control, and that 'the Vedic pantheon, with the exception of Indra and Vishnu, is composed of the functionaries of the government of the Asura empire having as its capital the Indus Valley.' All the gods of the Rig Veda are made into humans with specific roles, and the Harappans identified with five peoples: Asuras, Rakshasas, Yakshas, Gandharvas and Pishachas. She adds that the Asuras had a god called Asura. She goes on to trace a common heritage for the Asuras, Egyptians and Sumerians.[16]

The attempts to equate Asuras with the residents of the Indus Valley who were destroyed by the Devas or Aryans do not hold up to scrutiny. To start with, there is no evidence of mass burning or killing of people, so the invasion theory is untenable. The cities of the civilization self-destructed due to excessive siltation and flooding. Then, the Rig Veda is so obviously pantheistic in nature, that to pick out a few Devas and make them human is incomprehensible. Why should Indra and Vishnu alone be left out? It does not make sense. Finally, the Asuras are, initially, leaders of the Devas and are identified with the gods of the Rig Veda. The enmity comes much later. If the Aryan invasion theory were true, then the Asuras should have been enemies from the beginning. Most importantly, while several gods are called Asura, there is no single great god called Asura.

However, Shendge comes nearer the truth when she traces the Asuras to the Asurs of Babylon. But it is difficult to say that the latter ruled the Indus Valley cities. There is absolutely no archaeological or linguistic evidence, as in the case of the Mittanis.

ASURA = ASHUR/ASSUR?

K.R.V. Raja[17] and R.G. Bhandarkar[18] have related Asura to the Semitic word Ashur, used for the Assyrians, worshippers of Ashur, who conquered Persia, wondering whether they were the Aryans or whether they caused the migration of Aryan tribes towards India. Although there is enough to suggest similarities between the Iranians and Vedic Aryans, there is no literary or archaeological evidence of an eastward migration from Iran. But there is one group—the Mittanis—who provide a link between the Ashurs and the Aryans.

The Assyrians were originally vassals of the Mittani kings of Mesopotamia who had Aryan names and worshipped Indra, Varuna, Mithra and the two Nasatyas. The Mittanis were intermittent rulers of Mesopotamia from 1480 BC. Besides Indra, Varuna, Mithra, and the dual Nasatyas (Ashvins), they probably even worshipped Aruna (Uruwana). According to their Boghaz-keui documents, their kings included Dusratta (Dasharatha). Their language is recognizably Sanskritic, just as so many aspects of their culture were distinctly Aryan, such as chariot racing, which was a favourite Rig Vedic sport. Like the Vedic mārya or 'young heroes', the Mittanis had maryani, with the same meaning. Their words for language and the numerals are either similar or identical to Sanskrit.[19] Thième has linked in great detail the Mittanis, ruled by Mattivaza, son of Dusratta (Dasharatha) to the Rig Vedic Aryans, and asserts that the Mittanis were essentially Vedic, not even proto-Aryan, since the resemblances stop with the Veda and do not necessarily include the *Avesta*.[20] The Mittanis were also allies of the Egyptians with whom they made common cause to fight the Hittites, whose king was depicted as a ten-headed and ten-armed figure, the first time in art history.*

The *Shatapatha Brahmana* says that the Asuras speak a foreign language, while Patanjali, in his *Mahabhashya*, calls them non-Brahmanic foreigners and deficient in grammar. The *Bhavishya Purana* says that the Asuras came from across the sea of salt water.[21]

The Assyrian empire developed in the ancient city of the God Assur on the Tigris River in Mesopotamia—modern Iraq–Iran. The people worshipped the God Assur (or Ashur) after whom both the capital city and the country were named. So important was Assur (also Ashur, later Ashshur) that many of the kings—Assur-uballit, Asur-nasir-pal and Asur-bani-pal—bore his name.

The people were initially agricultural, but the city grew in importance till, by 2350 BC, the Assyrians had conquered Mesopotamia and parts of Asia Minor and Egypt, an empire that covered Iran, Iraq, Syria, Lebanon, Israel, Jordan and Turkey. Between 2000 BC and 700 BC, the Assyrians reached the zenith of their power. This was also the period when the Asuras of India passed from being gods to demons.

The Assyrians—or Asurs—were, initially, vassals of the Mittani kings. They were known to be devilish fighters and

* See Chapter 3—Demonized Enemies.

defeated the Mittanis and took away their kingdom. Then there is a blank. What happened to the Sanskrit-speaking Mittanis?

The Assyrians were, primarily, breeders and traders of horses. They were ruled by an alliance between the kings and warriors on the one hand and rich and powerful religious leaders on the other. What was remarkable about the followers of Assur was their total disregard for other cultures and civilizations. They expelled or killed the peoples of the lands they conquered and destroyed their cities. Their cruelty and punishments became legendary: they crushed out local culture and national identity. But they were also great builders: Queen Sammuramat is believed to have created the famous Hanging Gardens of Babylon and the Library at Nineveh where over twenty thousand cuneiform clay tablets were discovered. The finest example of Assyrian architecture is the palace of Asur-bani-pal at Nineveh, with its sculptured reliefs of battle scenes and animals. While the Assyrians borrowed much from Babylonia, they were best known for their mighty war machine, especially their horse-drawn chariots, along with the infantry, archers, cavalry and battle-rams (for breaking down walls). They were the most feared people of their times, living demons of the ancient world.

The symbol of Assur was the winged solar disc, in which the God is seated over a tree. The winged disc was also the symbol of Ahura Mazda. The Vedic Asura was similarly associated with the sun-bird.

Wilkins sees a bitter enmity between the Aryans of India, who hated the Assyrians and what they stood for—Asur or Ahura—and the Assyrians.[22] Mackenzie clarifies that although Indra may belong to this early Iranian period, Indra assumes a distinctly Indian character after localization in the Punjab.[23]

The Mittanis and Asurs were two tribes battling for supremacy over the same space—the land of contemporary

Iran. If the former are identified with the Aryans and the latter with the Iraqis-Iranians, the pieces fall into place: the gods and demons of the former were reversed as the demons and gods of the latter. It would have been most natural for each to demonize the other.

Nirad Chaudhuri believes there can be no doubt that the Mittanis were very closely related to the Aryans, and finally went to Persia and, thereafter, to India, if the two were not the same people, and that the Mitanni–Mesopotamian connection is the only certain aspect in the history of the Indo-Aryans before they came to India. The migrants, according to him, took about four hundred years to settle down in Iran and Aryanize the country. 'Then another eastward push began . . . This appears to have been due to a family quarrel, which is recorded in Hindu mythology as the war between the Devas and the Asuras, the Gods and the Titans. All Hindu texts are agreed in making the enemies closely related in blood and culture . . . The clash appears to have taken place in the first instance over land. The Devas, who lost the war, left Iran to the Asuras, and moved east. Hindu mythology represents the victory of the Asuras as an usurpation of the heaven of their own gods . . . The theme of paradise lost and regained is one of the major stories of Hindu mythology, and it must date from the Iranian sojourn of the Indo-Aryans . . . .

'There survives . . . a vague memory that the quarrel may also have been over a question of religion and beliefs . . . about the nature of truth, which probably involved a whole range of moral and religious notions. There is also a hint . . . that the Persians looked on the self or soul in a very worldly sense, and did not perceive the eternal over-soul in themselves. The thing which the true Aryan resented most . . . was the approach to the jealous and intolerant Semitic single God.' There are also

Avestan references to migrations from Iran to the land of the 'Hepta Hindu' or Sapta Sindhu.[24]

The final eviction of the Asuras was done with the aid of Agni or fire. According to the *Shatapatha Brahmana*, the Devas and Asuras, both alumni of Prajapati's school, were fighting for superiority. Yet, even when the Asuras were defeated, they rose up again and again. Finally, Agni offered to go to the northern border and bar their entry. 'Then they will not be able to fight again from that fourth land which is far distant from these lands' (*Shatapatha Brahmana*, 1.2.4. 8–12).

It is the inversion of the roles of Asura and Deva that points to a past conflict and the parting of ways.

ASURAS IN THE EPICS

It is in the epics, the *Ramayana* and *Mahabharata*, that the Asuras are totally synonymous with demons.

There is an important story in the *Shatapatha Brahmana*. The Devas and the Asuras both sprang from the Creator, Prajapati, and strove together. The Devas were defeated and the Asuras decided to divide the world among themselves and live on it. Hearing of this, the Devas decided to go to the spot where the division was taking place. Placing Vishnu, the sacrifice, at their head, they went to the spot and asked the Asuras to include them in their division of the earth and give them a share. As Vishnu was a dwarf, the Asuras offered as much land as Vishnu could lie on. The Devas went on working and worshipping the sacrifice by which means they acquired the whole earth.

The tenth book of the *Rig Veda* (10.124) has mentioned the struggle between the Devas and the Asuras, where several deities, including Agni, Soma and Varuna 'say a kind word to the father Asura', but choose Indra and abandon the father. This hymn suggests that some of the gods abandoned their parent Asura and came over to Indra. Agni's words 'I the Deva go from the ungodly (*adeva*) one' hold the key. This hymn indicates that the Vedic Devas were detaching themselves from the Asuras. The *Shatapatha Brahmana* incident seems to be an explanation for this development.

The *Shatapatha Brahmana* story next appears in the *Ramayana* when Vishwamitra tells Rama the story of Bali, son of Virochana, who conquered Indra, chief of the Devas, and enjoyed the three worlds. When Bali was performing a sacrifice, the other Devas told Vishnu that as Bali would grant everybody's desire, Vishnu should take the form of a dwarf and save them. Then Vishnu took the form of a dwarf and asked Bali for as much land as he, Vishnu, could cover in three paces. Having obtained his request, Vishnu assumed a miraculous form and, with three paces, covered the whole world: with one step he covered the earth, with the second he covered the atmosphere and with the third the sky. Thereafter, he assigned Bali to Patala, the underworld, and gave the world to Indra. The story is mentioned in the *Mahabharata*, but is elaborated in great detail in the *Bhagavata Purana*.

In the *Rig Veda*, Vishnu is the mighty sun who covers the world with his three mighty steps: two steps are visible (sunrise and sunset), while the third (the noonday sun) is known to the gods alone. This story combines the Rig Vedic character of Trivikrama Vishnu with the growing antagonism between the Devas and Asuras and the ultimate defeat of the latter. These three stories taken from the *Rig Veda*, *Shatapatha Brahmana* and *Ramayana* suggest how the Asuras deteriorated from being equals of the Devas to inferiors and enemies.

The opposition between the Devas and Asuras had already

commenced towards the end of the Rig Vedic period (Book 10, or the *Purusha Sūkta*, is a later interpolation in the Veda). Agni, fire, chooses the Devas, or Indra and his allies, over the Asuras. Fire is important for the sacrifice. In the *Shatapatha Brahmana*, the Devas place Vishnu, the sacrifice, at their head, and Agni, the sacrificial fire, in the east. The Devas had obviously chosen the worship of Vishnu and the sacrifice over the Asuras and their religion. The Ramayana story of Bali elaborates it and firmly establishes the superiority of Vishnu, the Deva, over the Asuras.

The new meaning of the term Asura, derived from a-sura, is explained by a myth whereby the gods drank sura (wine), now a synonym for soma and amrita, the nectar of immortality. The churning of the ocean and the consequent battle between the Asuras and Devas for the nectar establish the equality of their birth and the defeat of the demons. The churning of the ocean, an allotrope of the pressing of the soma in the soma sacrifice, is a ritualistic myth, which is based on an agonistic model, like a game.[25]

ASURAS IN LATER LITERATURE

Later literature tries to explain the change in status of the Asuras by their acts of commission and omission. According to the *Brahmanas*, the Devas and the Asuras performed a sacrifice at the end of which they were both equal. Then, the Devas performed the 'silent praise', the latent essence of the hymns, which was unknown to the Asuras. The Devas defeated the Asuras and became their masters.

Another explanation is that the Devas gave up falsehood and adopted truth while the Asuras gave up truth and adopted falsehood. Yet another explanation is that when the sacrifice was performed, the Asuras put the offerings into their own mouths, while the Devas gave the offerings to each other. According to the epics, pride made the Asuras sinful, so they were driven out of their celestial homes, forsaken by happiness.

Several battles were fought between the Devas and the Asuras, all leading to the annihilation of the Asuras. Indra attacks the Asura leader Keshin with his thunderbolt. The demon throws his mace against the god, but the weapon is broken into a thousand pieces. Then the demon throws a rock, but Indra cuts it up with his thunderbolt and it falls, wounding Keshin.

The Asuras lived beneath the waters, in the caverns of Mount Meru, and left their homes only to fight the gods and the inhabitants of Meru. Their city was Patala, identified with the nether world, which surpassed heaven in its splendour, but was also the home of all evil and extreme violence, a veritable hell. An Asura fire, fed by water, burns constantly in Patala. It is contained, but cannot be extinguished. When the end of the world comes it will burst forth and consume the three worlds—heaven, earth and the underworld. It appears to be a prediction of a gigantic volcanic fire of destruction.

Their teacher and guide was the wise sage Shukra, a descendant of Bhrigu, a Vedic sage and one of the Prajapatis.

Asuras and Rakshasas become indistinct by the end of the Brahmanic period. They no longer fight the gods alone: they can be chased away by the sacrifice, done properly.

CONTEMPORARY ASURAS

The ancient embankment at Karsota Lake in Mirzapur, the Bijaigarh Fort and the Asuren embankment at Patna are believed to have been created by Asuras—the last by Krishna's enemy Jarasandha. According to S.C. Roy, a Munda tribe called

Asura believes that they were a metal-using people who once occupied the country and are descended from the ancient Asuras.[26] The major problem with this theory is that the gods of the *Rig Veda*, and not people, are repeatedly called Asuras.

CONCLUSION

First, Asuras were gods. Thereafter, they were described as beings hostile to the Aryans. Then they became foreigners and finally, a mythical race of beings hostile to the gods and Aryans.

Who, then, were the Asuras?

The Rig Vedic Asura was obviously a leader—of men or gods as the situation warranted. Ancient people were catholic and eclectic in their adoption of different gods. The early Aryans worshipped Devas as well as Asuras.

There can be no doubt that there was a connection between Asura–Deva of India and Ahura–Daeva of Iran, with a reversal of roles. Asuras became disliked demons in India, while the Devas were the gods. The reverse happened in Iran. The followers of the god Assur of Babylon became the rulers of the Tigris–Euphrates region, which is now modern Iran and Iraq, established their religion there, and Assur became synonymous with Ahura. Identifying the gods with powerful rulers was a common feature of ancient religions. The tales of the cruelty and conquests of the Assurs were so well documented and prevalent through the ancient world that they have come down to the present day and have created an image of a terrible and cruel people, in fact among the worst ever known. The Assurs, like the Asuras, were initially mere leaders, who later overthrew their Aryan Mittani rulers. Their cruelty and their magnificent war machines were famous in the ancient world. Their

destructive nature made them prime contenders for the role
of demons. If we further relate them to the Aryan Mittanis,
to whom they were linked first as subjects and later as
conquerors, we see a repetition of the Asura–Deva relationship.
And the place where this confrontation took place was ancient
Iran, where Ahura or Assur or Asura became the chief god.

There is a gradual change: First, they were the highest of
the high, heroes and leaders of the *Rig Veda*. They were identified
primarily with Varuna, an important Vedic deity. Then they
became supernatural beings hostile to the Aryans, characters
constantly at war with Indra and the Aryan tribes. They spoke
a foreign language, being 'non-Brahmanic foreigners' who
were 'deficient in grammar', and who came from across the
sea of salt water.

It is likely that the Mittanis came to India, after their defeat
by the Assurs, with terrible tales of the Assurs, and described
the latter as living in fortresses in Babylon. Their interaction
and relationship with their Assur enemies is not unlike that
between Devas and Asuras.

There is some indication that the Asuras were native to
India and were driven out, but there is no corresponding
evidence in Iran. According to Renu, the *Shatapatha Brahmana*
story of the final banishment of the Asuras indicates that the
distant fourth land to which they were banished was Assuria,
named after them, a land beyond the northern border which
they reached via Central Asia. They retained their name Asura
in the name of their new country, which is still called Assuria
by the people of Syria.[27] The three share a symbol: the Assur
winged solar disc, the Iranian winged solar disc (of Ahura
Mazda) and the winged solar bird (suparna), symbol of the
Vedic Asura.

Significantly, Indra, hero of the *Rig Veda* who later became lord of the heavens, was generally antagonistic to the Asuras, although he was also described as Asura on a few occasions. The *Rig Veda*, which describes the Asuras as celestial beings, also suggests mantras to overcome them. It is important to note that while the word Asura changed in meaning from leader to demon, none of the gods identified as Asuras—Varuna, Agni and so on—were ever described as demons or evil. Some, like Agni, continue to be the most important to this day. This means that something else happened to make the Asura leader into a demon. The only event that fits this time-line, and with which there is an Aryan association in the form of the Mittanis, is the Assur rule over Babylon and their integration with the Iranians.

Dr Banerjea reconciles the various dichotomies by suggesting that the Asura-Pracheta or Asura-Vishvaveda of the Aryans was the Ahura Mazda (Wise Lord) of the Iranians. He adds that as Assur was the term used in Assyria for the Supreme Lord and the Assyrians were the rulers of the Iranians, the word found its way into the Persian language, where the epithet Mazda (wise or good) was added to the term Assur. The cruelty meted out by the Assyrians to their foes and the bitter hatred that the Aryan Mittanis cherished towards them made the term Asura, once used for leaders, become descriptive of the enemies of the Devas. Thus the word that was originally derived from *asu* meaning breath and spirit or 'the Great Spirit' became a compound of a- and sura, meaning a non-god, and therefore a demon.[28]

Time and again they are described as foreigners speaking a barbaric language, who came from across the seas. A verse in the *Kathaka Samhita* says that one born in the Asura varna was not fit to become a priest. Their disposal of the dead was also different: Asuras made round graves and mounds to the dead, according to the *Shatapatha Brahmana*. These grew into the stupas of India and the great tombs of Middle Eastern cultures.

While the Vedic Aryans could have been the Mittanis who were migrating from Iran and Mesopotamia, the changing fortunes of the Asuras run parallel to another important event: the drying up of the Sarasvati, the mightiest river of the *Rig Veda*, and the eastern movement of the Vedic civilization. In the *Rig Veda*, Sarasvati is the greatest river, mentioned more often than the Sindhu (Indus). According to scientific studies, the Sarasvati dried up between the second and first millennia BC.[29] This means the Mittanis, if they were the Vedic Aryans, should have migrated around this date. Archaeology tells us that they were ruling Iran–Iraq at this time, so it is more likely that they were an Aryan people who joined up with the Vedic Aryans after their banishment from their homes. As they moved to the East, they must have brought horror stories of the worshippers of Asura, making the latter into demons. In the ancient world, kings and their subjects were identified with their gods.

The gods of the *Rig Veda* are dynamic and powerful forces of nature, who shower rain upon a parched land undergoing desertification. In various ways, Indra, Varuna, the Ashvins and Maruts hasten the arrival of rain, and are beseeched to break open the clouds, destroy the demon of drought and so on. As the Aryans moved into the Yamuna–Gangetic plains where they became agriculturists and food producers, their lives were less nomadic and the requirements from the gods changed. Prosperity, settlements, a home and hearth became the key necessities. Simultaneously, indigenous gods and goddesses such as Shiva, Narayana and the Mother Goddess were also gradually absorbed into the Vedic pantheon.

The tribal practices of the Aryans gave way to a highly structured religion of sacrifices that gained prominence along with the worship of Shiva and Vishnu. The Devas or gods were necessarily a part of this religion, since the sacrifice was offered to them. The sacrifice was necessary to banish foes like Vritra, the drought, who became an Asura.

In spite of the frequent wars between them, the Devas and Asuras often worked together to achieve common goals. The story of the amrita manthana or the churning of the ocean is one such instance, when the Devas and Asuras churn the ocean for the nectar of immortality. Of course, they inevitably end up fighting each other for the amrita, which the Devas finally obtain by a clever ruse. Thus the world is saved from the horror of immortal demons.

The demonization of the Asuras also coincides with the rise of the worship of Shiva and Narayana and the increasing importance of the sacrifice. The Asuras were undoubtedly Aryans in the Rig Vedic period. There were two religious developments in the later and post-Vedic period: one respected and performed the sacrifice, the other did not. There is a suggestion in the *Shatapatha Brahmana* and the *Ramayana* that the land amassed by the Asuras was taken over by the Aryans with the power of the sacrifice. The combination of the Rig Vedic story of the three steps of Vishnu, the sacrifice, and the *Shatapatha Brahmana* story of the land covered by the three steps of Vishnu as the sacrifice, indicates the religious developments of the time.

There also seems to be a preference for a more benign and boon-giving deity over a swashbuckling hero, which the Asura came to signify. Even as the Asura fell from favour, religious preferences were changing. Tantric ritual, with which the Asuras were associated in the form of asuramāyā also became less popular, and Tantrists lived on the fringe of society.

Like the Greek Titans, the Norse Jotuns and the Irish Fomorians, the Asuras are giant demons who fight the gods. Confined to Patala, they will, one day, take part in a final battle like the Norse giants, and engulf the world in fire.

The Asura leaders of the Aryans gradually merged with all the negatives of the ancient world: the Assurs of Assyria and the horrors they were famous for; magic-practising Tantrists; refuseniks who rejected the sacrifice; worshippers of ancient gods who had given way to new ones. Let us not forget that we are speaking of a span of centuries, when the popularity of individual deities waxed and waned very slowly. It was in one such time of change that the Asuras passed from being gods to demons. Such a people could not be leaders in the Brahmanic world view.

Finally, the Asuras were associated with everything inauspicious. The *Maitrayani Samhita* identifies them with the night, the black spot in a person's eye, the second half of the lunar month, the fortnight of the waning moon, untruths and the left hand. The Asura marriage is the 'fifth' form of marriage described by Manu, in which the bridegroom gives as much wealth as he can afford to the girl and her family, and then takes her according to his pleasure.[30] Vritra, the Rig Vedic demon of drought, declares that he is the best of the Asuras while Indra is the best of the Devas. The two make a pact of non-aggression, but the other Devas kill Vritra. Thus Asura, the divine leader and monarch of the *Rig Veda*, is identified with the demon and villain of the sacred book, Vritra. Asura had come full circle.

Asura represents the ultimate demon. It was finally left to the gods themselves to destroy the demons who were their own creations. Thus they either incarnated themselves or came to the aid of their devotees to kill the demon, a larger-than-life figure whose main crime was that he was different or owned something that the victorious mortals wanted.

BUDDHIST ASURA SAMSARA

In Buddhist cosmology, the six lower realms are a part of the ten spiritual realms. The 'good' realms are the Deva, human and Asura. The 'evil' realms are the realms of the Hungry Ghost, (non-human) animals and hell. The Asura realm represents 'jealousy, struggle, combat and rationality'. Although their lives are more enjoyable than that of human beings, Asuras are said

WHEEL OF LIFE WITH ASURAS AND GHOSTS

to be plagued with jealousy of the Devas. In the Buddhist depiction of the Wheel of Life, the Asura samsāra is placed at two o'clock, flanked by the Deva realm to the left and the Hungry Ghost realm below.[31]

NOTES

1. *Bhagavad Gita*, 2. 19,20.
2. Sura-plant.
3. O'Flaherty, W.D., *The Rig Veda*, p. 29.
4. Bhattacharji, S., *The Indian Theogony*, pp. 32–38.
5. Monier Williams, *A Sanskrit—English Dictionary*, p. 811.
6. O'Flaherty, *op.cit.*, p. 199.
7. W. Norman Brown, 'The Creation Myth of the *Rig Veda*', *Journal of the American Oriental Society 62 (1942)*, pp. 88–91.
8. Macdonell, A.A., *A History of Sanskrit Literature*, p. 113.
9. Garrett, J., *A Classical Dictionary of India*, p. 49.
10. Hale, W.E., *Asura in Early Vedic Religion*, pp. 51–53; 66–67.
11. *Ibid*, p. 14.
12. *Ibid*, pp. 1–37.
13. Wheeler, R.E.M., *The Indus Civilization*, p. 127.
14. Kriwaczek, Paul, *In Search of Zarathustra*, pp. 219–220.
15. http://en.wikipedia.org/wiki/Talk:Ashurah
16. Shendge, *The Civilized Demons: Harappans in the Rigveda*.
17. *Ibid*, pp. 15–16.
18. R. G. Bhandarkar, 'The Aryans in the Land of the Asuras', *Journal of the Royal Asiatic Society of Great Britain and Ireland*, pp. 76–79.
19. Sethna, K.D., *The Problem of Aryan Origins*, pp. 30–35.
20. Thieme, P., 'The Aryan Gods of the Mittani Treaties', *Journal of the American Oriental Society*, Vol. 80, No. 4, October—December 1960, pp. 301–17.
21. R.G. Bhandarkar, *op. cit.*

22. Wilkins, W.J., *Hindu Mythology*, pp. 437–8.
23. Mackenzie, D.A., *Indian Myth and Legend*, pp. 3–4.
24. Chaudhuri, Nirad C., *The Continent of Circe*, pp. 43–4.
25. O'Flaherty, W.D., *The Origins of Evil in Hindu Mythology*, p. 61.
26. S.C. Roy (cf. Hale, *op.cit.*, p. 20).
27. Renu, L., *Vedic Records on Early Aryans*, pp. 75–6.
28. Dr. Banerjea, *Bengal Magazine*, April 1880, Wilkins, *op. cit.*, pp. 438–9.
29. Bakliwal, P.C. and Grover, A.K., 'Signaures and Migration of Sarasvati River in Thar Desert, Western India', *Vedic Sarasvati*, pp. 113–18.
30. Garrett, J., op.cit., p. 50.
31. http://en.wikipedia.org/wiki/Six_lower_realms

3

Demonized Enemies

*'The dark takes form in the heart of the white and
reveals it.'*

Rabindranath Tagore[1]

One set of demons—the Rakshasas, Daityas and
Danavas—is distinct from the Asuras, in that there is
no divinity attached to them. Whereas the Asuras were once
the equal of the Devas, the Rakshasas, Daityas and Danavas
were those who came into conflict with the ruling dispensation.

Several Rakshasas, Daityas and Danavas appear to have
been famous rulers of ancient India. Yayati, a descendant
of Manu Vaivasvata and ancestor of the Yadavas, married
Sharmishtha, daughter of Vrishaparvan, a Danava king. The
Shalvas who lived in Mount Abu, Bhima's wife Hidambaa and
their son Ghatotkacha, Ravana and the inhabitants of Lanka,
and Bhagadatta, king of Pragjyotisha all came under this
category. Krishna's maternal uncle Kamsa, and Madhu, his
ancestor, were called Daityas and Danavas, as were the Buddhists
and Jainas. Since many were enemies of the epic and Puranic

heroes, demonic qualities were attributed to them and, in time, they were identified with the Asuras and demons. Pargiter sees them as descended from the five great tribes of ancient India who peopled the subcontinent.[2]

If the epic heroes Rama and Krishna existed, as they probably did, their enemies would have existed too. There is evidence, in the form of local traditions, that Rama travelled from north to south India in search of his wife Sita and Ravana, king of Lanka, who had carried her away. Excavations at Kurukshetra and underwater excavations in Bet Dwarka indicate that the two sites were inhabited around 1000 BC, when the events of the epics took place, and the latter was submerged as per the epic descriptions, making the story of Krishna a very likely one. Rama's enemies are castigated as Rakshasas who, as we shall see, were probably a tribe of ancient India. However, it is the baby Krishna who takes on a multitude of demons, and that too in later works like the *Bhagavata Purana* and *Harivamsha*. It seems highly unlikely that a baby could have fought and survived so many demons and suggests that, as the cult of Krishna grew, the myths of the Ahir tribe were appended to Krishna, the Supreme Lord.

RAKSHASA

The word Rakshasa comes from the root raksha, meaning to guard. There is a myth according to which Brahma, when he created the waters, also created the Rakshasas to guard them. There are many individual Rakshasas who are good. Some are even born as Brahmanas. But they ask for such all-consuming powers that they end up being cursed and finally destroyed by the gods. Their origins were varied: they were descendants of Pulastya or Kashyapa, or are described as emanating from the foot of Brahma. They were killers, cannibals and drinkers of blood, who stole the sacrificial offerings.

Unlike the Asuras who were fallen gods, Rakshasas appear to have been sorcerers with magical powers who used magic to fight the Aryans. The word raksha in the *Rig Veda* means to guard, protect, save, take care of, preserve. The *Atharva Veda* uses it to mean ward off, guard against, keep away. In this, they help the gods. Yet these very guardians became enemies. Thus they also fight against the gods. They protect; they also harm. An illustration of the transference of functions is seen in Jara, a female Rakshasi who lives on meat and blood, and who was appointed by Brahma to destroy evil Danavas. Her image is painted on walls to keep away evil.

The word first appears in the early books of the *Rig Veda*: rakshas is growing or increasing (4.3.14), sneaking up (10.89.14), hidden and with deceitful speech (6.62.9) and grown great (4.3.14). He is an enemy of Brahman (brahmadviś) (3.30.17). Rakshasa may be a spell cast by a magician (7.104.23) and appears as a demon (Yatu) in the form of various animals such as the owl, dog, cuckoo, eagle and vulture, whom Indra is implored to grind as if with a millstone (7.104.22). Rakshasa is likened to a demon or Yatu (8.60.20). The Rakshasas are pāpa or evil; aśas or accursed; ājuata or repulsive; māyin or possessing magic; arāvan or greedy; and bhangurāvat or tricky. They even made fun of Brihaspati.

The Rakshasas are implacable enemies of the Devas in the *Rig Veda*, and their destruction is fervently prayed for. Rakshasa is an enemy of Indra, who is implored to overcome his enemies . . . and kill the Rakshasas (3.30.16). Agni has sharp weapons for killing the rakshas (5.2.10) and burns them everywhere (8.43.26). Soma kills the rakshas and drives away enemies (9.97.10); elsewhere he overcomes the aggressor, wards off rakshas and difficult ways, has a good weapon and overcomes the enemies. (9.110.12). Rakshas is described as the scorner, and mentioned along with Vritra (10.152.3), and hailed as the plague (8.35.16; 9.85.1; 10.98.12; 7.38.7).

The *Rig Veda* says that rakshas are frequently found in the company of sorcerers (7.104.25; 10.87.9, 10, 14) and with Pishacha (1.133.5) and godless māyās (4.3.14). They disrupt the sacrifice (7.104.18). This last is probably why several deities are invoked several times to kill the Rakshasas: Agni seventeen times, Soma ten, Indra seven, Indra-Soma three, Ashvins two, and Indra-Agni, Mithra-Varuna, Vajinah, Vashishtha and the Maruts one each. Agni invariably burns them. Soma 'streams into the filter killing rakshas, longing for the gods', and breaks them up. Indra burns, kills, breaks, grinds and smashes them. The rakshas are referred to in the singular and plural. *Rig Veda* 7.104 is an entire hymn dedicated to the destruction of Rakshasas, and the poet wills evil on those sorcerers who dare to call the poet a sorcerer. He ends with a call to hurl weapons at the demons, who are called 'idol-worshippers'. In a society where nature worship was the rule, it is likely that the Rakshasas were non-Vedic worshippers of images who were condemned and disliked by the Aryans. Among the many evils Agni is asked to drive away are hunger, Rakshasas, enemies and plagues (3.15.1).

In *Rig Veda*, 9.97, the priest 'in whom plants gather . . . is called a healer, slayer of Rakshasas'. Here disease is identified with the demons. *Rig Veda* 10. 87 is devoted entirely to denunciations of the Rakshasas, flesh eaters, a description repeated by the *Manusmriti* and the *Ramayana*. *Vajasaneyi Samhita* (2. 29) identifies the Asuras with the Rakshasas for the first time.

Some passages in the *Taittiriya Samhita* differentiate between Asuras and Rakshasas by including both in a list of beings (2.4.1.1). Other passages treat them as synonyms (6.3.7.1–2; 6.2.1.5; 6.2.11.1). The *Taittiriya Samhita* repeats the fact that the Rakshasas destroy the sacrifice.

The *Kathaka Samhita* (25.8) narrates a story of an Asura named Ghosha who tried to flee from the Devas into the trees, but was caught and bound. Then 'he growled in an asuric voice', to which the Rakshasas responded by attacking the sacrifice. Here the Asura is a leader and commands the Rakshasas to do evil.

The *Shatapatha Brahmana* is full of stories of battles between the Asuras and Devas. Asuras and Rakshasas are indistinguishable, and are constantly attacking the sacrifice of the Devas. In the *Kaushitaki Brahmana*, Asura-Rakshasa occurs thrice in the plural, treating the two as indistinct and the same (10.2; 17.9; 28.2). *Aitareya Brahmana* identifies Asura and Rakshasa in several verses. By the end of the *Brahmana* period, Asuras and Rakshasas are either compounded or indistinguishable. Panini, in his *Ashtadhyayi* (5.3.117) gives a list of warrior clans, which includes the Rakshasa, the name formed by adding an 'a' to Rakshas.

The word Rakshasa means 'destroyer' or 'harmer', and that is the chief function of this demonic class of humans. These demons disturbed sacrifices and harmed the rishis or sages. They were fiends who captured good people, cannibals who ate their enemies. In later literature, many were Brahmanas and Goddess Parvati gave them the power to attain maturity at birth. All uncultured behaviour is attributed to the Rakshasas. *Manusamhita*, Book 3, advises the housekeeper to begin his ritual with an offering to the gods, for the Rakshasas tear to pieces an oblation that has no such protection. The Rakshasa vivāha is described as a form of marriage wherein the family is killed and the girl is taken away forcibly from her house, crying and shouting (*Manusamhita*, 3.33).

The epics—Ramayana and Mahabharata—are replete with every kind of Rakshasa. They are the personification of evil, with every ignoble characteristic. They perform magic, changing their appearance, disappearing, flying and doing their will, drinking human blood and disturbing the sacrifice. Thus their defeat and submission heightens the mortal heroes' abilities as they battle these supernatural forces. They oppose Aryan rituals and threaten their existence—till the divine hero appears in a lowly mortal form and destroys them. Ravana is the Rakshasa par excellence, but there are lesser demons in both epics. As the epic heroes battled alien peoples with different mores who resented the expansion of the former into their territories, the latter were described as demons, an appellation indicating that they were hostile and hated enemies.

Rakshas was a nocturnal spirit, a demon of darkness, and therefore evil. They are also protectors of the night and darkness. They are called krodhavāśa, and guard paradise and the treasure of Kubera. The Rakshasas behave in a very anārya, or crude (and therefore objectionable) way. They disrupt the sacrifice and harass the rishis who are slowly moving beyond the established kingdoms.

They are generally described as abnormally built: oversized or dwarfed, fat or thin, tall or short, one-eyed, with protruding teeth, hump-backed and crooked. Some have a hundred heads and twice the number of arms. Yet they can assume beautiful forms and shapes, changing their appearance at will to assume any human, animal or divine form, smelling out human beings, flying in the sky and capable of any abnormal action. The

Rakshasas are constantly at war—with the gods, the Aryans and all 'good people'. Rakshasas are scared of the light, which is known as rakshogna, or destroyer of demons. They are active in the dark and disappear at dawn. When attacked by Nagas (snake people) they turn into Garudas (kites) and devour them. They are eaters of both raw (uncooked) and carrion flesh. In general, the Rakshasa is a hostile figure.

The female, the Rakshasi, is equally violent, drinking blood or demanding a daily offering of a human being. She is crude and uncouth. She even does the unthinkable—she proposes marriage to the man who has caught her fancy and is willing to do anything to obtain him, even carrying him away if necessary. Shoorpanakha, Ravana's sister, asserts herself and approaches Rama and Lakshmana with sexual proposals. Such behaviour is not Aryan—or genteel—and she is duly punished by Lakshmana, when she blames Sita for Rama's rejection. Her nose is chopped off, a terrible punishment justified by her behaviour. Rakshasis may fall in love and marry humans and bear children: but these are generally always Rakshasas. Rakshasis bear children as soon as they conceive, and their children are born as adults.

But there are indications that there were also respected and respectable Rakshasas. The Rakshasas had fortified kingdoms, beautiful palaces and enormous riches, which they used to create a vision of wealth and splendour. Many of them, such as Tripura, were renowned architects. At Ramtek, an old temple built of hewn stones fitted together without mortar is attributed to a Rakshasa named Hemadpant, believed to have been a giant physician who brought Marathi from Ceylon. In fact, the region is full of ancient buildings attributed to him.

The Rakshasas have social structures similar to those of the Devas. Some achieved fame for their knowledge and erudition. Ravana was a great scholar and musician, the composer of the Shiva stotra. His brother Vibhishana was Rama's friend, who disapproved of his brother Ravana's action of abducting Sita. Vibhishana is today regarded as a god to whom Vishnu delegated his powers in the Western Province of Sri Lanka[3]. The prime minister of the Nandas was a renowned historical figure named Rakshasa who, when his dissolute rulers were defeated by Chandragupta Maurya, was retained as prime minister by the new ruler on the advice of Chanakya.

Oppressive and cruel kings, such as Bisaldeva of Ajmer, were turned into Rakshasas by their subjects. At Bilsar in Etah district, there is the story of a Brahmana named Puran Mal who asked the local raja, whose house overlooked the other's, to change the position of his sitting room. When the raja refused, the Brahmana poisoned himself with opium and became a Brahma Raakshas, causing death to the raja and his family till his successors were forced to move out of their residence. According to Colonel Tod, the ghosts of some Muslim rulers of Rajasthan were called Mamduh (corrupted from Mohammed) Rakshasa, in an effort to conciliate them.[4]

Rakshasas were probably either a single tribe or a generic name for an alien people. There are many identified Rakshasas. Further, their wars are with human enemies, unlike the Asuras who fought the gods.

Rakshasas took on animal shapes, as did several totemic tribes. There is a dichotomy here in that they cannot be primitive totemic tribes and yet, at the same time, live in houses of gold. The supposed wealth of these Rakshasas was probably a myth.

The word raksha means to protect. It is amazing that protectors like the Rakshasas were demonized. There may be different reason for this. Many villages all over India are protected by supernatural powers such as Virs/Virans, Bhutas and other spirits who, it is believed, circle the village at night. Even as they frighten, they protect. Maybe the Rakshasas originally performed the same dual role.

Vajrayana Buddhism continues this odd alliance between the demon and the protector. Demons guard the four cardinal points of several temples, preventing evil spirits from entering. Several Hindu temples, particularly of Shiva, sport demons on the vimāna and gopura. In such cases, demons are once again expected to frighten away evil spirits.

Evil men, particularly those who hate Brahmanas, can become Rakshasas. Diseases and meteorological phenomena are also Rakshasas. Hopkins has divided them into two types of spirits: one as 'cloud and bolt and mirage', a type of beauty, and the other disgusting, representing personified diseases and other evils attacking man. This is apart from Danavas and men metamorphed into Rakshasas.[5]

There are several classes and varieties of Rakshasas. Nairrita Rakshasas come from the north but live in the south (nairrita disha) (Ramayana, 3. 64. 22). Their kings include Kubera and Ravana. The Krodhavashas are northern Rakshasas, also called Yakshas, who take away the merit of those who own dogs, and are killed by Bhima (Mahabharata, 3; 17. 3. 10).

The Kimkara Rakshasas are 'mind-born' and serve Ravana, although their name means servants of Yama or Rama or Shiva or Maya (Mahabharata, 2. 3. 28). Praising and feeding the Rakshasas with a share of the offerings on holy days is intended to flatter them in order to protect oneself, for it satisfies them and prevents them from injuring one (Ramayana, 2. 43. 5). To quote Hopkins, 'In the later moral epic the Rakshasa resembles the medieval devil, to be overcome by virtue, with book and bell, or the equivalent mantra, though in the narrative portion Rakshasas annoy and slay pious priests without fear of mantra

or of virtue. Kings are exhorted to have no fear of them.'⁶
The king who protects his people and cows, whose Brahmanas
are learned men and who constantly strives for virtue is not
afraid. And the Rakshasas leave him in peace for he is virtuous;
and kings who protect cows and Brahmanas need fear nothing
from Rakshasas (*Mahabharata*, 12. 77. 8–30).

The Rakshasas have a message: they do not care for gods
or wise sages. They have to be killed by superhuman heroes.
The epic Rakshasas were brutal, gluttonous and barbaric, living
in the wilds. They brought disease. In the *Ramayana*, the royal
Rakshasas are more like the Asura leaders.

YATU, YATUDHANA

They are a lower class of Rakshasas who lack the ability to
ride chariots, horses or elephants. They can change shape and,
along with the Paulastyas, are known as the Nairriti army.
Twelve Yatudhanas were born of Kashyapa and Surasa. They
are also described as the sons of Yadu and similar to the
Rakshasas: Ravana is a Yatudhanasya dauhitrah (grandson of
a Yatudhana on the maternal side) (*Ramayana*, 6. 114. 81), while
Hidambaa protests that she is not a Yatudhani (*Mahabharata*
(S), 1. 167. 17). But a Rakshasi created by an incantation is
a Yatudhani (*Mahabharata*, 13. 93, 78). Along with the
Rakshasas, they guard Kubera's mountain. They were created
by the fire mantra to kill the rishis and appear as demons in
battle. They appear in various forms, such as dogs, vultures
and hoofed animals. The terms Yatudhana and Rakshasa
samsi are used equally to describe the servants of Ravana.
They live in the mountains, while Shiva is a Yatudhana of
two forms.⁷

YATU, YATUDHANA

DAITYA AND DANAVA

The *Atharva Veda* (10.6.10) refers to the golden fortresses of the Asuras and Danavas (asurāṇām puro) and (dānavānām hiraṇyayīh). The *Atharva Veda* also mentions the fortresses of the Asuras, and those of the Danavas (*A.V.*, 16.77.7), but there is still no indication that Asura and Danava are synonymous.

By the epic period, genealogies had become essential and important, and the obvious contradiction between the good Devas and evil Asuras, both of whom find positions of honour in the *Rig Veda*, had to be explained. So they were described as the sons of Kashyapa Prajapati. The Devas were the sons of his wife Aditi, who gave them the name Aditya. The Asuras were born to two other wives, Danu and Diti. Danu's children became Danavas and Diti's children Daityas. Together, the Danavas and Daityas were the demons. Daityas and Danavas, being the sons of rishi Kashyapa and the hags Diti and Danu, were half-brothers of the Adityas who were celestial deities. Aditi and Diti were the daughters of Daksha, and the antithesis of each other. Their lifestyle is not unlike that of the gods, for they are half-brothers, although always hostile to each other.

Diti begged Kashyapa to give her a son with absolute power who could destroy Indra. Kashyapa did so, but with the rider that she should carry it with pure thoughts and body for a hundred years. She observed the condition but Indra, knowing what was in store for him, waited for an opportunity to catch her out. One night, she went to sleep without washing her feet. Indra then aimed his thunderbolt at the womb, dividing the embryo into seven pieces. The mutilated child cried out and, unable to shut it up, he divided each piece into seven, thus creating a whole race of Daityas or 'sons of Diti'.

The terms Daitya and Danava are matronyms, having been derived from the mothers Diti and Danu.[†] Daityas and Danavas appear to have been two large families of demons antagonistic towards the Aryans. Yet the fact that the Daityas are the sons of the rishi Kashyapa, one of the great lawgivers, and the half-

[†]Many Aryan heroes like the Pandavas are also called Kaunteya and Partha after their respective mothers, Kunti and Pritha. However, they are better known as Pandavas, after their father Pandu. Daityas and Danavas, on the other hand, have no patronyms.

brothers of the Adityas is in keeping with the nebulous state of the Asuras as fallen gods.

The early Danavas and Daityas were human. King Yayati marries Sharmishtha, daughter of Vrishaparvan, king of the Danavas (*Mahabharata*, I.80, 82, 83). The Shalvas, a tribe who lived around Mount Abu (now in Rajasthan), are described as Daityas and Danavas (*Mahabharata*, III. 4, 17, 22).

Madhu and Kaitabha 'who never told a lie' are Danavas. Madhu, the founder of the city of Mathura and an ancestor of Krishna, from whom the latter derives the patronym Madhava, is described as a Daitya. It is likely that he was confused with the demon brothers killed by Vishnu. In fact many powerful and defeated enemies like Jarasandha, king of Magadha, and Lavana Madhava, Madhu's descendant, are described as Daityas.

The words Daitya and Danava are interchangeable with Asura in epic and puranic literature, and the two are described as demons and giants of the ocean, confined to the region called Patala by Indra. They are enemies of the gods and of the sacrifice. They are sometimes victorious, most often vanquished. Their opposition to the Vedic sacrifice made the Danavas the enemy of the later Vedic people. The Daityas are described as giants who fought the gods and interfered with the sacrifice.

Danava women are gigantic, wear jewels 'as large as mountain boulders' and, when attacked by the Devas, they 'wail like cranes in autumn'. The abode of the giants is made of gold and precious stones. There are mansions equipped with seats and beds, gardens, forests and mountains resembling clouds. A Daitya tribe lives in the city of Hiranyapuri, which sometimes sinks under the sea or under the earth and, at other times, soars into the heavens like the sun, and like Indra's city in the sky. Hiranyapura, the 'city of gold', is the moving home of the Daityas.[8]

The worship of the Danava–Daitya is not seen very often. At Hazaribagh (now in Jharkand), the Dano (Danava) is worshipped in the form of stone daubed with five streaks of red lead installed outside the house. The Daitya lives in a tree in Mirzapur. It resembles a man from front, but is hollow at the back. He appears at midnight in his tree as a flash of fire and smoke. He is worshipped with kalaśas of water and greens, and is called Beohar Baba or 'Lord of Merchandise' in one village. Colonel Tod has mentioned a place called Daitya-ka-har in the Central Provinces, on which people desirous of having children leap. Talao Daitya, a famous demoness of Kathiawar, lives in a cave lit by a permanent lamp, which never goes out even in heavy wind or rain.

Some of the Daityas and Danavas have names like Sumati and Sumanas, meaning kind-hearted. The Danavas and Daityas were driven from heaven at the end of the Krita age and took refuge in the caves by the sea, in mountains, forests, under the earth but chiefly in the ocean. Their combined hosts, on losing the nectar churned from the ocean and on being defeated by the gods, first appear as mountain-hurling beings, then disappear into the earth and the sea (*Mahabharata*, 1. 18. 46).

The Danavas are opposed to the caste system, rishis and Brahmanas. Obviously, these demons were not a part of the Vedic hierarchy. Danavas like Ashvapati Kaikeya (Kekeya is in West Punjab), Kichaka, Kaleya Daitya, and the sons of Kekaya, king of the Sutas, represent ancient tribes who were obviously inimical to the Aryas. Arjuna is the killer of Danavas in the epics, taking over Indra's Vedic role.

The *Markandeya Purana* says that the Daityas, Danavas, Rakshasas, Asuras and Devas were cousins, constantly fighting with each other, till the Devas were defeated. Aditi, mother of the Devas, asked the sun to be born as her son, which he did, and Martanda was born. Then the Devas challenged the Daityas and Danavas to a war, in which Martanda fought on the side of the Devas, and defeated the others.

PISHACHA

In the *Rig Veda*, the female Pishacha is described as a reddish-yellow-haired roaring Pishachi, also a raksha (1.133.5). The *Atharva Veda* is full of references to them as implacable enemies, and to Agni's chasing them out of their villages and homes. Agni is invoked to 'devour' the Pishacha, obviously dispelling the forces by providing light and burning them to death. They are 'those who hound us in our chambers, while shouting goes on in the night of the new moon . . . the flesh devourers, who plan to injure us, and whom I overcome.' 'I plague the Pishacha as the tiger the cattle owners. As dogs that have seen a lion, these do not find a refuge . . . From villages I enter, Pishacha fly away . . . May Nairriti take hold of this one' (*Atharva Veda*, 4, 36).

The *Vedas* place them lower than the Rakshasas, as the 'vilest and most malignant order of malevolent beings.' The *Brahmanas* and the *Mahabharata* say that the Pishachas were created, along with the Asuras and Rakshasas, by Brahma, from the stray drops of water which fell out from the drops out of which gods, men and gandharvas were produced. While Manu says they sprang from the Prajapatis, the Puranas describe them as the offspring of Kashyapa by his wife Pishachaa (also Krodhavasha or Kapisha)[9].

The root piś means to carve, fashion or mould, so Pishacha could mean a carver.

Panini in his *Ashtadhyayi* describes Pishacha as a warrior clan. The *Mahabharata* also describes Pishacha as a warrior clan of north-west India, along with the Daradas (modern Dard tribe). The epic also calls them Khasha, identified with the Khasis of north-eastern India who probably came over from the west. The Mongoloid colouring of the Khasis resembles the description of the Pishacha as yellow-skinned. They were probably closely connected to the Nagas and Yakshas.

Could they have been the stone and wood carvers who occupied northwestern India, where many early carvings in stone were found? They seem to have definite human origins.

The *Ramayana* identifies them with Rakshasas and Yatudhanas. Later, the Pishachas became synonymous with devils, ghouls and evil spirits, as wicked as the Rakshasas and Asuras with whom they came to be identified. Like the Rakshasas, they danced and drank blood. The term Pishacha is also used to describe evil spirits and ghosts that haunt abandoned places and cemeteries.

Pishacha is described as the god of the Dasyus and typifies cruelty (*Mahabharata*, 12. 278. 33). There are good Pishacha who have ceased to be pishitāshana. They are the guards of Meru and Skanda, vegetarians living on the fruit mahashankha which grows on the wonder tree, along the Sarasvati (river). A female Pishacha wearing pestle ornaments gives advice about tīrtha sthāna (sacred watering places) to the wife of a priest. Another Pishacha is a tīrthapālika (guardian of a sacred watering place) and prevents impure people who do not love Krishna from approaching the place. After she makes a Brahma Pishacha woman follow Hari (Krishna), she becomes an apsaras.[10]

In the Pishacha form of marriage, a girl who finds herself at a disadvantage (such as being pregnant), could claim to have been victimized by a Pishacha. As a result, the term came to mean a wedding where the girl was taken at a disadvantage by a mortal.

In contemporary language, Pishacha has come to mean an evil spirit.

DEMON AS DEVOTEE

According to the *Agni Purana*, there were twelve major wars between the Devas and Asuras. They were: (i) between Narasimha and Hiranyakashipu; (ii) between Vamana and Bali; (iii) between Varaha and Hiranyaksha; (iv) during the amritamanthana; (v) between Skanda and Taraka; (vi) against the Ajivakas; (vii) Shiva's destruction of Tripura; (viii) the killing of Andhaka; (ix) between Vritra and Indra; (x) Vishnu's killing of Shalva and other demons; (xi) Vishnu's destruction of Halahala (poison), who had entered Shiva's body; (xii) Vishnu's destruction of the demon Kolahala (turmoil).

The demons worship Shiva, Vishnu or Shakti with an intensity born of their faith. Yet they must be destroyed if the gods are to survive. The destruction of people of equal faith and the alliance between humans and gods against the demons demand an explanation, which is often irrational. This is all the more so when several demons, such as the Bhutas, are objects of veneration in several villages. In fact, the propitiation of spirits is even more popular than the veneration of mainstream Hindu deities in several South Indian villages. Making them into devotees of Shiva may have been a way of integrating the demons into the Hindu theology.

Shulman tries to understand the relationship of a man devoted to a deity who is killed by the very god he worships. One possibility is that the demon is a polluted and polluting

DEMON AS DEVOTEE

figure, who joins issue with the humble devotees who are promised salvation by bhakti. The Puranic tradition is satisfied with the content of the devotion, for imperfect or self-centred bhakti causes the demon's death. But the demon's death also demonstrates another facet of bhakti, which is the affirmation of the social order, or caste system, with its hierarchy of relationships, sustaining the social fabric instead of undermining it. Thus the impure devotee becomes fit for the ritual death of sacrifice. He suffers a violent death which may bring him salvation.

The second possibility suggested by Shulman is that the demon relieves the god of the need to be polluted through the sacrifice and achieves the power to be derived from the sacrifice. The demon is a symbol of the power that justifies his worship, which he attains by his death in the sacrifice. As power is sacred, it enables the demon to maintain a hold over his devotees, and he derives it from the sacrifice. But he must also derive it from his bhakti or devotion, which he uses to achieve his desires, greater power, a better life and more. The demon devotee becomes symbolic of earthly rewards derived through bhakti.

The third is the identification of the demon with material success and unbridled power which, though derived initially through bhakti, justifies the demon's death. His death leads to an ideal state of salvation, suppressing the ego and possessiveness. When the ego is suppressed, the devotee identifies with the god within and is released from human bondage. The demon comes to symbolize the evil within, which must be destroyed before salvation is possible. The human devotee needs only a form of self-sacrifice. Ahaṅkāra or egoism and the consequent striving for power is the greatest crime and a stumbling block on the path to salvation. 'The demon exemplifies the evil of ahaṅkāra; his slaughter points the way to redemption ... Thus, the demon remains a mythic model for man; his death, however unwilling, at the hands of the god, is a recommendation for self-sacrifice, for the loss of self that accompanies the recognition of an inner identity with the god ... The myth has given way to allegory; clearly, our texts now possess a means of explaining why the devoted demon has to die'.[11]

In Shulman's interpretation, the demon represents the conflict between the self and the yearning for god. As a symbol of ahaṅkāra, the demon is destroyed by the god, the demon represents the processes of self-purification and self-extinction. There is a conflict between sacrifice and self-sacrifice. Man, like the demon, is trapped by his ego and seeks earthly power and goods through bhakti.

DEMON AS ANIMAL

Krishna, the protector of cows, is constantly battling animal demons, such as the bull demon, crane demon and so on. Considering the fact that the bull is the vehicle of Shiva, one wonders why it is also a demon. The much-loved elephant is also depicted as the demon Gajasura and the monkey, deified as Hanuman, is also the demon Dvivida.

It is a little odd that a religion like Hinduism, which gives a position of importance to animals, even deifying many of them, also makes them into demons. The answer lies in the probability that many of the animal demons were probably totemic tribes defeated by the Ahirs and Yadavas, worshippers

ANIMAL-HEADED DEMON

of Krishna, and other epic heroes. Many Indian tribes continue to be totemic and we shall see how the buffalo demon Mahisha was the totem of the defeated Gonds, Marias and Todas. To emphasize the fact that the animal itself was not an enemy, most animal demons have human bodies and animal heads, thus becoming monsters, rather than animals.

DECEIVING THE DEMON

There are no limits to the subversion of the demons. Vishnu often performs acts of māyā or trickery to destroy demon enemies. No trick is too much, nor is it condemned. After all, it is for the general public good.

In the Kurma (tortoise) incarnation, after an agreement to share the amrita or nectar with the demons, in order to use their strength and numbers to churn the ocean, Vishnu and the gods are horrified at the thought of immortal demons. So Vishnu assumes the form of Mohini to distract the demons and take away the nectar. This is also a means to prove the debased and frivolous nature of the demons who can be distracted so easily by a beautiful woman, when they have set out on the important task of obtaining the nectar of immortality. Thus, implies the story, they do not deserve the privilege of drinking the nectar of immortality.

Again, Vishnu incarnates as Vamana the dwarf to prevent King Bali from becoming too powerful. Bali was a 'good' Daitya king, grandson of Vishnu's ardent devotee Prahlada and great grandson of Hiranyakashipu. Bali performed several sacrifices, which led to his appointment as the King of Heaven. The gods appealed to Vishnu to restore their worlds, so Vishnu assumed the form of the dwarf Vamana, who appeared before Bali as a Brahmana youth and was offered wealth and lands and whatever else he desired. But all Vamana wanted was the ground covered by his three steps. In spite of his guru Shukracharya's caution, Bali insisted on redeeming his promise, and asked Vamana to measure out three paces. Immediately, the dwarf grew in size. With one step he covered the earth, with the second he covered the sky and the heavens. When there was no place for his third step, Bali offered his own head, and Vamana placed his foot on it, crushing it into the earth. It was only when Vishnu's devotee Prahlada appeared and begged Vishnu to spare his grandson who did not deserve to be punished that Bali was made king of Patala (the netherworld).

Bali's piety and goodness are undisputed and the only justification for his removal is the fact that he was a Daitya. It is more likely that he was a symbol of harvest and fertility, suppressed by the blazing sun god Vishnu. His annual revival is the annual return of fertility and bounty after a hot summer. Bali's defeat has been interpreted by some scholars as the defeat of the non-Aryans by the Aryans. But he is equally associated with the harvest and fertility, since he appears once a year at Onam (harvest) time in Kerala. He was, most likely, a non-Vedic harvest deity who makes his appearance once a year, as the harvest.

Vishnu corrupts the Tripura demons, who derived their power from the asceticism (and, in later texts, bhakti) preached by heretical doctrines described as Buddhist (or even a melange of Buddhism, Jainism, materialism and others). Once corrupted, they are killed easily. But the heresy taught by Vishnu often spills over on to the earth, thereby explaining the existence of heretics on earth. Vidyunmalin, Tarakaksha and Kamalaksha, the three Asura sons of Taraka who won Tripura (three cities), were granted a wish from Brahma that they could only be killed by a single arrow. The demons could not be killed because they were devotees of Shiva. Vishnu becomes Buddha and Narada his disciple. The two deceive the demons with sweet words and destroy the chastity of their wives by gifting them jewels. Vishnu persuades them to give up worshipping Shiva and worship him as the Buddha, giving inducements of money, jewellery, clothing and women to entice the demons. With the exception of three demons, Paramayogin, Shilapara and Viraktayogin, who refuse to be swayed from their devotion to Shiva, the rest become followers of the Buddha. Then, leaving a part of himself behind as Buddha, Vishnu goes to Shiva who agrees to battle the demons because they have left his fold. All the demons die, except the three steadfast devotees who hide in the sea and meditate on Shiva. The message is that they too would have been destroyed if they had followed the Buddha, and heresies must be avoided at all costs, even if they speak of dharma.

Of this method of using subversion to destroy the demons, Shulman says, 'The struggles of the gods and demons must never reach a final resolution if the world is to survive, for it is created and maintained through a dialectical alternation of pravritti and a negative backward pull of nivritti; the gods and demons gravitate to the opposite poles of this process and neither side can opt out, not even in the name of basic values of the tradition. If these values tend to be articulated in the 'negative' idiom of nivritti—that is, a 'demonic' universalism, or a universal detachment and salvation, as seems to be professed by the pious Tripura demons—then the tradition must somehow compromise itself and its goals. The nāstika (atheistic) preacher comes from within, in order to save the dhārmic order by defeating enemies who are also initially within its range, inasmuch as they uphold the traditional ideals of freedom . . . . In the Tripura myth it is this (dynamic) tension (between the gods and the demons) which is, in effect, the underlying source of heresy, seen as a divine intervention aimed at restoring a cosmic order threatened by a universal salvation.' Shulman then illustrates how iconoclastic groups are forced to their own ironic compromises and accommodation in order to survive as a group, becoming another caste (or group of castes). 'Having a history', he says, 'effectively denies the iconoclast the residual consistency of the mythical heretic: only the Tripura survivors retain a simple, pristine idealism at Shiva's gate.'[12]

The sectarian conflicts between the Shaivas and the Vaishnavas are reflected in the god–demon conflicts, particularly in the case of the incarnations of Vishnu. Nearly all the demons (except Bali) who opposed the various incarnations of Vishnu received their powers from Brahma or Shiva, more often the latter. Some, like Ravana, who is credited with the composition of the Shiva stotra, were ardent devotees of Shiva. Whether they were devotees of Shiva or Brahma, the demons who opposed Vishnu's incarnations on earth are invariably depicted with the vibhuti, the three horizontal lines of ash that identify a Shaivite in Indian art. Even today, in popular art, demons are depicted with the three horizontal lines on their forehead, a distinct Shaiva mark. Subverting ardent Shaivites, who were described as demons, was perfectly acceptable to their sectarian enemies, the Vaishnavites. Never are Vishnu's acts of trickery condemned. There is a persistent refusal to accept Shaivism and Shaivites, maybe because of the heretical nature of their teachings. For the bhakti movement and the belief in universal salvation for all began with southern Shaivism. This would have upset the social order, particularly the deeply entrenched caste system which placed different castes in hierarchial places in a queue. All of Vishnu's avataras revere the sacrifice and the caste system. Shaivas preached bhakti for all, a radical thought at that time. Finally, the heretical sects were absorbed into syncretic Hinduism, even as Vishnu himself became an object of the very bhakti movement his early followers derided.

With the exception of the Tripura incident, there is less Shaiva–Vaishnava sectarian conflict among the demons killed by Shiva. The demons who oppose Shiva represent negative actions and emotions, rather than followers of Vishnu. Apasmara purusha is the demon of ignorance, Andhaka is darkness or ignorance and so on. Obviously Vishnu's followers were more ardently anti-Shaiva than *vice versa*.

FAMOUS EPIC DEMONS

The *Ramayana* and the *Mahabharata* are extremely important in any study of demons. The demons come alive, becoming flesh and blood characters, with hopes and desires, happiness and sorrow. The very fact that there are good Rakshasas and bad ones means that they were not always regarded as demons.

Hiranyaksha and Hiranyakashipu

The two brothers are fallen celestial beings, Jaya and Vijaya, doorkeepers of Vishnu's heaven. The first tries to steal the earth, a euphemism for land grabbing and greed. The second is arrogant for power and wants to be proclaimed as god. This too is blasphemy. Both of them have to be killed for their arrogance and also for them to attain liberation from their demon incarnation.

These two are probably the most mythical of all the demons, being former gatekeepers of heaven. Further, their wars are more legendary than human: the former steals the earth and battles Vishnu as Varaha, who kills the demon; the latter fights Vishnu as Narasimha, the half-man, half-animal destroyer of the demon. It is interesting that even though there is a local tradition in Srisailam (near Vishakhapatnam) of the rule of Prahlada, it does not include Hiranyakashipu, who was supposed to be Prahlada's father.

Bali

The epics trace out genealogies for several demon families. A well-established line is that of King Bali, descended from Hiranyakashipu, brother of Hiranyaksha.

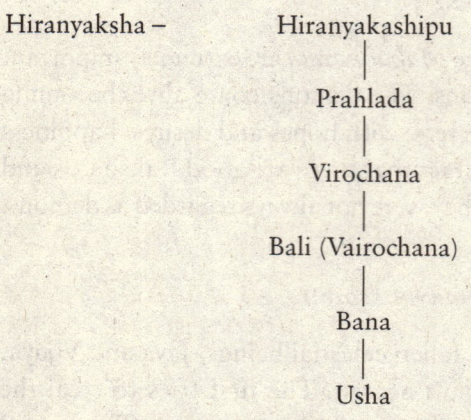

Hiranyaksha –   Hiranyakashipu
|
Prahlada
|
Virochana
|
Bali (Vairochana)
|
Bana
|
Usha
(marries Aniruddha, grandson of Krishna)

While Hiranyaksha and Hiranyakashipu seem to be legendary figures, the local tradition that Prahlada was the ruler of ancient Simhachala extends to his son Virochana, a vague figure, and his grandson Bali, a celebrated former ruler in Kerala, where he annually visits his subjects in a harvest ritual of thanksgiving. Bali is identified there with the harvest controlled by the blazing sun which is represented by the three steps of Vishnu, which push Bali under the ground. His triumphant return every year is the victory of the agriculturist over the rampaging forces of nature, the victory of the earth over the heavenly bodies. Thus demons can be good, for they are a part of our lives. Here a living tradition gets mixed up with natural phenomena. In the absence of recorded history, we have to rely on local traditions to establish the existence of past rulers.

The story of Bali absorbs the characteristics of the Vedic Vishnu as the sun who traversed the heavens in three steps, earning him the epithet Trivikrama. Bali is a true descendant of Prahlada: pious, truthful, performing sacrifices and an ardent devotee of Vishnu. He banishes all evil, ahankāra and lust from heaven, which he obtains after defeating Indra through the magic of mritasañjīvanī (life restoration) taught by Guru Shukra. But Bali's devotion to Vishnu is not sufficient to prevent his annihilation. After all, he seizes heaven and earth, indicating his attachment to power and wealth and the unselflessness of his devotion. He practises mritasañjīvanī, a non-Vedic and demonic form of magic. He is defeated by the dwarf Vamana, born to Aditi and Kashyapa, and possessed of true knowledge, which dazzles King Bali. Shukra tries to warn Bali that it is Vishnu, but Bali is still willing to risk giving the dwarf all that he asks for, in the hope of a greater reward. Even Bali cannot perceive that the final reward is his own redemption.

Prahlada, son of Hiranyakashipu, was a 'good demon' because he was a devotee of Vishnu, going to the extent of arranging for the killing of his own father. His grandson Bali's devotion to Vishnu could not prevent his removal from his throne and kingdom.

Finally, the line merges with Vishnu's human incarnation

when Usha, granddaughter of Bali and daughter of Bana, marries Aniruddha, Krishna's grandson.

Ravana

The *Ramayana* is a major source book about Rakshasas, who play a major role in the epic. Rama and Lakshmana are taken by the sage Vishwamitra to his Siddhashrama hermitage in the forest to fight Rakshasas. Here they kill Tataka and drive away Maricha. Tataka was the wife of Shunda and mother of Maricha, who haunted the forests on the banks of the river Sarayu, destroyed the sacrifices of the sages and the cities of Malada and Karusha. Tataka tried to confuse them with her magic, raining stones and rocks and clouds of dust, but Lakshmana cut off her nose and ears. Finally, Rama killed her with his skilled archery. Maricha was the son of Tataka and Shunda. Along with Subahu, he attacked and destroyed the sacrifices of the sages at Siddhashrama, till the young prince Rama defeated but did not kill him.

Siddhashrama was the hermitage of the demon king Bali till it was taken over by Vishwamitra who was Bali's devotee. Obviously, Tataka and Maricha were trying to drive away the sages and reclaim what belonged to the Rakshasas. Later, Maricha tries to dissuade Ravana from pursuing Sita, describing his earlier experience. He warns the king that Rama and Sita are protected by the dharma that guides their actions. Thus, he acknowledges the superiority of Aryan dharma and the Aryan war machine.

The *Ramayana* is very clear that the Rakshasas are enemies of the rishis, spoiling the sacrifice by polluting it, throwing human and animal flesh in the fire and so on. Rama's entire birth and life on earth was to rid the land of Rakshasas.

Yet, finally, he does not usurp their land. He installs Vibhishana, a 'friendly' Rakshasa, as king of Lanka and goes back to his kingdom at Ayodhya. If Vibhishana is a good man, he cannot be a 'demon', in the sense of an evil person or imaginary quality. This means that Rakshasa could not have meant 'evil' demon in the period of the Ramayana.

According to the Ramayana, Rakshasas were created by Brahma to guard the water. Descendants of the sage Pulastya, they were most effective at night. Many Rakshasas were of human and even divine origin, condemned to the state of demonhood because of their evil actions. During their fourteen-year sojourn in the forest, Rama and Lakshmana killed several Rakshasas, culminating in the war against Ravana, king of Lanka, and his demon army. The Rakshasas are the sons of Pulastya, while the Nairritas are the sons of Nirriti (Destruction). The *Ramayana* distinguishes between the prākṛita (common) Rakshasas and the aristocrats and 'princes of evil' (*Ramayana*, 3.29.16).

Some genealogies, like that of Ravana in the *Ramayana*, are well delineated. According to the *Ramayana* (7.4.31), Ravana, Kumbhakarna, Vibhishana and Shoorpanakha are the children of Kaikesi, daughter of the Rakshasa Sumali and wife of Vishravas. Vishravas, son of Pulastya, had a Brahmana wife Ilavida who gave birth to Kuvera, a Yaksha. Through his Rakshasa wife Kaikesi or Nikasha, daughter of Sumali, he had three sons, Ravana, Kumbhakarna, Vibhishana and a daughter, Shoorpanakha, all Rakshasas. The *Mahabharata* has a variation of the story in which Kubera gave his father three Rakshasi women: Pushpotkata who was the mother of Ravana and Kumbhakarna, Malini, mother of Vibhishana, and Rāka, mother of Khara and Shoorpanakha. (*Mahabharata*, 3. 275. 5). Ravana's wife Mandodari is Maya's daughter; Kumbhakarna's

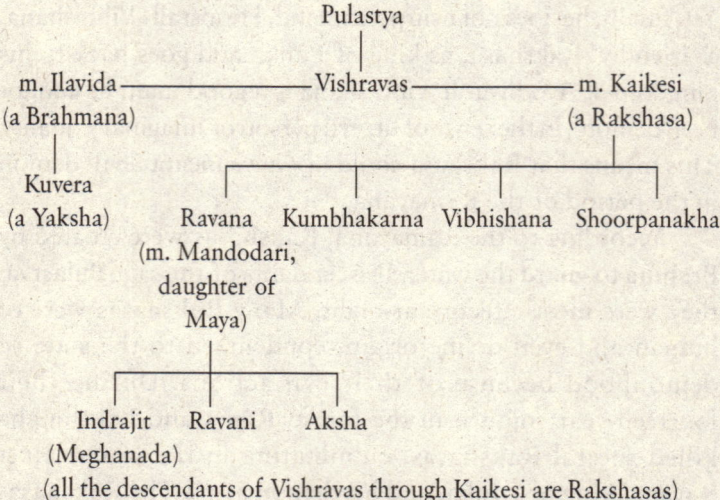

(all the descendants of Vishravas through Kaikesi are Rakshasas)

wife is the daughter of Vairochana (or Bali); and Vibhishana's wife is Sarama, daughter of the gandharva Shailusha.

Did Rama exist? There seems very strong reason to believe that he did. The story is geographically very correct, besides which there are any number of local traditions and temples all along Rama's route. It is unlikely that 3000 years ago somebody could have travelled around the country inventing local traditions regarding Rama's visit. If Rama existed, it is equally likely that Ravana also existed.

Some scholars opine that Ravana's Lanka was situated in central India, along the Godavari. The names Ravannamma and Ravannappa are very common among the lower castes of Andhra Pradesh and Karnataka, areas through which Rama travelled. But it seems unlikely that Lanka was in central India, since a geographically perfect work like the *Ramayana* would have known the difference between a river and the sea which was crossed by Rama to reach Lanka. The discovery of

a man-made shoal bridge in the Palk Strait between India and
Sri Lanka is also significant, as Rama is the only claimant to its
construction. To quote H. Parker, the author of the *Ramayana*
'possessed more than the slightest knowledge of Ceylon . . .
most of the geographical outlines referring to the island are
accurately portrayed.'[13] Sri Lanka also has local traditions such
as the cave at Ravana Ella Falls where Ravana is believed to
have hidden Sita from Rama, and the garden of aśoka trees
(aśokavana) at Nuwara Eliya, now the Sitai Amman Temple,
where Ravana once kept Sita prisoner. There is a record in an
early issue of the Bellary District Gazetteer of a Vanara tribe
in the region. According to the *Ramayana*, *Mahabharata* and
the Sinhalese Buddhist *Mahavamsha*, ancient Sri Lanka was
once occupied by Yakkhas (Yakshas) and Rakshasas.

Ravana is the archetypical Rakshasa, gentleman yet ogre.
He carries away Sita out of revenge; and a marriage where the
woman is forcibly carried off, against her wishes, has come to
be known as *Rakshasa vivaha*, or the demon form of marriage.
He is not the only one who covets Sita: a demon named Viradha,
clad in a tiger's skin, proposes to keep her, till his arms are
cut off by Rama and Lakshmana.

But there are several dichotomies, like the fact that Ravana
the Rakshasa is the son of a Brahmana, a great scholar of
Sanskrit and a devout worshipper of Shiva. Many obviously
non-Aryan tribes such as the Vanaras were associates of Rama
the Aryan, not Ravana the Rakshasa. It is obvious that there
was no racial preference. It was cultural and political. Those
who accepted the popular cultural and religious practices were
Aryan; those who did not were demons.

Interestingly, at the height of the Dravidian movement in
Tamil Nadu, E.V. Ramaswami Naicker floated a proposal to
build a temple for Ravana as the quintessential Dravidian hero

defeated by a marauding foreign Aryan, until he belatedly learned that Ravana was the son of a Brahmana and dropped the project! Further, Rakshasas are never described as Dravidas. It would be easy to term all demons as non-Aryans. But anārya means ungentlemanly, not non-Aryan.

The Lanka of Ravana was a maternal inheritance from his mother Kaikesi. According to the matrilineal system (still in prevalence as marumagatayam among communities in Kerala), inheritance is through the mother, and the eldest male is the karnavān (manager) of the joint family property, with others as holders of an equal share. If the family is a ruling dynasty, as were the Maharajas of Travancore and Cochin, the eldest male is king, followed by his younger brother(s). The next generation of rulers comes from the eldest sister of the maharaja, whose son is the king, followed by his brothers and the sons of the other sisters. Thus the Maharani is the king's sister, not his wife, and the sister's son is the next king. There is no doubting the power of Shoorpanakha who sends Ravana to capture Sita and orders him to fight Rama, even as Ravana's wife Mandodari advises him against such an action. But it is the sister who is heeded, not the wife. Finally, Ravana's successor is his brother Vibhishana, reaffirming the matrilineal inheritance.

Till recently, women of several Malayali communities chose to have a *sambandham* or association with a Brahmana who fathered their children, while the women continued to live with their own family. The children born of this alliance are proud of their Sanskrit heritage, even while they live within a matriarchal system. Ravana was also a great Sanskrit scholar and equally proud of his paternal genealogy.

Ravana's maternal grandfather's name is Malayavan, which means inhabitant of the mountains, a synonym for Malayali. Malayavan sees portents predicting the destruction of the

Rakshasas and recognizes that Vishnu has been born as Rama. He advises his grandson to return Sita to Rama and to make an alliance with Rama. The name Malayavan is of Tamil origin and means a mountain-dweller of the Malabar region; malai/ malaya = mountains, generally referring to the hills bordering Malabar;[14] avan = he (Tamil). Could the name be an indication of Ravana's origin?

There are two other reasons to support this belief. Firstly, the *Dipavansha*, the Sinhala Buddhist chronicle of Sri Lanka says that the last Buddha's first visit to the island was to 'dispel the Rakshasas and put away the Pishachas'. Lanka was covered with great forests and full of horrors: 'frightful cruel blood-thirsty Yakkhas of various kinds and savage, furious and pernicious Pishachas'. He sent down 'rain, cold winds and darkness' and later 'intense heat, to escape from which the Yakkhas could merely stand on the shore'. Finally, he permitted the Yakkhas and Rakshasas to escape to an island called Giridipa, 'the Island of Hills', a name, according to Parker, 'which may possibly indicate Malayalam, "the Mountain Region". The *Rajavaliya* terms the place Yak-giri-duwa, "the Island of Demon Hills", described as beautifully adorned by rivers, mountains and lakes . . . full of excellent food and rich grain, with a well-tempered climate, a green, grassy land . . . adorned by gardens and forests; there were trees full of blossoms and fruits . . . around it there was a chain of mountains, towering, difficult to pass.'[15] To continue this theory, there are the Eelavas of Kerala who are believed to have come from ancient Lanka or Eelam, and are even named after the island.

The Rakshasas and the Yakshas are born of the same mother, Khasa, daughter of Daksha, thus accounting for the siblings Ravana and Kuvera, the latter described as a Yaksha. Both Ravana and his half-brother Kuvera claim their inheritance from their mothers. Such an arrangement would have seemed extremely strange and anārya to the patriarchal society of Ayodhya. Many of the Rakshasas and later Asuras are fathered by Aryas or Devas. Naraka was the son of Varaha, the boar; Mahisha was also the son of Varaha, Vishnu's boar incarnation. But they chose to take the mother's family name.

In the *Mahabharata*, the Rakshasas are described as mountain-dwellers, disturbing sacrifices, rituals and the meditations of sages. Just as the Asuras are the enemies of the gods, the Rakshasas are the enemies of people. They come out at night, their greatest strength after 'the first forty seconds of grey twilight preceding nightfall'. They are called sorcerers and evil mortals and dangerous. They travel faster than the wind and can change shape. Sometimes they appear as tigers, bears or monkeys—or even a deer—in a myriad colours. In the *Ramayana* they are associated with the Rakshasas of Lanka, grotesque dwarfs and ugly giants. The *Mahabharata* says that they feast on human beings and cattle. The Devas or gods help the Aryans defeat the evil Rakshasas: Agni burns them or Indra kills them.

Ravana's ten heads are his distinguishing feature, something to which no other god or demon can lay claim. His ten heads make him so powerful that, every time one head is cut off, another appears. Rama has to destroy all ten heads to kill the demon king. There is one precedent for this unique feature: the ten-headed and ten-armed Hittite (Hatti) king who fought Ramses II at the Battle of Kadesh. Although the scene on the wall of Ramses II's temple at Abu Simbel depicts a tall Ramses looming over and attacking a crouching ten-armed Hittite, in reality the Egyptians could not defeat the Hittites and entered into a peace treaty in 1269 BC. The Aryan Mittanis, mentioned earlier, were allies of the Egyptians against their common

enemy, the Hittites. Ramses II built a temple for his beloved
wife Nefertari, the first time in ancient Egyptian history, besides
building her statue equal in size to his own, the only occasion
in Egyptian art. He is regarded as Egypt's greatest and most
powerful pharaoh, and has inspired several works of art and
literature, including Percy Bysshe Shelley's famous poem
Ozymandias, and the film *Prince of Egypt*, a legend where he is
portrayed as Moses's adoptive brother.[16] While the similarity
between Ramses and Rama is restricted to their names, for the
two led very different lives, did the ten-headed enemy of Ramses
inspire the image of Ravana? Maybe—we will never know.

Kamsa

The most important demon of the *Mahabharata* is Kamsa,
Krishna's maternal uncle, the wicked king of Mathura. He
imprisoned his sister Devaki and her husband Vasudeva when
he heard the prophecy that their eighth child would kill him.
But the baby Krishna was taken away to the home of Nanda in
Gokul. Kamsa ordered the death of all male babies, but Krishna
escaped. Kamsa tried to have Krishna killed several times, but
Krishna escaped every attempt, till he killed Kamsa. Kamsa
was not born a demon—after all, he was Krishna's uncle and
a Yadava—but he is referred to as the Asura Kalanemi, who
was a descendant of Hiranyakashipu. This was obviously a
case of the deeds overtaking the man.

Ghatotkacha

Half Pandava, half Rakshasa, Ghatotkacha is certainly no evil
demon. In fact he is a lovable giant and his death is one of the
most tragic events of the Kurukshetra war. Bhima the Pandava

marries a female Rakshasa (Rakshasi) named Hidambaa and the couple have a son, Ghatotkacha, the lovable giant who fights alongside the Pandavas and is killed in the Kurukshetra war. The association of Bhima and Hidambaa is very important. Her brother Hidamba is a ferocious and fearless fighter who takes on Bhima in combat. Hidamba is defeated and killed, after which his sister Hidambaa proposes marriage to Bhima. Bhima accepts, after obtaining permission from his mother Kunti. Initially, Kunti is shocked to see her son live in a tree house with his Rakshasi wife, but after Hidambaa builds Kunti a house on the ground and behaves like a good daughter-in-law, Kunti is won over. Unlike the complicated and powerful Draupadi, Hidambaa is a simple wife for the gentle and simple Bhima. Yet, when the time comes for the Pandavas to leave the forest, Hidambaa chooses to stay behind with her son Ghatotkacha, while Bhima leaves with his brothers, leaving the son whom he has brought up himself with his Rakshasi wife. In a patriarchal society this would be unthinkable. And Bhima never sees his son again till he returns to ask his help for the war.

Bhima's association with Hidambaa also brings into focus the many alliances that the Pandavas made to prepare for the war they had every intention of fighting to reclaim their kingdom. The unfriendly brother Hidamba is disposed of, the Rakshasi married and a half-Pandava child placed in line for the throne. Here again the undemonic quality of the Rakshasas and their strategy comes in. If the Rakshasas had really been evil demons, it would be unthinkable for Bhima to marry one and father another. For Ghatotkacha is always called a Rakshasa, never a Pandava, in typical matrilineal fashion. They were obviously a powerful tribe with whom a marriage alliance was sealed as future security.

Mahisha

The next important epic demon is Mahisha, son of Rambha (not to be confused with Rambhā, the apsaras), demon son of Kashyapa and Danu, and a Mahishi (female buffalo). Rambha and his wife were killed by a giant buffalo. The son grew up to become the king of the mahishas.

The demon lived in the Vindhya Mountains and, by the practice of severe austerities, gained the strength to drive the gods out of the heavens. So Brahma, Vishnu and Shiva issued flames from their mouths. Durga emanated from these flames as a beautiful woman with ten arms, riding a lion (sometimes she is depicted riding a tiger). She held each deity's special weapon in each of her ten hands: discus, conch, club, trident, spear, flame, bow, arrow and quiver, snake and the thunderbolt. As Durga approached the Vindhyas, the demon tried to capture her. Unable to do so, the demon attacked her under several forms, each of which was destroyed by Durga. Finally, Durga killed Mahisha.

Mahisha is associated with the town of Mysore (formerly Mahisha-*ūrū* or city of Mahisha the buffalo), named after him. In fact, it is locally believed that he was a local ruler killed by the goddess, and a huge statue of a mustachioed male figure of Mahisha holding a sword and a snake stands at the foot of the Chamundeshvari Hill, at the top of which stands the temple of Durga as Chamundi, killer of Mahisha.

Whom did the goddess defeat? Less than 100 kilometres from Mysore are the Nilgiri Hills where the Toda tribe lives, a tribe that worships the buffalo as a god and whose origins are shrouded in mystery. The Todas venerate the buffalo, whose horns adorn their temples. The Todas are buffalo herders and, until recently, supplied milk to the other tribes through a tribal barter system. So sacred are the buffaloes that no other tribe was allowed to own any. The Toda buffaloes are enormous, handsome animals who are fierce fighters if approached by strangers. It is likely that the Todas were buffalo worshippers who were defeated by the followers of the goddess. The Todas also have a tradition of being the palanquin bearers of Ravana, from whose atrocities they fled. Besides the buffalo-worshipping Todas, there is also a sub-caste called Mahishi in Karnataka, whose followers still worship the buffalo and the Goddess Chamundi.

There is also a sexual tension between Durga and Mahisha, who was a suitor and wanted to marry her. Mahisha was obviously a leader of a buffalo-totem tribe, destroyed by the goddess. Were the Todas the followers of Mahisha the buffalo, and therefore were known as the Mahishas/Mahishis or buffalo people? Were they driven out of the fertile green banks of the Kaveri River by a new people worshipping a new goddess? Very likely.

In Maharashtra the demon Mahshoba (Mahisha + bā or father), who was killed by Parvati, is held in high esteem and venerated by the lower castes, particularly cultivators. Fowl and goat are sacrificed to Mahshoba.

The cairns of the Nilgiris, believed to have been deserted by the Todas, are called *moriaru manay* or house of the Morias. The word could also be synonymous for the Marias of central India.[17] Besides the Nilgiri hills in south India, central India is also famous for buffalo totem tribes like the Marias and Gonds, who even wear the buffalo horns on festive occasions. The Marias also worship Danteshvari Devi, besides the buffalo. Here both the goddess and the buffalo deity are revered.

Mahisha is also associated with the town of Mahishmati, situated south of the river Godavari, on a tributary of the river Krishna, and was founded by King Mahishmat, whose name imples that he was rich in buffaloes. The region was ruled by King Nila of Dakshinapatha, and his subjects were called Mahishakas.[18] This is also the region of the Gond tribes.

The destruction of the demon by the goddess shows that the demonization of the defeated ruler was a universal trait not restricted to the Aryans. Durga was a non-Vedic goddess. Apart from the lack of similar goddesses in the Vedic tradition, early references to Durga associate her with the Vindhyas, giving her the epithet Vindhyavasini; tribes such as the Shabaras were her worshippers, and they had non-Vedic habits such as drinking blood and eating meat or offering flesh. She creates helpers such as Kali and the bloodthirsty Matrikas, who are wild, bloodthirsty and particularly fierce. She is not submissive, does no household duties and excels in battle, being a fierce independent warrior. The word durg means fortress, and the goddess is as formidable as a fortress.

The sacrifice of the buffalo to Durga is practised all over India, particularly during the festival of Navaratri which celebrates the war between the goddess and the demon. Mysore is particularly famed for the celebration of Navaratri, when the image of Goddess Chamunda, whose temple is on the Chamundi hill, is taken out in ceremonial procession on an elephant.

Like the Rakshasas of the *Ramayana* and *Mahabharata* who were distinctly human, Mahisha is also an example of the demonization of a god or ruler whose people were defeated by the worshippers of Devi.

DEMON WOMEN

Demon women are described as unkempt, uncouth, ill-mannered and so on. But they are emancipated and fight for their rights, like Tataka who haunted the forests of the river

Sarayu, destroyed the sacrifice and even the cities of Malada and Karusha. She tried to recapture Siddhashrama, hermitage of King Bali, till it was taken over by Vishwamitra. Her sticks and stones are no match for Rama's skilled archery, and she is finally killed.

Two women stand out in particular. The first is Shoorpanakha or the long-nailed one. She is the opposite of Sita. She is initially described as ugly, pot-bellied, cross-eyed, harsh-voiced, crude, evil and cruel, while Sita is good and pure, beautiful, shy and retiring. However, the epic also adds that she took on a beautiful appearance, so her appearance could not have been too bad. Shoorpanakha is daring and bold, and takes on a beautiful form to proposition Rama and then Lakshmana. Sita would never make overtures to a man or approach him sexually. When Sita is abducted, she waits patiently for her husband to rescue her. Shoorpanakha, when attacked by Lakshmana, requisitions her brothers' help to kill Rama, Lakshmana and Sita for insulting her, and wants to drink their blood. She is overtly sexual, 'forward' and aggressive, traits not appreciated in women in the patriarchal Aryan world. She is the undesirable female and the epic is scathing in its criticism of her behaviour. She forms the antithesis to Sita who is held up as the model woman and a role model for feminine behaviour.

Shoorpanakha is a very powerful woman. She is able to persuade her brother to abduct Sita and fight Rama, even against the advice of his gentle wife Mandodari, who appears to have little or no influence on her husband. There is already a strong hint of the matrilineal in Ravana's origins. As the ruler's sister, Shoorpanakha would have been the all-powerful queen. As one of the villains of the epic, she was condemned to be a demon. On the other hand, Mandodari, though also born a

Rakshasi and daughter of Maya, architect of the demons, is never demonized but is praised for her gentleness (and ineffectiveness) and immortalized as one of the panchakanyas. Thus, it was not the geneology but behaviour that characterized the demon.

The other important Rakshasi is Hidambaa, sister of Hidamba and wife of Bhima. Bhima's years in the forest, married to Hidambaa and parenting Ghatotkacha, were among the happiest in his life. Hidambaa gave birth to a powerful—but good—demon Ghatotkacha, who took part in the Mahabharata war and killed several Kaurava warriors.

HIDAMBAA

Hidambaa had the ability to look into the past and the future—apparently she was a soothsayer. Such women, in Christian Europe, were called witches. Hidambaa's proposal of marriage to Bhima does not take away from the epic's general approval of her, but it is mentioned as being different and unwomanly. Her Rakshasa background is used to explain away her different behaviour. When the Pandavas leave the forest, she takes the decision to stay behind with her people and give Ghatotkacha the inheritance that is rightfully his as the son of King Hidamba's sister. However, she also promises her own and her son's help if ever they are called. Marriage to Hidambaa gives the Pandavas a powerful ally.

What is striking about Rakshasa women is their independence, their assertion of their sexual urges, their ability to decide on the men they wished to marry and to make all the moves. Whereas the establishment women were demure like Sita or complicated like Draupadi; neither was independent nor did they make their own destiny.

Rakshasa women had no hesitation in bringing up their children on their own and giving them their name. Famous Rakshasas like Mahisha and Jarasandha are named after their mothers. It was the non-Aryan Dravidas, Mundas and other tribals who had matrilineal systems that must have seemed very strange, even immoral, to the patriarchal establishment.

CONCLUSION

The distinct social structures and the good qualities of many demons distinguish them from supernatural demons or negative natural phenomena. Thus they can only be demonized human beings.

It would be easy to dismiss Rakshasas as demons. However, the word demon presumes something evil. People like Vibhishana and Bali belie such a meaning. Ravana, a great Vedic scholar, and Rakshasa, the Nanda and Mauryan prime minister, were certainly no demons. Yet they were all Rakshasas, leading us to conclude that the term Rakshasa meant something else, not an evil character. The strongest clue is the historical prime minister of the Mauryas, Rakshasa, who was surely no demon. The frequent appearance of names derived from Ravana among certain communities and the great qualities of certain Rakshasas like Bali and Hidambaa also prevent their demonization. If they were still classified as Rakshasas, the word surely meant something else.

The killing of the buffalo is as ancient as Indian civilization. In a terracotta tablet found at Harappa, a character wearing a bun is slaughtering a buffalo before a figure seated in a yogic posture wearing the same 'tricorn' headdress as the so-called Pashupati figure. On the other side of the tablet is a female figure holding two tigers apart, with a wheel above and an elephant below. The various associations of the goddess are unmistakable: the slaying of the buffalo, and the tiger, which is her vehicle in later art. The killing of the buffalo in front of a yogic figure suggests that it was a ritual sacrifice[19].

The *Rig Veda* calls the Rakshasas sorcerers and magicians. It is likely that they were Tantrists, more so since most were worshippers of Shiva or Shakti. Maybe their utilization of the occult did not endear them to either the pantheistic Vedic people or the ritualistic and philosophic Aryans. It was not that their manners and customs, their social structure and moral values, were so alien to the Aryans that Rakshasa, the name of a tribe, came to mean demon. Those tribes that continued to threaten the people of the later Vedic and epic period were demonized, even as epic heroes continued to be related to them as were the Devas and Asuras.

NOTES

1. Norman, D., *op.cit,,* p. 5.
2. Pargiter, F.E., *Ancient Indian Historical Tradition*, pp. 291–300.
3. Parker, H., *Ancient Ceylon*, p. 668.
4. Tod, J., *Annals and Antiquities of Rajasthan.*
5. Hopkins, *Epic Mythology*, p. 43.
6. *Ibid*, p. 46.
7. *Ibid*, p. 44.
8. Mackenzie, *Indian Myth and Legend*, p. 65.
9. Dowson, pp. 234–235.
10. Hopkins, *op.cit.*, p. 45.
11. Shulman, D.D., *Tamil Temple Myths*, pp. 317–320.
12. Shulman, D.D., *The King and the Clown in South Indian Myth and Poetry*, pp. 100–108.
13. H. Parker, *op. cit.*, p. 8.
14. Dowson, *op. cit.*, p. 195.
15. Parker, *op.cit.*, pp. 12–13.
16. http://en.wikipedia.org/wiki/Ramesses_II.
17. Oppert, G., *The Original Inhabitants of India*, pp. 183–187.
18. Kinsley, D., *Hindu Goddesses*, pp. 96–97.
19. Kenoyer, Jonathan Mark, *Ancient Cities of the Indus Valley Civilization*, p. 114.

4

Non-Demonized Enemies

There is a definite distinction between the demonized and non-demonized enemies of the Aryans. Not all enemies were demonized.

The demonized enemies were of divine, supernatural or spiritual origin, be they Asura, Rakshasa, Pishacha, Daitya or Danava. The Dasas, Dasyus and Nagas were groups who either integrated with the Aryans or were overpowered by them, so they ceased to exist as a distinct genre. Those who did not integrate were also called Asuras.

Later, as the integrated peoples of the post-Vedic period came across new tribes, those who were antagonistic were labelled demons—Asuras and Rakshasas—while the rest were known by their tribal names. Thus Vanaras, Savaras and Ahirs are respected, while the Rakshasa tribe disappeared: they probably integrated with some other tribe rather than be labelled demons. Many tribes disappeared into the forests of India where they preserved their ancient cultures.

The epics Ramayana and Mahabharata are a cornucopia of information about the various demons that plagued the gods and people. The gods invariably defeated the demons, reaffirming the triumph of good over evil. This was essential to maintain social harmony.

DASA, DASYU

Dasas, Dasyus and Nagas were constant enemies of the Aryans but were never demonized.

The *Rig Veda* describes the Dasyus/Dasas as without rituals (akarma), inhuman (amanushah), vowless (avrata), without Brahmanas (abrāhmana), possessing māya (māyāvat) and more. There are specific names of Dasas and Dasyus such as Pipru, Namuchi, Varchin, Sambara, Chumuri, and Sushna in the *Rig Veda*, indicating that they were actual people. The Veda distinguishes between the Aryans and the Dasyus, and Indra specifically aids the Aryans against the Dasyus. It is clear that they are a separate people distinct from the Aryans and against whom the Aryans fought. Dasyu is also synonymous with Dasa and Daha, the latter a word of Iranian origin meaning robber, and probably describing the food gatherers. Indra is their implacable enemy in nearly every verse in which they appear. The word Dasyu becomes rare after the *Atharva Veda*. They had probably been absorbed by the Aryans and the term was no longer used for them.

The word Dasa has come to mean slave. But the earliest use of this word described people who opposed the Aryans of the *Rig Veda*. They are described as dark, evil, and enemies of the Devas (gods) and Aryans. Dasa meant robber, savage, barbarian, while its variant meant fisherman, ferryman, mariner, occupations that would have been common along the Sindhu (Indus) and Sarasvati rivers. The clan father of the Dasas was Dasa: *dāsasya apatyam puman iti dāsah*.

The related word in the Persian language is dāha (s in Sanskrit is h in ancient Persian), which means robber. It is likely that the Dasas or Dasyus, who are described as robbers and barbarians, were food gatherers who helped themselves to the cattle of the pastoral people of the early Vedic period. This is substantiated by the Rig Vedic story of the Dasyu Pani, described as 'senseless, false, evil-speaking, not believing, not praising, not worshipping' and every nasty epithet that one can use for an enemy. They stole the cows and hid them in caves. They were pursued by Sarama, Indra's dog, who recovered the cows.

Dasas are described as jealous-hearted and repulsive in appearance. They steal the cloud-cows held captive in the cave of the demon Vala. This is probably a reference to the cattle thieves who would have harassed the pastoral Aryans.

It is interesting that, in spite of the obvious enmity between the Dasas and the Aryans, the former were never demonized. The reason is to be found in the changed meaning of the word. Dasas were conquered and enslaved. The Rakshasas, on the other hand, continued to be powerful and prosper.

The *Rig Veda* and *Atharva Veda* equate Panis with Dasas and Dasyus. They are enemies of the Aryans, and their cows are robbed by Indra. Yet Pani is described by Yaska in *Nirkuta* as *Pani vanij*, or Pani the trader.

NAGA

Nagas are semi-divine mythical beings, with human heads and snake bodies. Yet they were also a historical people of the same name, probably snake-worshipping Shakas (Scythians) of the trans-Himalayan region. Their symbol was the hooded

NAGAS

cobra or cobra-capella, which appears time and again in Indian art and religion.[1]

According to mythology, Nagas were the sons of rishi Kashyapa and his wife Kadru, their step-brother being Garuda, son of Kashyapa and Kadru's sister Vinata. The Nagas and Garuda were constantly at war till the Nagas were all destroyed at Janmejaya's sacrifice. The Nagas were born in Patala, also called Nagaloka, probably in the Himalayan foothills, or in Kashmir. Several towns in the north are still named after them, like Taxila or Takshashila, the town of the Naga Takshaka.

The Nagas were believed to be armed with deadly venom, but possessed the nectar of life and immortality. They appear frequently in Epic literature (rather than in the Vedas) where they are constantly at war with the Aryans. Indra's arch-enemy, the demon Vritra, is also described as a Naga and an Asura although he was a mythical figure.

Kashyapa and Kadru are credited with the founding of the nation of Nagas. Takshaka and Vasuki were the greatest of their seven children, and were cursed to be born on earth and burned alive for not obeying their mother's command. The story of the Nagas is delineated in the *Vishnu Purana*. Kadru and Vinata were the two wives of Kashyapa, Kadru the mother of twelve (the *Vayu Purana* mentions forty, some accounts say one thousand) Nagas including Shesha, Takshaka and Vasuki, and Vinata, mother of Garuda. The two wives bet on the colour of the tail of Uchchaishravas, the divine horse. Kadru ordered her sons to cover the tail to make it look black. Takshaka the eldest refused and was cursed by his mother to be burnt to death. Shesha is another who became the king of Patala, the netherworld and is closely associated with Vishnu. He forms Narayana's couch in the bottom of the waters. In fact Shesha has come to represent water itself. Another Naga is Vasuki who was used as the rope that was wound around Mount Mandara during the churning of the ocean. Their sister is Manasa Devi or Vishahara, who had the ability to neutralize the venom of the serpents.

Takshaka became very arrogant and bit King Parikshit to death. Parikshit's grandson Janmejaya held a snake sacrifice (sarpa yajña) to rid the earth of snakes, especially Takshaka. The latter hid beside Brahma, but was brought out by the magical spell of the chief priest Uttanka who consigned them to the fire. As they were being burnt alive, the Brahmana Astika appeared and was offered any boon of his choosing. Astika asked for an immediate end to the sacrifice, and Janmejaya acceded to his request.

Ulupi, princess of the Nagas and daughter of Kauravya, king of the Nagas, married Arjuna when the Pandavas were banished to the forest. She gave birth to his son Iravat.

The Nagas were a historical people who, after they lost their lands, moved to the Narmada river, which they called their sister, and which is also the location of Nagpur, the city of Nagas. Modern Taxila (ancient Takshasila) in Pakistan is named after the Naga king Takshaka (although sometimes it is said to be named after Taksha, son of Bharata and nephew of Rama). The Nagas were an ancient and respected tribe of India, obviously snake worshippers, and often play a historical role. Several ancient dynasties claim origin from them.

But there were good Nagas and bad ones. The thousand sons of Vinata are an example of evil Nagas, while Shesha (Ananta), Vishnu's couch, is a good Naga. Many later rulers of south India, including the Cholas, claimed descent from the Nagas. Many towns are named after them, such as Nagpur, Nagapattinam and Nagarkovil.

MLECCHA

They were foreigners, barbarians and non-Aryans.[2] They were uncouth and did not follow the Vedic religion. The *Vishnu Purana* says that many Kshatriya races who were deprived of the study of the Vedas and of religious rites had been degraded by Sagara, and thus became Mlecchas. But they were not regarded as demons because they did not disturb the Vedic rituals.

Bhagadatta, king of Pragjyotisha (north-east India), who took part in the great Kurukshetra war with a contingent of Chinas (Chinese) is called a Mlecchha (*Mahabharata*, 2. 18. 25), although his city is referred to as belonging to the Daityas, Danavas and Dasyus (*Mahabharata*, 5. 47; 12. 341).

NISHADA, PULINDA AND BARBARA

They were a mountain tribe of the Vindhyas who are identified with Nala, the Bhils and forest tribes. The term is also used to describe outcastes, born of a Brahmana father and Shudra mother.[3]

When the childless king Vena of the Angas died, the sages rubbed the thigh of the dead man, from which rose the flat-faced, short and dark Nishada, from whom came the Nishada tribe of the Vindhyas, famed for their wicked deeds. From the right arm of Vena came Prithu, another son (*Mahabharata*).

According to a later version in the *Padma Purana*, Vena fell under Jaina influence. For this he was pummelled by the sages till the Nishadas came out of his thigh and Prithu from his right arm.

Prithu was the first king and father of Prithvi or Earth. Thus we see a repetition of the tribal association with Mother Earth as a supreme deity. Although this is a repetition of the Bhuta imagery, Nishadas were never identified with demons.

Barbarians who lived in the forests and mountains of northern and central India, and along the Sindhu River were known as Pulindas and Barbaras.[4]

They were non-Aryans and foreigners, described as barbarians, who lived outside the Indian subcontinent and who did not follow Sanatana Dharma or Hinduism (*Mahabharata*).

CONCLUSION

Why were some enemies demonized and others not?

The character and nature of the enemy were the deciding factors. Dasas or Dasyus were food gatherers who were easily overpowered, defeated and enslaved. Nagas were powerful allies, both political and matrimonial, though obviously non-Vedic. Mlechhas were uncouth foreigners and barbarians, but not enemies. Tribes like the Nishadas and Pulindas moved away to the hills and forests and kept to themselves.

On the other hand, enemies like Ravana and Kamsa were great warriors and defeating them was a matter of pride. Their lands were also coveted and taken over. The battles were long and hard-fought.

Further, when heroes such as Rama and Krishna were deified, demonizing their enemies was an automatic corollary, for gods could only fight demons, not people. The gods were invoked to help people against their own demons and enemies, so they could not be seen as antagonistic to human beings. Demonizing their enemies enhanced the stature of the deified heroes, especially if the enemy was a ten-headed monster who could shake the Himalayan mountain Kailasa, like Ravana, or was the ruler of the northern heartland like Kamsa, or was the powerful buffalo-king of the Deccan Plateau like Mahisha. It was also an Indian way of attributing the victory to supernatural forces, to humble oneself before the actions of the divine.

REFERENCES

1. Dowson, J., *A Classical Dictionary of Hindu Mythology and Religion*, p. 213.
2. *Ibid.*, p. 209.
3. *Ibid.*, p. 224.
4. *Ibid.*, p. 244.

5

Spirits, Ghosts and Others

DEMONOPHOBIA

Khanam, in the book *Demonology* (2003), traces Indian demonophobia to demonolatry, or demon worship, 'a form of belief in its origin independent of Brahmanism or the orthodox form of Hinduism'.[1] While the vast mythology surrounding the Asuras, Rakshasas and others would prevent them from coming under Khanam's definitions, there are undoubtedly many demons who are malevolent spirits and ghosts of the dead.

BHUTA

The Bhutas are spirits of the dead, some of whom become malevolent due to the form of their death, either by murder, execution or suicide. They live in cemeteries, haunt trees, enter dead bodies and attack human beings whose flesh they eat. They are malignant beings, fiends who owe allegiance to Shiva, their lord and ruler, who is often called Bhuteshvara and

Bhutanatha. They are born from Krodha, or anger. The Vedas and Puranas warn against the worship of Bhuta (or spirit worship). The *Bhagavad Gita* warns people against the worship of Bhutas or spirits, saying 'those who worship me (God) come to me and those who worship Bhutas go to Bhutas after death.'

Bhu means earth and the suffix ta means give (in Tamil), so Bhuta means 'given by' or 'formed' or 'created' from the earth. Yet the Bhuta never rests on the ground. Bhuta was a deity of the earth who was and still is worshipped in rural India, by castes outside the pale of the conventional caste system, by people who feared their gods as creatures of malevolence. Not unnaturally, he became a demon who haunted cemeteries, a veritable ghost who has plagued the mind of people from time immemorial. He is an earth spirit, who inspires fear and dread.

Bhutas inhabit crematoriums, burial grounds and deserts. They also inhabit old houses, especially ruins, which is why there is great reluctance among local people to excavate an old ruin or ancient site, for it will disturb the resting souls who will then attack the grave diggers. They are night wanderers, found in the company of Rakshasas and Yakshas. Mines and caves are also the natural abode of spirits, many of whom, such as Saptashri Devi of the Konkan, live in caves. Bhutas are also guardians of treasure, which is believed to be hidden in caves and beneath the ground of ancient buildings and ruins.

But the Bhutas, even as they live on the fringes of Vedic culture, are an essential part of folk tradition. They are the recipients of offerings or bali, which are offered to them after the gods and between the guests and the pitṛs (forefathers), in that order. In the forest, Sita makes her offerings first to the Bhutas who inhabit the wild. Shiva is the Bhutapati, the lord of the spirits, as he is of the ganas (dwarfs). His constituency is made up of the unknown: spirits of the dead and dwarfs, a world of magic and fantasy. The non-Vedic Bhutas lived on the fringes of the heavenly host, as demonic spirits. Their leader Shiva became Bhutanatha, one of the primary deities of composite Hinduism.

Bhutas are found at crossroads and on the boundaries of villages. It is customary, all over India, to plant an iron stake at a crossroad and bury grains beneath it for crows to eat. An image of Ganesha may also be installed as a deterrent to spirits who could otherwise haunt the place.

Bhuta generally denotes the spirit of a person who has died an unnatural death, such as an accident, suicide or even capital punishment, or of one for whom the funeral ceremonies were not carried out, thereby denying the spirit rest. For example, a man who dies without any male offspring or competent persons to carry out his death rites becomes a Bhuta and, in particular, harasses young sons of others. To offset the evil effects of such spirits, a blessing is wrapped in a silver foil and tied around the boy's neck, or a coin engraved with a dog (as a protector) may be tied around the waist. A widow who remarries may be haunted by the spirit of her first husband.

They are not ghosts: they occupy a space between ghosts and the eaters of raw flesh, but evil Bhutas are closely associated with ghosts. Bhutas are most feared by women and children whom they haunt. They are also used to scare little children away from areas that may be physically dangerous.

The *Vishnu Purana* says they were fierce eaters of human flesh, and that they were created by Brahma in a moment of anger, while the *Vayu Purana* says that their mother was Krodha or anger. But in North Indian folk culture, Bhutas are particularly fond of fresh milk.

Most folk and tribal demons are Bhutas or spirits. Bhutas inhabit a sub-world of magical spells by which they possess unwary people. They must not be provoked, for they are quick to anger and can cause untold harm and hardship to their captives. They can only be driven away by more powerful beings that are invoked by witch doctors with special powers and training. They are ghosts, goblins and imps who lurk in wait to capture human beings.

The Bhuta is identified by three characteristics: firstly, he does not cast a shadow; secondly, he speaks with a nasal twang; thirdly, he stays away from the sight and smell of turmeric, particularly burning turmeric. He enters the body through the mouth, hands, feet and ears. Therefore, the first three must be kept scrupulously clean, while the ears must be covered with cloth on early or chilly mornings.

No discussion of Bhutas will be complete without an examination of Shiva's role as Bhuteshvara or Bhutanatha, lord of the spirits. One of his names Sharaveshvara (derived from shara or sharu meaning arrow) means 'the god who kills with arrows'. In the *Avesta*, Sharva is a daeva or demon, a malevolent being symbolizing the tyrant. In the Shakta, Tantric and Mahayana Buddhist cults, Shiva is identified as Kala and becomes Mahakala, Bhairava and Bhima. Death had to be symbolized by a major god, and Shiva assumed the role. His Vedic followers are the Rudrah, Rudrasah and Marutah (not Maruts), who make up his troops. They are associated with death and are identified as spirits hovering around cremation grounds. According to the *Mahabharata*, their wrath is feared, and the retinue consists of deformed beast-faced creatures, devouring human flesh, praising Shiva and making merry. They are red in colour, dwarfish, deformed and resemble various abhorrent and ferocious creatures, with obnoxious, funny and repulsive manners. They roam the earth, but their permanent home is Varanasi, where Shiva and Gauri live. Says Bhattacharji, 'One has the impression that they do not belong to the world of the living or to the plane of normality. Hence one is driven to the conclusion that this sombre and dread god is surrounded by spectres, spirits who have passed on—a belief which lingers even now, for Shiva is Bhutanatha, and the word Bhuta . . . has come to mean ghost, as Shiva is also Pramathesha—lord of the Pramathas (tormentors), and these are undoubtedly spirits. These terms connect Shiva with the spectre world, where the ghosts roam at his bidding, ghosts with whom he lives in the cremation ground . . . At the back of these spirits, metempsychosis may have been at work . . . these ancestor spirits became the constant companion of Pramathesha.'[2]

One aspect which sets Shiva apart in the epic period is his fondness for flesh, or rather, the continued practice of his followers to propitiate him with flesh—even human—at a time when sacrifices were losing their popularity. The Tantric animal and human sacrifices to Shiva in the northern tradition were anathema to the vegetarian Vaishnava cult. According to the *Harivamsha* (a sectarian Vaishnava work), Shiva is the lord of Pishachas and it was his dreaded spirit retinue which perpetrated the destruction at Daksha's sacrifice. In fact it was left to southern Shaivism, particularly the Shaiva saints of Tamil Nadu, to bring out the more ascetic and peaceful nature of Shiva. Many of the demons are given boons of immense power by Shiva, and Vishnu is forced to incarnate himself to rid the world of the scourge. While much of the negative image of Shiva was due to Vaishnava–Shaiva rivalry, the practices of the Kapalikas and Kalamukhas, their invocation of spirits and demons and their use of skull mendicant bowls and garlands of skulls would undoubtedly have added to his fearsome image. Shiva is often seen on the threshold of demonhood through his association with demons, although he himself is a killer of several.

The creation of Duryodhana is attributed to kritya, a sorcery ritual, by which the villain of the epic is an accomplice of Bhuta demons and is created by Shiva's magic (*Mahabharata*, III. 240). The Bhutas play an important role in the 'Sauptikaparva' of

the *Mahabharata*. Ashvatthama, son of Drona, is devastated
by the death of the Kauravas, especially his friend Duryodhana.
He decides to avenge the death of his father and friend. His
friends advise him to get a good night's sleep and fight the
Pandavas the next day. But Ashvatthama, in a combination of
grief and cowardice, cannot wait. He rushes off to the enemies'
camp to kill them as they sleep. But, before he enters, he
encounters a Bhuta with flames coming out of his eyes, who
prevents his entrance. Immediately, Ashvatthama worships
Shiva and offers himself in sacrifice. The offer has its effect:
Shiva gives Ashvatthama a glittering sword, and says that the
Pandavas' time was running out. The divine weapon frightens
off the Bhuta, and Ashvatthama enters the camp to commit his
dastardly deed of killing the allies, children and grandchildren
of the Pandavas as they sleep. In this story the Bhutas appear
to be the watchmen of the Pandavas, and could be defeated
only by the sword of Shiva.

Khanam has recorded several spirit traditions. The headless
horsemen or Dund are believed to be the ghosts of warriors
of the *Mahabharata*. Like the Bir, each Dund also rides around
the village at night, his head tied on the pommel in front of
him. In Mirzapur he is known as Baghesar or the Tiger Lord.
Many are the tales, in North India, of brave warriors whose
heads were cut off, yet their headless bodies continued to fight
till they could reach their village or even burial places. Faizabad,
Ajmer and elsewhere in North India are sites of headless
horsemen wandering around, generally the relics of Hindu-
Muslim wars. A similar figure in Bengal is the Skandhakata,
headless beings living outside villages in swamps and marshland.

The Masan (derived from the word smashan or
crematorium) of the Himalayan region could be the ghost of
a child or a low-caste man or an animal. It has a black and

hideous face, and inhabits crematoriums and burial grounds. This spirit takes possession of innocent people and can only be driven away by a benevolent spirit. A similar spirit from the same region is the Khabish. The Himalayan Airi is the ghost of a hunter who was killed during the hunt and haunts the forest where the accident occurred. Anyone who sees the Airi is burnt to ashes or torn to pieces by his dogs, but whoever survives it receives hidden treasures from the spirit. Other spirits of the hills are Acheri, the ghosts of little girls, the Deo (from Deva) who harass men and cattle, and the Runiya who uses a rock as his vehicle and haunts avalanches and landslides.

MASAN

In 1820, it was reported that the population of the Kumaon was divided into human beings and ghosts. The Tharus of the Himalayan terai believe that bhuts haunt the trees in the forest, especially the cotton tree (*Bombax heptaphyllum*), and the Pretas, or spirits of the dead, give them a tough time. When darkness descends on their villages, they all huddle together inside their huts and will not come out except for fires. Even during the day, no Tharu man, woman or child will go into the forest without casting a leaf, branch or piece of old rag upon the bansati (Sanskrit vanaspati or 'lord of the woods') at the entrance to the forest which can save them from the diseases and accidents the malignant spirits of the forest can cause.[3]

In south India, spirits are deemed to be responsible for every unfortunate event and infectious disease, for the deaths of animals, human beings and every malignant event. They are all-pervading, waiting to enter the home, individual and even the soul when a rule is broken. So the Mother Goddess Amman is propitiated to drive away the evil Bhutas or spirits who would otherwise make life a misery. Every village has its spirit—some malignant, others protectors. They are propitiated by bloody animal sacrifices which, in pre-Independence India, included human, especially child, sacrifice. The religion of the Indian village is one of fear, leading to propitiation of spirits to leave the propitiators alone.

PRETA

The Preta is the spirit of the newly dead, the departed soul, the 'deceased' (unlike the pitṛ or ancestor who has been long dead and is a divinity). Between the moment of death and the conclusion of the funeral rites, the soul wanders around its original home. Pretas are ghosts who are not malevolent, but malevolent spirits are occasionally referred to as Pretas.

However, they appear in battle scenes where there are large numbers of dead, dancing with the Pishachas and Bhutas amid the carnage. They appear as hosts and troops. The Preta partakes of the annual rituals to the ancestors, but is never cruelly disposed towards living persons, especially its own family members who live under the Preta's protection.

The *Mahabharata* is replete with information about Pretas. The Preta is worshipped at the Pretashila hill at Gaya. The special food for the Preta is pinda or cooked rice offered at the funeral ceremonies. Yama is the lord equally of the pitṛs and Pretas. If jīvaloka is the world of the living, pretaloka is the world of the dead. They appear in gory scenes of battle and in burial grounds, dancing with the ghostly Pishachas and Bhutas, shrieking like ghosts. The voices of the wounded are likened to Pretas. Those who are killed in battle are said to have gone into the power of the Pretas. A person who is carrying out the ceremonies for the dead (pretakrityani) is impure until the ceremonies are completed and the Pretas join the pitṛ.

While Pretas are the ghosts of all the dead, they seem to have a connection with the non-Aryans in that they haunt burial grounds that are used by the non-Aryans, since the Aryans cremate their dead.

Later, the term Pishacha becomes more commonplace for ghosts. They too love to frighten people, causing nightmares and appearing in different forms. The *Garuda Purana* is full of information about ghosts and how to ward them off.

BIR, VIRAN

This malignant village demon is found all over India. He is known as Bir in the north and Viran in the south, taking his name from the Sanskrit vira meaning 'brave' or 'hero'.

VIRAN

This demon is more of an ogre, produced by evil nature, characteristics and vices, such as the ghost of a criminal or murderer or liar or adulterer and so on. They consume dead bodies in burial grounds and are extremely vile and malignant.

Most South Indian villages have a temple to the Mother Goddess or Amman, situated in the middle of the sacred grove. She is assisted in her protective duties by a host of Virans, fierce, mustachioed spirits who have to be propitiated with blood and animal sacrifice, failing which they will let loose their malignant powers in the form of diseases and evil happenings. The Virans have names like Madurai Viran, Muniyandi, Muniyappa, and so on. They are propitiated with bloody offerings of animal (and earlier, human) sacrifices.

In Uttar Pradesh there are several Birs, such as Kharbar, who will bring disease on people and cattle unless propitiated; Kera and Genda who are worshipped at Jaunpur and Nagpur respectively; and the seven Birs of Maharashtra who haunt the fields at night.

The Jilaiya of Bihar resembles a Bīr, and sucks the blood of any person whose name it hears. It is a birth fiend that can affect the health of the child in the womb in the same way as the cat-demon Chor Devan of the Oraons of Chota Nagpur, the cat or hen shaped Satvai of Maharashtra, the spirit Sathi of the Marathas of Nasik and the Vadvals of Thane, all of whom may attack either the child in the womb or the newborn infant. Villagers have developed various strategies and magic to counter them. All these involve bloody animal sacrifices.

SHAKTIS

Shakti is the energy or force manifested in the female principle through the consorts of the male deities. But the Shaktis are female, non-Vedic, non-Aryan spirits who control their constituents with a mixture of terror and blood-letting. They are malevolent spirits representing all the evils that could befall a person, such as disease, death and ill luck. They are generally found in villages and are worshipped out of fear and propitiated with gory acts of animal sacrifice to prevent malevolent effects of their activities. They are forms of the Mother Goddess, the Earth Mother who is also the Gramadevata, the guardian deity of the village. They may be called Amman (Tamil), Ammavaru (Telugu), Mata (Hindi) and so on. Each village has its own

SHAKTI

goddess with her own mythology. Spirits of disease such as Mari, malevolent goddesses who command by causing fear, like Kali, and many others, are a part of this host of frightening village goddesses who have captured the soul of rural India.

There are several stories regarding the origin of the Shaktis. One story makes them the one hundred and one daughters of Shiva, born when their mothers, wives of one hundred and one demons, embraced a pipal tree, which was actually Shiva. They went out to torment people, who then propitiated them with food and thus supported them. Every bloodthirsty and tormenting female goddess is regarded as a form of the Shaktis.

Another story traces them to Parvati. Giriraja had several sons, but no daughters, so he prayed long and hard to Shiva. Taking compassion on him, Parvati agreed to be born as his daughter, took a human form and hid in an anthill. That night the king had a dream that a daughter had been born to him in the anthill. He directed his servants to dig up the anthill, and found a girl sitting inside, next to a golden lamp, whom he later named Renuka. Immediately, he sacrificed an elephant to her, followed by five hundred cartloads of each type of food. Thereafter he sacrificed a sheep at every foot. Renuka changed herself into the one hundred and one Shaktis who became village goddesses. In this story, various features of non-Vedic worship are accounted for, such as the lit lamp, the worship of the anthill, the sacrifices and the worship of the Shaktis.

In South Indian tradition, the origin of the Shaktis is popularly attributed to Renuka, wife of sage Jamadagni and mother of Parashurama, an incarnation of Vishnu. The story goes that the Rakshasas lived in the mountains and forests. Giriraja wanted to get rid of them, but was unable to do so. Then Narada informed him that only his daughter Renuka could defeat them, but the king refused to hide behind his daughter. He attacked the Rakshasas again, but was unable to withstand their onslaught. Then Renuka decided to go to her father's aid and asked her aunt (and mother-in-law), the raja's sister, for permission to do so. The aunt refused, but said she could go if her husband gave her permission. Renuka set out to ask her husband. On the way she saw a little boy and laughed at him. Jamadagni considered this to be an act of wickedness as he was undergoing penance. He commanded his sons to behead their mother, but all except one refused, for which they were cursed with idiocy by their father. The remaining son was Parashurama who carried out his father's desire. When offered a boon by the sage for his implicit obedience, he asked for his mother's life back. Then Renuka asked her husband for permission to fight the Rakshasas. When her husband refused, she decided to show him her true self—a frightening spectacle of a Shakti with a thousand arms, each arm holding a spike with a body impaled at the end of each spike and, beside each body, was a demon holding a torch in one hand and a sword in the other. Renuka now obtained Jamadagni's permission to fight the Rakshasas whom she killed in large numbers. But for every demon she killed, sixty thousand new ones arose. Finally, she asked her brother to spread out his tongue and not let a drop of Rakshasa blood fall, for which he would receive a sheep and an enormous pile of rice. This was done and the Rakshasas were killed by Renuka.

In the original *Mahabharata* story there is no mention of the Shaktis or Rakshasas. But Renuka is a headless goddess, popular in South India, who is identified by the common people as a bloodthirsty demoness.

There are several local Shaktis all over India. They are propitiated with sacrifice and impalements of buffalo, sheep and fowl, with blood flowing freely till the person 'possessed' by the demoness speaks out and declares that the spirit is satisfied. Then she leaves the village for another season and day.

The Shaktis belong to rural India and live outside the pale of mainstream Hinduism. Their army is made up of the Birs and Virans discussed earlier. The spectacle of a Shakti with a thousand arms is quite frightening. It is rare to find a Brahmin priest in a Shakti temple in South India; the officiating priest generally belongs to the lower castes, even the scheduled castes (Harijans). They are malevolent spirits who are propitiated out of fear rather than love.

It is important not to confuse the malevolent Shaktis that haunt every village and are propitiated out of fear with the great goddess Shakti of mainstream Hinduism, although the latter undoubtedly owes her origin to the village Shakti. The Shaktis are female spirits who take different names in different villages. It was obviously a method of absorbing lower-caste deities, with their very gory rituals. The stories of the origin of the Shaktis were obviously created to enable the absorption of a very alien and frightening religion that was totally at variance with the Vedic prayers for peace and prosperity. The Shaktis were propitiated so that they may leave people alone. By absorbing the local gods and goddesses, the people themselves were also absorbed into mainstream Hinduism.

YAKSHA

Yakshas are referred to as a people (yakshāvah) in *Rig Veda* VII.18.9 and as an epithet of Turvasa (turvāsayaksha, a purodāsa) in *Rig Veda* VII. 18.6. It has three different uses in the *Rig Veda*. Firstly, it is a person or group of persons. Secondly, it is a status perceivable by Agni (*Rig Veda*, I.190.4). Thirdly, it is a secret (*Rig Veda*, VII.61.5; IV.13.3; X.88.13). There is a spirit-like quality which is transferable.

In the *Jaiminiya Brahmana* (III. 203, 272) Yaksha means 'a wondrous thing'. In the *Grihya Sutras*, they are classed as Bhutas. Yaksha is a Rakshasa and lord of robbers and evil-doers in the *Shatapatha Brahmana*. In the *Ramayana*, Tataka, a Yakshi, becomes a Rakshasi, and this is considered a fall. Yakshas and Rakshasas are classified as rajasik, while Pretas and Bhutas are tamasik, according to the *Mahabharata* (6. 41. 4). Says Coomaraswamy, 'There is some confusion of Yakshas and

YAKSHI

Rakshasas, who according to one tradition have a common origin; both have good and evil qualities, benevolent and malevolent as the case may be; very often the same descriptions would apply to either, but the two classes are not identical, and broadly speaking we find the Yakshas associated with Kubera, the Rakshasas with Ravana, who is their chief. Yakshas as a rule are kindly, Rakshasas bloodthirsty.'4

In fact it is the relationship between Ravana and Kubera—Kubera's kingship over the Rakshasas in Lanka, his role in the birth of his Rakshasa half-brothers by sending over Rakshasa women to his father Vishravas, the Rakshasas among

Kubera's attendants, and Kubera's residence in the company of Rakshasas—that associates him inexorably with the demon horde. With Kubera being the lord of Yakshas, his association with the demons automatically associated the Yakshas with the demons. According to the *Ramayana*, when Brahma created the guardians of the waters, some cried out 'let us guard' (rakshāmah) while others cried out 'let us gobble' (yakshāmah). Ravana, king of Lanka, is also the brother of Kubera. Since Ravana is a Rakshasa, and Kubera is a Yaksha, Rakshasas and Yakshas became siblings. There is a tie binding the two. According to the later *Harivamsha*, both are born of the same mother, Khasha, daughter of Daksha, and both are red-eyed and dark-skinned.

According to the Buddhist *Mahavamsa*, the aboriginal inhabitants of Sri Lanka are called Yakkhas. Vijaya marries a Yakkhini whose two children become the ancestors of the Pulinda, perhaps the Veddas who still worship the Yakkhas as ancestors. In the *Digha Nikaya*, Varuna is called a Yaksha.[5] Buddhist mythology relegates Yakshas to demonhood, demanding sacrifices of flesh, including human flesh. They are also doorkeepers of shrines, the original role of the Rakshasas as protectors or *raksha*s. Buddhists converted some Yakkhas, made others ineffective and ignored the powerful ones.[6]

Yakshas may be good or bad, powerful or timid. They are spirits of trees and plants. They are guardians of hidden treasure, not unlike the dwarfs and giants of Teutonic legend. They are supernatural beings attending on Kubera, their leader, whose treasure they defend with frightening yells, feeding on human flesh and armed with weapons and the speed of the wind. According to Coomaraswamy, Yakshas lost their importance in popular folklore and came to be classified with the Rakshasas, as did the Daevas at the hands of Zoroaster, or that of the older European mythology under the influence of Christianity. The *Ramayana*'s explanation for the name Rakshasa and Yaksha, of those who cried rakshāmah (let us guard) and others who cried yakshāmah (let us gobble) may be derived from the big stomach which defines the Yaksha.[7]

However, there is a dichotomy between the classification of the Yakshas with the Rakshasas and the *Atharva Veda* (X. 7. 38) reference to 'A great Yaksha in the midst of the universe, reclining . . . on the back of the waters, therein are set whatever gods there be, like the branches of a tree about a trunk.' The association of the Yaksha with the tree of life is most appropriate, for the Yaksha is a spirit of the tree. But the Yaksha was also the prototype of Narayana. Narayana was not a Vedic god, although he was later identified with the Vedic solar deity Vishnu. In Buddhist theology, Devatas were the spirits of trees and nature, the role of Yakshas in Vedic theology. Like the ambiguity of the early Asuras, the Yakshas also veered between the realm of good, represented by the gods, and the realm of evil, represented by the demons.[8]

THE EVIL EYE

Belief in the evil eye is common to nearly all Indians—Hindus, Muslims and Christians. The evil eye may befall anybody from a pregnant mother to a newborn baby to an adult. It is generally the result of jealousy and covetousness. The evil eye can invite demons, spirits or bhutas to enter the body of the child and harm it.

Adding an imperfection can ward off the evil eye. Thus a baby will have lampblack (kājal) smeared in its eyes or added as a dot on the cheek. Metals, precious stones, red chillies and

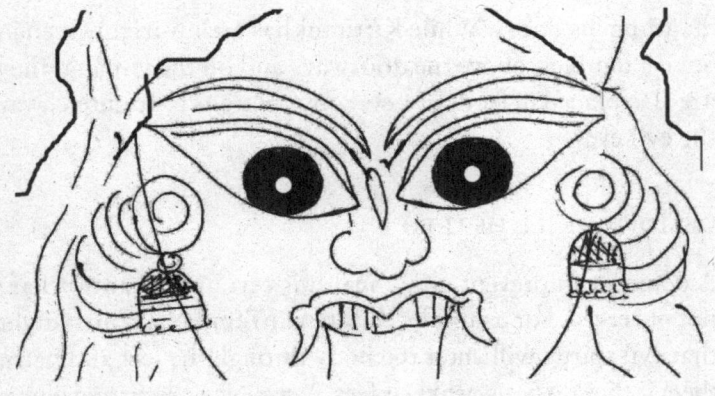

THE EVIL EYE

salt are other antidotes. The belief is that there are innumerable
evil spirits waiting to do harm.

There are several spells to remove the evil eye. Fire, red
chillies, lime and many other objects are used to ward off the
evil eye, accompanied by incantations in local languages. The
most effective is believed to be fire, into which the bewitched
object is thrown. Thus, from the period of the Vedas, Agni is
called upon to destroy demons.

Kirtimukha, or gorgon heads, are placed above doorways
to keep away evil spirits. According to legend, the demon
Jalandhara sent a message through Rahu demanding the
beautiful Parvati. Hearing Rahu, Shiva sent a huge, lion-faced
gana, with flaming eyes and long arms to rush out and catch
Rahu. Rahu begged for his life, so Shiva ordered him to be
set free. The gana let go of Rahu, but pointed out that he had
been deprived of his food. So Shiva ordered the gana to eat
his own limbs, which he did. Then Shiva named the bodyless
gana Kirtimukha (face of fame) and gave him the job of

guarding his doors. While Kirtimukhas are invariably seen in Shaiva temples, above the doorways and on the vimāna, they are also placed in front of new constructions to frighten away the evil eye.

DEMONS OF ILL HEALTH

A demon can prevent good health if certain precautions are not observed. For example, children in Tamil Nadu are taught that evil spirits will enter the body through the feet and harm them if they do not wash their feet. A chronic or recurring illness is described as a captivation by an evil spirit. Simple health rules like washing one's teeth and hands keep away evil spirits.

Common people, particularly the superstitious, were controlled through fear. If you do not do this, evil will befall you. If you do not do that an evil spirit will capture your heart and soul. Similarly, if certain rituals were not observed, the person would be captured by spirits. Evil spirits or demons were used for general social good.

REPELLING OR CONCILIATING EVIL SPIRITS

Family spirits are generally benevolent, and funeral rites and the annual shrāddha ensure that the souls of the departed are on the path of rebirth. But the malignancy of hostile spirits makes their conciliation very important. Each tribe, caste and community has charms and spells to propitiate and repel evil spirits. Castes who bury their dead generally place charms with the dead bodies. Even those who cremate form an image of the body with either plants or cooked rice, and then break it apart with their arms and throw it into water, to ensure that the spirit does not return. Malignant spirits must be scared away, and fire, earth and water are used singly or together to scare away such a spirit.

Possession by spirits is also attributed to demons. The possession is of two types. The first type of possession by spirits manifests itself as a form of hysteria. An uneducated people may not be able to handle mental sickness and attribute it to possession by demons. Such demons are driven away by various forms of exorcism, using drums, spells, fire and leaves of the neem tree. Often, the person is beaten soundly—with a branch or broom or slipper—until the demon speaks to the exorcist and agrees to depart. Sometimes it can result in serious injury or even death, as in the case of witches who are even deliberately killed.

Food is often left by the wayside for mischievous spirits: anyone touching it will be attacked by spirits. Thus, even pumpkins, lime or coconut broken in front of houses, to drive away evil spirits, are not touched since they are left for the evil spirits and demons. Kuttichattan of Travancore (Kerala) is a famous spirit who, if propitiated properly, takes good care of his master, but who can go haywire if mishandled.

Diseases and illnesses are also attributed to various demons. Since the demon is bloodthirsty, threatening to take a life, animals are often sacrificed to propitiate the demon's lust for life. The buffalo is preferred as the luckless sacrifice, but goats and fowl cost less and are therefore sacrificed more often than buffaloes.

Devil dances and magical incantations are popular all over India. The theyyam and kudiyattam of Kerala are examples of devil dancing. Other forms of shamanism are very popular all over rural India and in the Himalayas. Sometimes the shaman drinks the blood of the sacrificial victim, before or after the sacrifice.

DEMON NAKSHATRAS

The nakshatras (generally translated as stars, but actually lunar mansions) are divided into three gunas or temperaments: deva (divine), manushya (human) and rakshasa (demonic). While the first represents a spiritual, charitable and good nature, manushya gunas are worldly, with both positive and negative qualities. Rakshasa gunas are dominant and self-willed, with a potential for violence. Of the twenty seven nakshatras, the following are demonic:

- ❖ Krittika
- ❖ Ashlesha
- ❖ Magha
- ❖ Chitra
- ❖ Vishakha
- ❖ Jyeshtha
- ❖ Mula
- ❖ Dhanishtha
- ❖ Shatabhisha

The function of the guna is to find a compatible spouse, which is only possible within the same guna. The woman's guna is required to be more elevated than the man's. A woman with deva or manushya guna can marry a man with a lesser guna, but a woman with the Rakshasa guna can marry only another of the same guna. Thus the guna kuta is regarded as essential for a happy marriage.[9]

DEMON MARRIAGE

The asura or Rakshasa *vivaha* was of two types. One was marriage by abduction, when a man carried off the girl of his choice and married her, with or without her consent. Krishna's marriage to Rukmini and Bhishma's abduction of the sisters Ambika and Ambalika, to marry his half-brother Vichitravirya, are instances of Rakshasa vivahas. However, neither Krishna nor Bhishma are demonized for their actions.

The second form of demon marriage refers to the practice of paying a bride price to the family of a girl, who is then taken according to the man's pleasure.

Sometimes the 'abduction' is staged, with the bride's consent, and is thus actually a love marriage, against the family's wishes, such as Krishna and Rukmini or Arjuna and Subhadra. However, the 'Rakshasa' marriage generally did not have the bride's consent.

DEMONS AND THE VEDIC RELIGION

The opposition between the magic-makers and the priests who invoke the aid of the gods is one of the primary facets of Hinduism. Every tribe and community acknowledges the supremacy of the god over the demon. The opposition between demonolatry and orthodox religion is little more than nominal, and popular Hinduism is made up of a veneer of higher beliefs overlying demon worship, often making it impossible to distinguish between the two. This phenomenon is particularly apparent in southern and eastern India and the Himalayan foothills, where Brahmanism has been forced to come to terms with local beliefs. Brahmanism has ritualized the old demon worship, bringing in processions and ritual washing (abhishekha). The amalgam with Brahmanism has also eliminated or at least reduced the blood sacrifices, in deference to Brahmanic feelings. In fact, one of the signs of the upgradation of a spirit into a god is the abjuration of blood sacrifice, making the god Shaiva, or vegetarian.

In those South Indian temples where animal sacrifices are conducted in full view, the priests are rarely, if ever, Brahmanas. In some transitional places, Brahmanas may perform the main rituals and the sacrifices may be conducted in a separate enclosure at the back, but Brahmanas who work in these places are looked down upon as very low in the hierarchy. In several places, the sacrificial animal has been replaced by breaking open a pumpkin and smearing it with kumkum, recreating the visual image of the sacrifice. The fusion of the vegetarian Brahmanic form of worship and the violent worship of the village gods usually manifests itself in the acceptance by the Brahmanic orthodoxy of the demons as the followers or assistants of their gods. This is particularly noticeable in the Shakta and Shaiva cults. The village goddesses are the Shaktis or manifestations of the female energy; ferocious spirits are subdued by Shiva as Bhuteshvara.

The process of the absorption of demonolatry by orthodox Hinduism has resulted in the decrease of overt demon worship, as intelligence, education and the active missionary efforts of the orthodox priesthood extend. According to Khanam, the numbers of Bhuts in Bengal ran into several millions some years ago. Some of the most dreaded spirits of Kolhapur disappeared during British rule: the Brahman spirits because they disliked the killing of cows, and the Muhammadan spirits because pork was freely eaten, leaving only the low-caste spirits whose influence was much reduced. In Travancore, the home of demon worship, it gave way to Hindu deities like Shiva, Vishnu, Subrahmanya and Ganesha.[10]

THEOLOGY

Demons are born in troubled minds, out of human vices and deliberate acts of evil. Guilt becomes an evil demon possessing the mind and the thought process. Those vices that afflict men and women and turn their minds away from righteousness are described as demons. They also act as lessons to show that when they enter people's minds and hearts, they are demonic, overpowering the individual and enveloping him in darkness and ignorance. Demons flatter the ego, the ahankāra. Such evil must be destroyed.

Demons represent all that is negative in the minds and actions of people, and the victory of good is intended to decide the choice of good over evil. Demons also know magic, and magic has been disliked by mainstream Hinduism. The Asuras employ a life-restoring magic. The ocean is churned to obtain the nectar of immortality. But immortality is reserved for the gods alone, and neither humans nor demons may dare to aspire to it. Arrogance, pride, greed, anger and delusion are demons.

The demons destroyed by Shiva represent qualities of ignorance, darkness, ego, greed and so on. But it is in the worship of Ganesha that human imperfections are personified as demons. The enemies of Ganesha are human failings that must be conquered by each individual. Each vice is a demon, destroyed by a different form of Ganesha:

❖ Lust, love or Kama is described as an asura, who was destroyed by Ganesha in the form of Vikata

❖ Vicious and unjust anger is the demon Krodha, subdued by Lambodara

❖ The demon Lobha represents avarice and greed, and is defeated by Gajanana

❖ Moha is the demon of infatuation and delusion, vanquished by Mahodara

❖ Mada is vanity, a demon defeated by Ekadanta Ganesha

❖ Envy and jealousy are Mata, a demon destroyed by Ganesha as Vakratunda, riding a lion

❖ Mama is the demon of attachment or desire, removed by Vighnaraja riding a serpent

❖ Abhimana is egoistic pride, an Asura subdued by Dhumravarna[11]

Those qualities regarded as inimical to Hindu dharma or values of righteousness and the road to moksha or salvation are described as demons. The demons destroyed by Vishnu and Shiva represent similar qualities, which makes their destruction imperative. As long as the vices remain, Ganesha—or one's personal favourite deity—has to return time and again to destroy them.

Finally, in the destruction of the demon lies the redemption of the individual. The demons obtain their power from their karma. Kalanemi, brother of Bali, is reborn as several demons and finally as the wicked Kamsa, uncle of Krishna. Kamsa is killed and his karma burns out in the presence of the Lord. Demons and demonic forces try to destabilize the dharmic order, so they must be destroyed. Even as they are destroyed for our security, they find their own liberation.

NOTES

1. Khanam, *op.cit.*, pp. 17–29.
2. Bhattacharji, S., *The Indian Theogony*, pp. 130–133.
3. Khanam, *op.cit.*, p. 18.
4. Coomaraswamy, A.K., *Yakṣas*, Part I, pp. 4–8.
5. Ibid., Part I, pp. 13–14; Part I, p. 2.
6. Misra, R.N. *Yaksha Cult and Iconography*, p. 37
7. Coomaraswamy, Part I, p. 4; p. 5, f.n. 1.
8. Ibid., p. 47.
9. Harness, D.M., *The Nakshatras*, pp. 121–122.
10. Khanam, *op.cit.*, pp. 46–49.
11. Jagannathan, S. and N. Krishna, *Ganesha*, p. 17.

Demons of Jainism and Buddhism

Demons appear in the mythology of Jainism and Buddhism, which are offshoots of the Vedic religion. Since both these theologies have a high content of Brahmanical deities, they also include demons in their mythologies.

JAINA DEMONS

Demons in Jainism are divided into Naarakas (inhabitants of hell) and Kudevas. The former cannot leave the place where they are condemned to live, nor can they harm anyone other than another Naaraka. When a person who has committed a heinous sin dies, his soul is taken away to one of the seven hells, where it undergoes great privations and horrors. It dies at the end of its allotted time, after a miserable life in hell.

The Asurakumaras (Asuras) reside beneath the surface of the earth. Fifteen are extremely wicked and delight in wanton cruelty.

The vyantaras include demons, goblins, ghosts and spirits who live above or below the earth. They are divided into eight

142   The Book of Demons

classes: Kinnara, Kimpurusha, Mahoraga, Gandharva, Yaksha, Rakshasa, Bhuta and Pishacha. While the last four in particular include demons and ghosts, some Rakshasas are actually good, and worship the Tirthankaras. Demonic characters are known as dushta vyantaras.

Jaina attitudes towards demons are very similar to that of the surrounding Hindu communities.[1] The Jainas believe that beneath this world is adhogati, or abyss, the Jaina hell, above which there are seven infernal worlds. Above these are ten pavanalokas or purifying worlds, above which is situated the earth.[2]

BUDDHIST DEMONS

Demons play an important role in the life of the Buddha himself. In his final incarnation as the Buddha, he undergoes a personal struggle with the demon Mara and his three daughters—Desire, Unrest and Pleasure. Buddhism absorbed many of the aboriginal pantheons both in India and in the countries where it spread.

Buddhist demons are different from Brahmanical demons in that most are local spirits, not necessarily Buddhist or Brahmanical. Mara was the personification of evil, a tempter. Hariti is a famous she-devil. Rudra in his destructive mood, the Asuras, Rakshasas and Pishachas are among the many demons of the Buddhist pantheon. Asuras are giant demons, titans headed by Rahu, the personification of the eclipse. Rakshasas are ogres and fiends who are capable of assuming siren-like forms. They include Daityas, Kumbhandas, Pishachas and Pretas or ghosts and ghouls like the Pingala. Sometimes the evil spirits may become friendly, but Buddhist ritual includes incantations to exorcize the harmful ones. Buddha's disciple,

Maudgalyayana, is credited with exorcizing spirits by reciting the paritta or pirit sutra, which is still recited to combat sickness and misfortune, particularly in Hinayana or Theravada Buddhism of Sri Lanka, Burma and Thailand. Some of the celestial Bodhisattvas, such as Marichi, were fiendish. Tantric Buddhism, which appeared around the tenth century AD introduced a 'rampant demonolatry, with exacting priestly rites, into a religion which in its origin was largely a protest against worship and ritual of every kind.' The chief demons of Mahayana or Vajrayana Buddhism are Vajra-Bhairava or Yamantaka, Samvara, Hayagriva and Vajra-kala,

GUARDIAN DEMON OF BUDDHIST MONASTERIES

who stand watch over monasteries and stupas and prevent the attack of the minor demons.[3]

The guardian demons of the four cardinal points are a prominent sight on the temples and monasteries of northern Buddhism, seen in Ladakh, Tibet and Mongolia. They include Vaishravana, king of the north, Virudhaka, king of the south, Dhritarashtra, king of the east and Virupaksha, king of the west. Chitipatis are dancing skeletons or corpses who accompany Yama, the god of death.[4]

NOTES

1. Khanam, R., *op.cit.*, pp. 57–9.
2. Garrett, J., *A Classical Dictionary of India*, p. 5.
3. *Ibid.*, pp. 61–6.
4. Dorjey, T., *Reach Ladakh*, pp. 74–5.

7

Demonic Lands

While Lanka is the home of the demons of the *Ramayana*, the home of the demons of the *Mahabharata* is Patala or Hiranyapuri. Other homes are Pragjyotisha, where Naraka kept the earrings stolen by the Nagas from Aditi, and Asmanagara, city of stone. These were real cities. On getting back the earrings from Naraka, Arjuna brings back the Asura women as wives, not unlike conquerors who capture local women as prizes and loot. Naraka is a synonym for hell: his city floats beyond the sea and was destroyed by Arjuna. Pradyumna destroys Saubha, a Daitya city belonging to King Shalva which was sometimes described as an aerial city and as a city of human beings at other times.

Arbuda is the original name of Mount Abu in Rajasthan and of the people who lived in that country. It is named after a serpent demon of the same name killed by Indra. Avatarana was the land of the Rakshasas. Hiranyapuri, meaning 'city of gold', is the peripatetic home of the Daityas. It can sink beneath the sea, or under the earth, or fly in the heavens like the sun. It was a city of imagination and it is unlikely that it can be identified with any known place. Madhuvana, Mathura, is the grove of Madhu, a famous demon who, along with his brother Kaitabha, was killed by Vishnu. Madhu is also described as the ancestor of Kamsa and Krishna. After Madhu's death, his son Lavana was killed by Shatrughna, brother of Rama, who rebuilt the city and renamed it Mathura. It was here that Dhruva performed his penance (*Vishnu Purana*).

Mathura, an ancient city on the banks of the river Yamuna, was the birthplace of Krishna. Kamsa was king of Mathura where, much later, he was killed by Krishna. Like several other cities associated with Rakshasas, Mathura is also named after a non-Vedic king of ancient India.

Megasthenes, in his *Indika*, mentions that the queen of the Pandaias (Pandavas) founded a city in the south called Madura. Written in Tamil, Mathura would be pronounced as Madura. Thus Madhu was immortalized all over India.

NARAKA (PRAGJYOTISHA)

Naraka is synonymous with hell, where tortured souls go and where the Rakshasas dwell (*Manu Samhita*). It is another name for Pragjyotisha, kingdom of Naraka, a rich and powerful demon king, son of Mother Earth (Bhumi Devi) and the boar Varaha, whose paternity was hidden from Vishnu by his mother. His kingdom was the impregnable fortress of the demons, Pragjyotisha. Naraka stole Aditi's earrings and brought them to Pragjyotisha, so the gods approached Krishna, who killed Naraka and returned the earrings to Aditi (*Mahabharata*, *Vishnu Purana*). Pragjyotisha was situated in the east in Kamaroopa, on the borders of Assam. It was obviously annexed from the Rakshasas.

According to the *Harivamsha*, Naraka assumed the form of an elephant and carried off and violated the daughter of

Vishwakarma, the gandharvas and apsarases, a total of 16,000 women for whom he built a beautiful residence and filled it with jewels, garments and valuables. No Asura before him had ever been so awful.[1] Naraka had seven sons—Tamra, Antariksha, Shravana, Vibhavasu, Vasu, Nabhasvan and Aruna.

The demonization of the non-Aryan Naraka, who was associated with the Earth, justifies the annexation of his kingdom. Naraka or hell was relegated to the nether regions. It was impregnable, yet rich and prosperous, a prosperity bestowed and represented by Aditi, the solar mother of the Devas, and agriculture. After Pragjyotisha was annexed, Naraka ceased to exist on earth and became hell, a land of fire and brimstone. Presided over by Yama, god of death, Naraka is full of fire and poison (*Brahma Purana*).

Adhoshiras was one of the divisions of Naraka, or hell, in which people are punished for bribery. There are several types of Naraka, each earmarked for a different type of sinner. They are listed by the *Vishnu* and *Shiva Purana*:

Rourava:	For false witnesses, Brahmana killers and alcoholics
Shukara:	For thieves and killers of cattle, Kshatriyas and Vaishyas
Taptalauha:	For those who commit infanticide
Taptakhala:	For one who insults his teachers or criticizes the Vedas
Krimibhaksha:	For those who insult Devas, Brahmanas or kings
Lalabhaksha:	For those who eat without offering food to the gods
Vishasana:	For Brahmanas who eat forbidden foods
Rudhirandha:	For sellers of wine

Vaitarani:	For killers of bees
Krishna:	For cheats
Asipatravana:	For destroyers of trees
Vahnijvala:	For hunters of deer
Agnimaya:	For one who burns property
Sandamsha:	For a person who fails to complete a vrata
Shvabhojana:	For a person who accepts his son as his teacher
Lavana:	For those who associate extensively with immoral women
Mahajvala:	For those who commit the crime of incest

As demons are also sinners, the above hells would apply to them too. In any case, the various hells are presided over by demons. But these places can be avoided by praying to Shiva, says the *Shiva Purana*.

The *Bhagavata Purana* has a slightly different list, and suggests worship of Vishnu to avoid them:

Tamishra Naraka:	For thieves
Raurava:	Populated by snake-like beings called Ruru, who return violence with violence.
Kalasutra:	For those who harm Brahmanas
Asipatravana:	For those who oppose the Vedas
Shukaramukha:	For those who punish the innocent
Krimibhoja:	For those who eat without offering food to the gods, Brahmanas or guests
Suchimukha:	For misers

The *Agni Purana*'s list of the different types of hell has some variations:

Mahavicha:	For cattle thieves
Amakumbha:	For killers of Brahmanas and for land thieves

Raurava:	For killers of women, children and old men
Maharaurava:	For arsonists
Tamishra:	For thieves
Mahatamishra:	For thieves
Asipatravana:	For those who kill their parents
Karambhavaluka:	For those who burn people to death
Kakola:	For those who eat only sweets
Kuttala:	For those who do not perform sacrifices
Tailpaka:	For oppressors
Mahapata:	For liars

The *Brahmavaivarta Purana* describes eighty-six hells, but these are presided over by Yama, Lord of Death, and are not the dwelling of demons.

The *Bhagavata Purana* has a graphic description of Pragjyotisha, a well-fortified city constructed by the demon Mura, which defied penetration. Four forts guarded the four directions, with formidable armies. The next boundary was a water-filled moat (canal), in addition to which the city was surrounded by electrified barriers. Thereafter, a gaseous substance (anila) and a network of barbed fortification surrounded the city. Krishna broke the walls of the forts with his club, scattered the armies with his arrows, counteracted the electric boundary with his chakra, nullified the waters and gaseous boundaries and cut the barbed wire to pieces. The sound of his conch, pānchajanya, filled the hearts of the great fighters of the city with terror, even as it broke the great fighting machines.

PATALA

This is the netherworld, peopled by Asuras, Rakshasas, Daityas, Danavas, Yakshas, Nagas and others, in fact by every unwanted being of the ancient world. They may be seven or eight, depending on the source. Each Purana gives a different number and set of names:

Vishnu Purana	Padma Purana	Shiva Purana
Atala	Atala, ruled by Mahamaya	Patala
Vitala	Vitala, ruled by Hatakeshwara	Tala
Nitala	Sutala, ruled by Bali	Atala
Gabhastimat	Talatala, ruled by Maya	Vitala
Mahatala	Mahatala, home of the great Nagas	Tala
Sutala	Rasatala, where the Daityas live	Vidhi Patala
Patala	Patala, ruled by Vasuki	Sarkara
		Bhoomi
Avichi		Vijaya

Narada, after visiting the infernal regions of hell, returns to the heavens and praises them, saying that they are far more delightful than Indra's heaven in the skies, possessing palaces and jewels, where the sun rises but does not radiate too much heat, where the moon shines but is not cold, with forests of beautiful trees and ponds with lotus flowers, and the song of the cuckoo everywhere, with every kind of luxury and sensual gratification. Below Patala sleeps Ananta the great snake with a thousand hoods covered with jewels (*Brahma Purana*).[2]

OTHERS

Puran, the city of the Daityas, was situated in the western region which was conquered by Kakutstha, who took the title of Puranjaya, or 'conqueror of the city of Puran' after a war against the demons, in which the latter were defeated.[3] Saubha was a magical aerial city, situated on the shore of the ocean and protected by the Shalvas, which belonged to the Daityas. It was destroyed by Krishna, according to the *Mahabharata*. Shonitapura was the kingdom of the demon Taraka who was killed by Shiva.

The word Tripura means triple city, and is another name for the demon Bana who received three cities from Brahma, Vishnu and Shiva. He was finally killed by Shiva, who was thus given the appellation Tripurantaka, or the destroyer of Tripura. The *Harivamsha* describes Tripura as an aerial city that was burnt in a war with the gods.[4]

According to the *Padma Purana*, the demon Taraka had three sons, Vidyunmali, Tarakaksha and Viryavana who performed severe austerities to obtain immortality. When Brahma refused, they asked for three forts: one of gold, another of silver and the third of iron, where they would live for a thousand years, at the end of which the forts would become one that could only be destroyed by a single arrow. Brahma granted their boon and Maya, the demon architect, built the three forts. The demons lived there and flourished, but the gods did not like this. They asked Brahma and Shiva to destroy the cities, but both refused, since the brothers were not doing anything wrong. They asked Vishnu who suggested that they should be made to sin and accordingly, created a man with shaven head and his mouth covered with a piece of cloth and taught him a religion, completely against the Vedas, called Jainism. The brothers followed the religion and stopped worshipping the Shiva Linga. Thereafter, Shiva, accompanied by Brahma, agreed to destroy the city, whose thousand years were now over. He aimed a single pashupata weapon which burnt down Tripura in a second. Obviously, Tripura was a city of Jainas which was burnt down by the worshippers of Shiva.

Like Mount Abu and Mathura/Madura, many cities carry the names of the Rakshasa rulers. The original name for

Badami in Karnataka was Vatapi, named after its Rakshasa ruler, while Thanjavur is named after the Rakshasa Thanjan and Mysore after the demon Mahisha. The length and breadth of the country carry many more such names.

RIVERS AND PLANTS

Towns are not the only geographic spaces named after ancient demons. Rivers such as the Prabhavati (modern Gandaki) are also named after demons. Finally, plants, such as the tulasi, neem and banyan were also once identified as demons. Thus the demons of India have left their imprint on every aspect of Indian life and culture.

NOTES

1. Dowson, J., *A Classical Dictionary of Hindu Mythology and Religion*, p. 220.
2. Ibid., p. 233.
3. Ibid., p. 247.
4. Ibid., p. 321.

The Battle Never Ends

Sometimes the end of a book can be as inconclusive as its beginning. The subject of Demons would certainly seem so.

The problem is that a melange of characters became the demons of India—gods who fell from grace; Assur warriors of West Asia; enemies like the Rakshasas, Danavas, Daityas and Pishachas; and, finally, the actual demons themselves—ghosts, spirits and other unpleasant beings.

The Rig Vedic Asura, a leader of the gods, fell from grace as the cruel and violent Assurs of Babylon drove out the Aryan Mittanis. The fact that the gods themselves—Varuna, Agni, the Maruts and others—did not fall from grace means that the term Asura alone became impolitic, with a meaning so terrible that it became synonymous with demon. So Asura became foreign to, and disliked by, the Aryans, demons hostile to the gods of the Aryans and to the Aryans themselves, people who had once hailed the Asuras as leaders. Something terrible had happened to transform the Asura leader into a demon. The Assur capture of Babylon, their confrontation with the Aryan Mittani and the identification of their god with the

Iranian Ahura are the most likely reasons for this total change of character.

Asura-Deva of India and Ahura-Daeva of Iran were undoubtedly connected, with their roles reversed. Even as Asuras became disliked demons in India and Devas the gods, the reverse was happening in Iran, where the Daevas or gods of the Indus had become demons and Ahura the supreme god. The followers of the god Assur of Babylon became the rulers of the Tigris–Euphrates region—modern Iran and Iraq—and established their religion there. Assur became synonymous with Ahura. The cruel and victorious Assurs created a terrible image for themselves, of a cruel people with war machines that terrorized and a destructive nature that made them ideal demons. This image obviously merged with the Asuras, if they were not the Asuras themselves. Like the Asuras, the Assurs were initially mere leaders. Later, they overthrew their Aryan rulers, the Mittanis, to whom they were linked first as subjects and later as conquerors. The Mittanis came to India with horrific stories of the Assurs or Asuras. The Asura-Deva confrontation took a different direction in ancient Iran, the land of the Assurs, where Ahura or Assur or Asura became the chief god of the victors.

The drying up of the Rig Vedic river Sarasvati, the eastern movement of the Vedic civilization and the growth in importance of Shiva and Vishnu meant that a more settled version of the Vedic religion was being preferred, a religion for food producers and settled communities rather than nomadic. The earlier religious practices of the Aryans were being substituted by a highly structured religion of sacrifices that was gaining prominence. The sacrifice was offered to the Devas or gods. There is evidence that the Asuras rejected the Vedic rituals, for there are frequent references to Asuras disrupting them. The memory of the alien and cruel Assurs merged with the rejectors of Vedic traditions. Both the *Shatapatha Brahmana* and *Ramayana* say that Asura land was taken over by the Aryans with the power of the sacrifice.

The eastern movement of the Vedic civilization coincided with the rise of the epic age, an age of great heroes, new pacts and violent wars in different parts of the Indian subcontinent, from Ayodhya and Mathura in the northern Gangetic plains to the southern island of (Sri) Lanka. They came across people whose manners, customs, social structure and moral values were so alien that Rakshasa, the name of one powerful tribe, came to mean demon. But these were demonized human beings. Many demons came from developed societies, while others were good and honourable persons. Ravana was a great Sanskrit scholar and devotee of Shiva. His brother Vibhishana was so honourable that he preferred to oppose his brother rather than support the abduction of another man's wife. Bali was a much loved king, a man of his word. So the word Rakshasa could not have meant a supernatural evil demon. The strongest clue to their human existence is the historicity of Rakshasa, an able minister of the Nandas and of Chandragupta Maurya, praised by Chanakya himself. Derivatives of the name Ravana also appear often among certain communities. The fact that so many cities are named after Rakshasas is also an indication that they were once rulers of those lands, for nobody would consciously name a town after an evil spirit.

Magic, with which the Asuras and Rakshasas were associated, has always been unpopular, and practitioners of magic have never found acceptance in Indian society. Their utilization of the occult did not endear the Asuras and Rakshasas to either the pantheistic Vedic people or to the later ritualists or to the Upanishadic philosophers. It is obvious that these were native demon worshippers who used magic to frighten and control, and were, therefore, frowned upon by Vedic society.

It is also interesting that great surgeons and physicians like Charaka and Chyavana are called Asuras and Rakshasas. The secrecy associated with traditional Ayurvedic healers, which continues today, probably associated them with some sort of magic, which their medicines were believed to invoke. Thus, even as they were essential for the greater good, there were apparently grey areas in people's attitude to these healers, which earned them the appellation of demons. While it is tempting to assume that they were of non-Vedic origin, the fact that their works are in the Sanskrit language and tradition belies this theory.

While some enemies like the Rakshasas were demonized, others were not, depending on their character and importance. As the epic heroes were deified, their enemies had to be demonized, for gods fight evil supernatural beings, not human beings. Making them animal-headed enhanced their magical qualities and powers. It may also be a throwback to a period when men had to battle wild animals in their struggle for survival. Enemies like Ravana and Kamsa were great warriors and defeating them was an unparalleled achievement for the hero-god. The gods and demons often worked together to achieve common goals. During the *amrita manthana* (the churning of the ocean), they worked in tandem.

God and demon need each the other; one is the antithesis of the other. They are similar in many ways and even share a paternal ancestry. But they also differ because the Asuras are evil. The Devas must destroy them. It is the eternal battle between good and evil. The final message is clear: Good always triumphs.

The demons serve as a lesson that evil shall be destroyed and good shall triumph. This is also a motivator for those who are up against insurmountable odds, that there is hope only for good and none for evil.

By including ghosts, spirits and other unpleasant beings

among demonized enemies, we enter a subterranean world of malignant spirits who cause disease, death and other calamities, incited by a sorcerer or witch or even acting on their own out of sheer malevolence. The non-human and human spirits appear in the dark of the night, in thick forests or dark caves, waylaying a lonely wayfarer with fear in his heart or a woman praying for the birth of a healthy child. They prey upon the fears of human beings trapped in situations beyond their knowledge or control. Spirits of the murdered, spirits of those who died with unsatisfied desires and spirits of dead warriors and kings who were notorious for the cruelties they perpetrated left a lasting impression on the minds of a subject people. Pre-animistic beliefs, fears of uncontrollable powers and impersonations of the terror of night and nature were common to Aryans and non-Aryans. They were invented to describe what fell outside the ordinary, the world of the unexpected and unknown, created by the imaginations of people with fear and superstition in their hearts. Such spirits could only be controlled by those with a special knowledge of witchcraft and the means to drive away the spirits.

Demons can survive only if they find receptive minds. If an enemy is feared as something beyond the ordinary, he becomes a demon. If human beings could control their thoughts and tendency to make the awesome into an object of eternal fear, there would be no demons.

Finally, the demons represent the alter ego. Asuras and Devas are brothers. They represent two sides of a coin. They reside in the hearts and minds of people. They can be defeated only if the person chooses to drive the demon away. The final message is that we can choose between good and evil. But we must remember that good must, and shall ultimately, win. Hindu tradition makes the choice easier.

A Note on the Paintings (Plates 1 to 8)

Since most works of art celebrate gods and heroes, finding stand-alone demons in art was a difficult task. Further, I wanted them to be as contemporary as possible, to remind the reader that demons are metaphorically as relevant today as they were several millennia ago.

❖ Plates 1, 2 and 8 are oleographs of the early twentieth century, inspired by Raja Ravi Varma's style of painting.
Plate 1 is a print from the Ravi-Udaya F. A. L. Press, Ghatkopar, Bombay.
Plate 2 comes from the Bolton F. A. L. Works, Tardeo, Bombay.
Plate 8 is a print from the Ravi Varma Press, Malavli, G. I. P.
(Courtesy of The C. P. Ramaswami Aiyar Foundation, Chennai)

❖ The paintings in Plate 4 are taken from a nineteenth century painted Tamil paper manuscript narrating the story of Rama.
(Courtesy of The C. P. Ramaswami Aiyar Foundation, Chennai)

❖ Plate 5 consists of two drawings from the illustrated *Scenes from the Ramayana* published by R. Venkateshwar & Co., Ananda Press, Madras, in the early twentieth century. The company is now defunct.
(Courtesy of Mr. T. Gopalakrishnan)

❖ The artwork in Plates 6 and 7 are illustrations of the childhood of Krishna, in the colourful Oriya style of patta chitra painting on tussar silk.
(Courtesy of the author)

❖ Plate 3 is a photograph of a 16-foot high statue of Mahisha at the foot of Chamundi hill, where Mahisha's killer, goddess Chamunda (or Chamundi) is worshipped in a charming temple.
(Photo courtesy of Mr P. Sudhakar).

—Nanditha Krishna

Rama fighting the ten-headed Ravana

Hanuman carrying Rama and Lakshmana and walking
over the Rakshasi Surasa, guardian demon of Lanka

16-foot statue of Mahisha at the foot of the
Chamundeshvari Hill, Mysore (Mahisha-ur)

Rama fighting Kumbhakarna

Vibhishana, a good Rakshasa

Lakshmana cuts off Shoorpanakha's nose

Kumbhakarna fighting the monkey army

Depiction of Krishna and the wrestler Chanura
in an Oriya pattachitra painting

Baby Krishna suckling the demon Putana to death

Krishna killing the bull demon Arishtanemi

Krishna fighting Baka, the crane demon

Rama aims his bow at the demon Tataka

PART 2

In the following section, names of individual demons are in bold type and can be referred to in alphabetical order. The literary source for more information is given in brackets. While the same story may appear in several books, only the first book where it appears is mentioned.

A Dictionary of Demons in Sanskrit Literature

❖ **Abhimana**

The demon of egoistic pride, conquered by Ganesha as Dhumravarna. (*Mudgala Purana*)

❖ **Aadi**

The son of **Andhaka** who was killed by Shiva, Aadi was waiting for an opportunity to avenge his father's death. Aadi could change his appearance at will, but could also be killed when he used this power. In the form of a snake, he slid past Shiva's bull Nandi, then assumed the form of Parvati and approached Shiva. But Shiva and Parvati had just separated after an argument, so Shiva searched for body marks to prove that this was his wife. When he found them missing, he killed the demon. (*Shiva Purana*)

❖ **Aghaa**

General of **Kamsa** and brother of **Putana** and **Baka**, Aghaa took the form of an enormous serpent. Mistaking it for a cave, Krishna's cowherd friends entered his mouth. Krishna rescued them and killed the demon. (*Bhagavata Purana, Harivamsha*)

❖ **Agnishvatta**
Descendants of **Maaricha**. Also, spirits (pitṛ) of the forefathers who did not maintain their domestic fires or offer sacrifices. (*Vishnu Purana*)

❖ **Ahi**
Another name for the Vedic **Vritra**, demon of drought. Ahi takes the form of a serpent. His name means a cloud formation, or water vapour, and he is continuously at war with Indra, the Vedic god of thunder and rain (*Rig Veda*). Rig Vedic religion was pantheistic, the personification of various forces of nature, with natural happenings described as clashes or alliances between the various natural phenomena. The Ahi-Indra war describes the thunderbolt releasing rain from the cloud and ending the spell of drought.

❖ **Akampana**
Ravana's general who was killed by Hanuman in the Ramayana war. Akampana advised Ravana that, in view of the strength and invincibility of Rama, he should instead try to steal Rama's spouse Sita instead of openly abducting her. (*Ramayana*)

❖ **Aksha**
The eldest son of **Ravana**, king of Lanka. When Hanuman visits Lanka as Rama's messenger, Aksha is one of the Rakshasas who is sent by Ravana to kill him. He attacks Hanuman with a volley of arrows till the latter grips his feet, twirls him around in the air and throws him on the ground, smashing him to death. (*Ramayana*)
    Not to be confused with Aksha, another name of Garuda.

❖ **Akuli**
1. An **Asura** priest, along with **Kilaata,** who had a special influence on Manu. (*Shatapatha Brahmana*)
2. Spirits (pitṛ) of the demons. (*Harivamsha*)

❖ **Alakhadipa**
King of the **Nairrita,** one of the four **Rakshasa** clans. (*Bhagavata Purana, Brahmanda Purana*)

❖ **Alambusha**
Rakshasa son of Rishyashringa. He supported the Kauravas in the Mahabharata war and fought Satyaki who defeated him. Of part-human ancestry, he was finally killed by **Ghatotkacha.** (*Mahabharata*)

❖ **Alarka**
Another name for the Asura **Damsha.** (*Mahabharata*)

❖ **Alayudha**
Brother of **Baka** who was killed by **Ghatotkacha** in the Mahabharata war. (*Mahabharata*)

❖ **Anarya**
Ignoble or unworthy. While it initially stood for vile behaviour, it later came to denote those who were not Aryans, including demons.

❖ **Andhaka**
The word means 'blind darkness'. Andhaka is sometimes called the son of Shiva and Parvati, conceived when Parvati stole up behind Shiva and playfully covered his eyes. The world was

plunged in darkness and his third eye opened in anger. From the heat and the sweat of Shiva and Parvati rose the demon Andhaka, dark, dishevelled, dancing and walking like a blind (andha) man. Rejected by Parvati, he was brought up by the childless demon **Hiranyanetra** and lived on Mount Mandara. He performed severe austerities, chopping away parts of his flesh, which he would throw into the sacrificial fire. Finally, Andhaka did the unthinkable and desired his own mother Parvati. He even disguised himself as Shiva to deceive her. Parvati hid in an arka flower. Furious, Shiva danced his tandava

ANDHAKA

till he was ready to destroy the demon. He pierced Andhaka with his trident and held him high till he was scorched to death by Shiva's third eye.

But Andhaka is also described as the son of **Kashyapa** and Diti. He had a thousand arms and heads and two thousand eyes and feet. Since Andhaka tried to carry away the pārijāta tree from heaven, he was killed by Shiva, who was thus known as Andhaka samhāra (destroyer) or Andhaka ripu (enemy). (*Kurma Purana*)

Shiva's destruction of Andhaka represents the destruction of darkness or ignorance and a host of negative qualities.

Durga also kills an Andhaka, part of **Mahisha**'s army, with her arrows. Since Andhaka was killed on ashtami, the eighth day of the lunar fortnight, the day is set aside for the worship of the Sapta Matrikas or the Seven Mothers (forms of Devi). (*Devi Mahatmya, Markandeya Purana*)

Andhaka the demon must not be confused with Andhaka the Yadava, who was an ancestor of the Vrishni tribe to which Krishna belonged.

❖ **Anjaka**
Son of **Viprachitti**.

❖ **Anuhlada**
The son of **Hiranyakashipu**. He seduced Shachi, wife of Indra. (*Mahabharata*)

❖ **Apasmarapurusha**
The demon of ignorance, with the body of an infant, crushed by the left foot of Nataraja, a form of Shiva symbolized by the dance that set in motion the continuous process of creation, preservation and destruction of the universe. The word

apasmāra means forgetfulness and symbolizes the ignorance that makes us lose our balance and consciousness.

❖ **Arbuda**
1. A Rig Vedic demon of the atmosphere.
2. A serpent (Naga) demon who lived in Girivraja and was killed by Indra. Mount Abu in Rajasthan and the people who lived there were named after him (*Mahabharata*). In the *Rig Veda*, he is described as a powerful Dasyu who was defeated by Indra, who stepped on him.

❖ **Arishta/Arishtanemi**
A wild bull-demon, son of **Bali**, and servant of **Kamsa**. The animal terrified the cowherds and tore up the hills and mountains around Vrindavan. He was finally killed by Krishna. (*Harivamsha, Bhagavata Purana*)

❖ **Asamanjas**
Son of Sagara, a king of Ayodhya, and Keshini, a princess of Vidarbha. He was a wild and immoral young man. He later lived in the sea in the form of a conch shell and was known as **Panchajana**, in which form he was killed by Krishna. (*Harivamsha*)

❖ **Ashiras**
Headless spirits or demons.

❖ **Asura**
See Part I, Chapter 2: Fallen Gods—Asuras.

❖ **Ashvapati**
Name of a Kaikeya or resident of Kaikeya (Western Punjab), (*Shatapatha Brahmana*) who was an **Asura** (*Mahabharata*).

❖ **Atikaya**

Ravana's mountainous son who was granted a boon by Brahma. He was finally killed by Lakshmana with Brahma's weapon (the brahmastra). (*Ramayana*)

❖ **Avindhya**

A good **Rakshasa** who advises **Ravana** not to kill Sita. (*Ramayana*)

❖ **Ayomukhi**

A **Rakshasi** deputed by **Ravana** to guard Sita and persuade her to marry Ravana. (*Ramayana*)

❖ **Baleya**

Descendant of **Bali**.

❖ **Baka**

1. The **Rakshasa** brother of **Putana, Kamsa** sent him to Vrindavan to kill the child Krishna. He took the form of a giant crane, carried away Krishna in his beak and then swallowed him. However, his throat started burning, so he threw Krishna out and tried to kill him by biting. But Krishna caught hold of the beak and tore it apart, thus killing Baka. (*Bhagavata Purana*)

2. He was a Rakshasa king with red hair and pointed ears, who lived in a cave. He was given one human being a day to eat till Bhima the Pandava killed him. (*Harivamsha*)

❖ **Baki**

Sister of **Baka**.

❖ **Bala**

An **Asura** who lived in Atala. He taught ninety-six kinds of magic to trouble the Devas. He created three women who gave an aphrodisiac called *hataka* to men, enjoyed them as long as they liked and then discarded them after draining off their energy.

Bala defeated Indra in battle. Cleverly, the god sang the Asura's praises till Bala offered Indra a boon. Indra asked for Bala's body, which the Asura gave, and which Indra cut into pieces and threw about. Gold (or diamond) mines appeared wherever the body fell, as a result of Bala's merit of keeping his promise to Indra. After his death, Bala's wife **Prabhavati** asked **Shukra** to bring him back to life, which Shukra said he could not do. He suggested that Prabhavati should leave her body and join her husband. Prabhavati did so, and became the river of the same name. (*Mahabharata*)

❖ **Bali (Danavendrah, Asurasattamah)**
He was a 'good' **Daitya** king, son of **Virochana**, grandson of **Prahlada** and great grandson of **Hiranyakashipu**, who was present at the amrita manthana (churning of the ocean). Bali performed the Vishvajita sacrifice, after performing one hundred Ashvamedhas (horse sacrifices), and was appointed the King of Heaven, another Indra. The pious and much loved ruler defeated Indra and the gods through his penance and piety and the magic of mritasañjīvanī (life restoration) taught by his guru **Shukra**. The gods then appealed to Vishnu to restore their worlds, so Vishnu assumed the form of a radiant-faced, dwarf-sized, Brahmana youth, Vamana. Vamana appeared before Bali who, impressed by his appearance, offered him wealth and lands and whatever else he desired. But Vamana said a good man should not ask for more than his needs, and all he wanted was the ground covered by his three steps. Bali's preceptor Shukra cautioned him against acceding to Vamana's request, but Bali insisted on redeeming his promise, and asked Vamana to measure out three paces. Immediately, the dwarf

grew in size. With one step he covered the earth, with the second he covered the sky and the heavens. When there was no place for his third step, Bali offered his own head, and Vamana placed his foot on it, crushing it into the earth. Then Vishnu's devotee Prahlada appeared and begged Vishnu to spare his grandson who did not deserve to be punished. So Vishnu made Bali the king of Patala (the netherworld).

The origin of the three steps of Vamana is to be found in the Rig Vedic allusion to the three steps (trivikrama) of Vishnu, the solar god. The three positions of his three steps are the rising, midday and setting sun. (*Mahabharata, Harivamsha*)

Bali's story lives on in Kerala, whose people claim him as an ancient ruler whose rule was one of peace and prosperity. He was, it is believed, pressed into the earth at Mavelikara. Bali was permitted by Vishnu to visit his people once a year, and this he does during the annual harvest festival of Onam. (See Part I, Chapter 3: Demonized Enemies)

BALI AND VAMANA

❖ **Bana**

The thousand-armed son of **Bali**, Bana was a devout Shaiva and an enemy of Vishnu, who had suppressed his father. His daughter **Usha** fell in love with the portrait of Aniruddha, Krishna's grandson, drawn by her companion. With her magical abilities, Chitralekha kidnapped Aniruddha and brought him to Usha. When Bana learned of Aniruddha's identity, he tried to kill him, but Krishna, Balarama and Krishna's son Pradyumna went to Aniruddha's rescue and a bitter fight took place, in which Shiva and his warrior son Karttikeya assisted Bana. But Karttikeya was wounded, Shiva was overpowered by Krishna and the thousand arms of Bana were cut off by Krishna. Then Shiva interceded on Bana's behalf and Krishna granted him his life. (*Harivamsha*)

The story of Bana's defeat reflects the animosity between the Vaishnavas and Shaivas, which had reached epic proportions by the Puranic period.

❖ **Barhanashva**

Son of Nikumbha. (*Bhagavata Purana*)

❖ **Barhishad**

Spirits (pitṛ) of the demons. (*Harivamsha*)

❖ **Bhurunda**

They are soul-seizing sirens and harpies, birds with strong beaks and bodies who bury the bodies of the Kurus. They sing with pleasant voices and have human faces. (*Mahabharata*)

❖ **Bhasakarna**

Ravana's general. When Hanuman went to Lanka in search of Sita, he killed Bhasakarna by hurling a mountain peak at him. (*Ramayana*)

❖ **Bhasmaka**

A demon who, through his austerities, obtained the power to kill any creature by touching it. The demon decided to test his powers on Shiva himself, who had to run away. Then Vishnu took the form of a beautiful woman called Mohini who invited the demon to dance and imitate her movements. Bhasmaka did so. In the course of the dance, Mohini touched her head, which the demon imitated, forgetting his boon. His body burst into flames, and the demon was destroyed. (*Harivamsha*)

This is another example of Shaiva–Vaishnava rivalry, for Vishnu had to 'save' Shiva's life.

❖ **Bhauma**

Another name for **Naraka**.

❖ **Bhima**

He was the **Rakshasa** son of **Kumbhakarna** and **Karkati**, who was determined to take revenge on Vishnu. He got a boon of great strength from Brahma, after which he attacked and imprisoned the king of Kamaroopa who was a devout worshipper of Vishnu. Thereafter, the king and his wife prayed to the Shiva Linga. When Bhima raised his sword to cut off the king's head, Shiva came out of the Linga and killed the demon. This is the origin of the Bhimashankara Linga, one of the jyotirlingas. (*Shiva Purana*)

Bhima the demon must not be confused with Bhima the Pandava.

❖ **Bhrigu**

A great priest and teacher of the Asuras, and father of Chyavana. (*Aitareya Brahmana*, *Shatapatha Brahmana*)

❖ **Bhuta**

See Part I, Chapter 5: Spirits, Ghosts and Others.

❖ Baital

Another pronunciation for Vetal. See Part I, Chapter 5: Spirits, Ghosts and Others.

❖ Brahmadaitya

A Brahmana who becomes a demon.

❖ Chamara

A member of Mahisha's army killed by Durga's lion. (*Devi Mahatmya, Markandeya Purana*)

❖ Chanda

Chanda and his younger brother **Munda** were Asura allies of the demons **Shumbha** and **Nishumbha**. Munda was better known as **Mahisha**, and was killed by Kali or Chamunda, an emanation from the forehead of Goddess Durga. As the goddess killed Chanda and his brother Munda, she was named Chamunda. (*Devi Mahatmya, Markandeya Purana*)

Chanda could have been the name of an ancient tribe defeated by worshippers of Durga, just as Munda was, and continues to be, the name of a central Indian tribe.

❖ Chandodari

A **Rakshasi** deputed by **Ravana** to guard Sita and persuade her to marry Ravana. (*Ramayana*)

❖ Chanura

A wrestler-demon in **Kamsa**'s employment who was commandeered by the latter to kill Krishna in a public competition in Mathura. Instead, Chanura was killed by Krishna. (*Mahabharata*)

❖ **Charvaka**

A friend of Duryodhana, he was a **Rakshasa** who disguised himself as a Brahmana when Yudhishthira entered Hastinapura in triumph after the Mahabharata war. He accused and abused Yudhishthira for war crimes, till the Brahmanas identified him as an imposter and scorched him to death with the flames from their eyes. (*Mahabharata*)

Charvaka is also the name of a philosopher who advocated materialism and was the founder of a school of skepticism and materialism named after him. It is likely that he was the same Charvaka who met Yudhishthira after the war, and was labelled a Rakshasa for subscribing to an unacceptable philosophical system.

❖ **Chikshura**

Mahisha's general, killed by Durga with a spear. (*Devi Mahatmya, Markandeya Purana*)

❖ **Chyavana**

1. Name of a disease-causing demon. (*Paraskara grihyasutra*)
2. The son of Bhrigu, the great priest and teacher of the **Asuras**. Once a great magician, he grew old and blind till the Ashvins cured him of both old age and blindness. After regaining his vision and his youth Chyavana was extremely happy with the Ashvins and, when they were denied soma (a ritual drink) by Indra, he offered to get it for them. He organized a soma sacrifice to which he invited all the Devas including the Ashvins. Indra was furious and ordered the Ashvins to leave. Chyavana started a fight with Indra. Out of the sacrificial fire, he made a demon called **Mada** to kill Indra. Indra tried to use his vajra in reply, but found that his limbs were paralysed. Finally Indra prayed to his guru

Brihaspati who advised him to apologize to Chyavana. As Chyavana was accepting the apology, Indra tore him into four pieces, which became wine, women, hunting and the game of dice, which still retain fascination for men. (*Aitareya Brahmana*, *Shatapatha Brahmana*)
3. Chyavana was also a great Ayurvedic physician. (*Brahmavaivarta Purana*)

❖ Daitya
See Part I, Chapter 3: Demonized Enemies.

❖ Dakhini
A female demon attendant of Goddess Kali, who drank blood and ate human flesh. The name is derived from the word Dakshayani.

DAKHINI

❖ **Daksha**

Father of the **Daityas** (demons) and Adityas (gods or shining ones), sons of **Diti** and Aditi respectively. Daksha also appears elsewhere in the *Puranas* as the father of Sati, wife of Shiva. (*Mahabharata*)

❖ **Damsha**

He was an **Asura** who was cursed by a rishi to be born as a blood-drinking octopod (worm). On being released from the curse he appeared not as an Asura but as a red Rakshasa, **Alarka**, riding a cloud (*Mahabharata*).

❖ **Danava**

Son of **Kashyapa** and **Danu**. See Part I, Chapter 3: Demonized Enemies.

❖ **Dantavaktra**

This was the final birth of **Vijaya**, one of the doorkeepers of Vishnu's heaven Vaikuntha who, along with his brother **Jaya**, was cursed by some sages to take three lives as a demon. He was the king of Karusha and son of Vriddha Sharman, a **Daitya** who fought Krishna and was ultimately killed by him. (*Bhagavata Purana*)

With the Brahmana appendage Sharman to his name, Dantavaktra was a Brahmana who opposed the hero-god Krishna.

❖ **Danu**

Mother of the demons or **Danavas**. Her sons include **Shambara, Namuci, Puloman, Keshin, Svarbhanu, Ashva, Viroopaksha, Naraka** and **Vatapi**. (*Mahabharata*)

❖ **Darba**

Another name for **Rakshasa**, meaning 'tearers'.

❖ **Daruka**

He was a demon who lived with his wife **Daruki** in the ancient forest of Darukavana near Dwarka in Gujarat, whence the name Dwarka. Parvati had granted Daruki the boon that forests would follow wherever she went. The couple began to oppress the world and destroyed the sacrifice. So the people went to sage Ourva who cursed the **Rakshasas** with death if they committed any violence on earth. The gods then attacked them, leaving the demons in a fix. If the demons did not fight they would be killed and if they did fight they would also die. So they decided to go and live under the ocean, where the forest followed Daruki.

Daruka imprisoned and nearly killed Supriya, a devotee of Shiva, when Supriya's ship was caught in a gale and sought shelter at Darukavan. Daruka asked Supriya to teach him the Shiva panchakshari and the method of doing the Shiva puja, which Supriya refused to do, as he was afraid that the demon would abuse his knowledge. Shiva gave Supriya the pashupata weapon, with which he finally killed Daruka. The linga that Supriya worshipped was the Nagesha or Naganatha. (*Shiva Purana*)

This myth probably refers to the submerging and desertification of western Gujarat, particularly in and around Dwarka.

❖ **Daruki**

The wife of **Daruka**, she went about killing people after her husband's death. Shiva appeared before his devotees to save them and, at the request of Supriya, lived on near Dwaraka in the form of a jyotirlinga, also known as Nagesha or Naganathaswami. This linga protects the people and the region against the evil machinations of demons. (*Shiva Purana*)

❖ **Dashanana**

'Ten-faced', another name for **Ravana**, demon king of Lanka and the main villain of the Ramayana war. (*Ramayana*)

❖ **Devantaka**

1. **Ravana**'s general who is killed by Hanuman in the Ramayana war (*Ramayana*).

2. A demon who was harassing the three worlds and was destroyed by Mahotkata, an earlier incarnation of Ganesha in the krita yuga, who was born as the son of sage **Kashyapa** and his wife Aditi for the purpose. (*Ganesha Purana*)

❖ **Devayani**

She was the daughter of **Shukra**, priest-preceptor of the Asuras. She fell in love with Kacha, her father's student, who rejected her advances. She cursed him and was cursed in return that she, a Brahmana's daughter, would marry a Kshatriya. One day, when she and **Sharmishtha**, daughter of the Daitya king **Vrishaparvan**, were bathing, their clothes were mixed up and each came out wearing the other's clothes. They quarrelled, so Sharmishtha slapped Devyani and pushed her into a dry well, from which she was rescued by King Yayati. Devyani married Yayati, and demanded that Sharmishtha become her maidservant. But Yayati fell in love with Sharmishtha and the latter bore him a son, the discovery of which made Devyani so angry that she took her two sons Yadu and Turvasa and left Yayati. Shukra cursed Yayati with old age, but later offered to transfer the curse to any of Yayati's sons who would accept it. All the sons of Yayati refused, and were cursed by their father that their heirs would receive no inheritance. All except Puru, Sharmishtha's youngest son, who bore his father's curse for a thousand years, succeeded his father as ruler, and was the ancestor of the Pandavas and Kauravas. (*Bhagavata Purana*)

❖ **Dhanyamalini**
A wife of **Ravana**. (*Ramayana*)

❖ **Dhenuka**
The ass-demon killed by Balarama. Krishna and Balarama were picking fruits in the demon's forest-garden, called Talavana, when Dhenuka and his fellow demons, all in the form of an ass, came running towards Balarama and began to kick him. The latter caught Dhenuka by his heels and twirled him in the

DHENUKA

sky till the demon was dead. Then Dhenuka and his friends were thrown into the palm trees till they were all dead. (*Bhagavata Purana*)

❖ **Dhumraksha**
1. **Ravana**'s general who was killed by Hanuman in the Ramayana war (*Ramayana*).
2. A demon who was destroyed by Mahotkata, an earlier incarnation of Ganesha in the krita yuga, who was born as the son of sage Kashyapa and his wife Aditi for the purpose. (*Ganesha Purana*)

❖ **Dhumralochana**
Shumbha's general who was sent by the demon to capture Durga, who destroyed him with a roar. (*Shiva Purana*)

❖ **Dhundhu**
While the sage Uttanka was in meditation, Dhundhu hid beneath the sands to harass him. Then King Kuvalashva, son of Vrihadasva, and his sons attacked him for seven days, while Dhundhu spat out flames. Finally, the king dug out the demon, unfazed by the hot fire that killed nearly all of them, leaving merely three sons. For this feat the king received the epithet Dhundhu-mara. The king's grandson Haryashva, after whose five (pancha) sons the country Panchala was named, killed the demon (*Brahma Purana*). Draupadi, heroine of the Mahabharata war, was a princess of Panchala and was known as Panchali.

This appears to be the story of a volcano, or a great fire, that burnt itself out.

❖ **Diti**
Daughter of **Daksha**, wife of **Kashyapa** and mother of the **Daityas** or demons. (*Ramayana*)

❖ **Drishana**
Another name of **Virochana**, son of **Prahlada** and father of **Bali**. (*Vishnu Purana*)

❖ **Druhyu**
Grandson of the Daitya king **Vrishaparvan** and son of the **Daitya** princess **Sharmishtha** and Yayati, whose descendants became the 'princes of the lawless barbarians of the north'. Since he refused to part with his youth for his father's gratification, he was cursed by Yayati to have no pleasures in life and to wander over countries and oceans, with no settled kingdom. The Bhoja line begins from him. (*Matsya Purana*)

❖ **Dundubhi**
A wicked and proud buffalo demon possessed of great strength, he was sent by Himavat, lord of the mountains, to challenge the invincible monkey king Vali to a fight. But he was defeated and killed by Vali in a hand-to-hand combat. (*Ramayana*)

❖ **Duradura**
Ravana's general who was killed by Hanuman when he went to Lanka in search of Sita. (*Ramayana*)

❖ **Durga**
The destruction of the demon Durga, meaning fortress, gave Devi her name Durga. The demon overcame the three worlds and drove Indra and the Devas from heaven and into the forests. He abolished all religious ceremonies and the Vedas and forced the Devas to worship him. He made the stars disappear and the rivers change their course, produced rain out of season and crops when he wished. The burden was too much for the earth and its inhabitants to bear. The gods asked Shiva to help, and he directed them to Devi.

Devi created·**Kalaratri** and sent her against Durga, but she was unsuccessful. So Devi set out herself, to face the demon army consisting of 10,000,000 horses, 120, 000,000,000 elephants and 100,000,000 chariots. He attacked her with arrows, rocks, trees and clubs. But Devi, who had grown 1000 arms and produced 9,000,000 beings out of her body, destroyed the demon's army. The demon threw a mountain at her, which she cut up. The demon took the form of an elephant and then a buffalo, but Devi destroyed each form till the demon took his natural form, a demon with 1000 arms and a weapon in each. Then Devi held down the demon's 1000 arms with her own, threw him down and pierced his breast with an arrow till he died. After her victory, Devi assumed the demon's name, and became Durga. (*Devi Mahatmyam*)

❖ **Dooshana**

1. One of the generals of **Ravana**. He was the companion of **Khara**, Ravana's brother, and was killed by Rama in the Dandaka forest, when Khara attacked Rama in retaliation for the disfigurement of **Shoorpanakha**. (*Ramayana*)

2. There is another story of another Dooshana who lived in the Ratnamala hills near Avanti, the present Ujjain. He was a killer and a cannibal, who ate the flesh of the people he killed. The local people were terrified and went to a pious Brahmana living nearby for help. The Brahmana performed a mahāyagna to Shiva who appeared and destroyed the demon. Thereafter, at the request of the Brahmana and the local people, Shiva took residence in a jyotirlinga at Ujjain in the form of Mahakala. (*Shiva Purana*)

❖ **Dvivida**

An ape demon who was an enemy of the gods. He stole Balarama's plough and thus started a terrible battle in which

DVIVIDA

Dvivida was killed and the mountain on which his body fell shattered into a hundred pieces. (*Harivamsha*)

(Not to be confused with the Vanara or monkey allies of Rama).

❖ **Gajamukha**

An elephant-faced demon who performed severe austerities under the advice of the demon guru **Shukra** and obtained powers of invincibility from Shiva. Gajamukha then used his powers to harass the gods who could not subdue him because of Shiva's boon. Then they rushed to Ganesha who broke his right tusk and threw it at the demon, cursing him to change into a mouse.

He quickly got on to the back of the mouse and made it his vehicle, thereby keeping it under control. (*Ganesha Purana*)

❖ **Gajanibha**
Creatures who look like elephants and draw **Ghatotkacha's** chariot. (*Mahabharata*)

❖ **Gajasura**
The elephant demon harassed gods and men, and even tried to conquer Kashi. The constant battles weakened Shiva's ganas, forcing his intervention. Gajasura regarded his death as

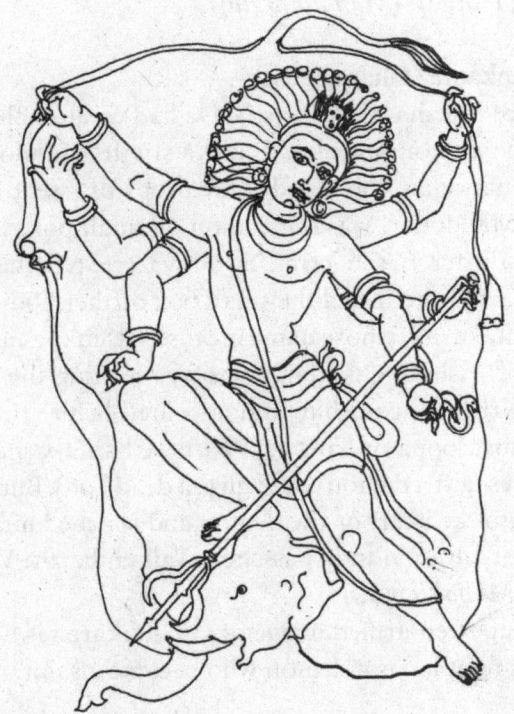

SHIVA DANCING ON THE SKIN OF GAJASURA

deliverance and asked that his skin should be stripped to shade Shiva's head, while his elephant head should be strung on Shiva's garland of skulls. Thus Shiva as the destroyer of Gaja—*Gaja samhara murti*—is portrayed dancing with an elephant's skin held over his head and the elephant head either beneath his foot or strung on a necklace of skulls. (*Shiva Purana*)

The temple of Shiva at Viluvur in Tamil Nadu, containing a beautiful bronze image of Shiva as Gajasamharamurti, is believed to have been the location where this incident occurred.

❖ **Gautami**
A fierce **Rakshasi** (not to be confused with Gautami, another name for Durga). (*Mahabharata*)

❖ **Ghantakanta/Ghantakarna**
They were **Rakshasa** brothers. Shiva had created Bhadrakali to kill the demon **Daruka**. Daruka's wife **Mandodari** did severe penance and obtained some drops of sweat from the god. As Mandodari was the demon of small pox, she made Bhadrakali her first victim. So Shiva created the demon Ghantakarna who licked the small pox off her body.

Ghantakarna, whose name means bells in the ears, was a devotee of Vishnu. One day, as he was reciting the name of Vishnu, Krishna heard him and appeared before the demon in his Vishvaroopa or Universal Form. Ghantakarna offered him the best gift a demon could give: a dead body. But Krishna looked into the heart of the demon and touched him, giving him instant salvation and a passage to Vaikuntha, the Vaishnava heaven. (*Mahabharata*)

The eighteen-armed image of Ghantakarna is honoured in Vishnu temples as a demon who became a saint.

❖ **Ghatotkacha**

Son of the Pandava Bhima and the demoness **Hidimbaa**, he is
brought up by his mother. Although he is only half **Rakshasa**,
the paternal half being Aryan, he is called a Rakshasa, indicating
the matriarchal nature of his tribe.

Ghatotkacha was unstoppable in the Mahabharata war.
So Karna, son of Kunti and friend of the Kaurava prince
Duryodhana, was forced to use the invincible lance given to
him by Indra to kill Ghatotkacha. Thus Karna forfeited the
opportunity to use the lance to kill Arjuna, and sealed his
own fate. (*Mahabharata*)

Ghatotkacha is a 'friendly' demon belonging to the family
of the victorious Pandavas. But he is sacrificed to ensure the
ultimate victory of his father's brother Arjuna who, thanks to
Karna's use of the divine lance against Ghatotkacha, could kill
Karna and ensure the victory of the Pandava princes (See Part
I, Chapter 3: Demonized Enemies).

❖ **Hari**

Son of **Taraka**, he obtains, as a boon from Brahma, a lake which
restores life to anyone who bathes in it. (*Mahabharata*)

❖ **Havyaghna**

He was created from the smoke of the sacrificial fire of Rishi
Bharadvaja and began eating the leftovers. Bharadvaja sprinkled
Ganga water, ghee and soma over him and released him from
Brahma's curse, which had made him live as a demon.

❖ **Hayagriva**

At the end of the kalpa, Brahma was asleep, and the Vedas
fell out of his mouth. Hayagriva, 'the horse-necked' **Asura**,

stole the sacred books. But Vishnu took the Matsya (fish) incarnation and recovered the Vedas, killing the demon.

Sometimes Vishnu himself is identified with Hayagriva, a form he assumed to recover the Vedas from the **Daityas** who had stolen them. (*Harivamsha*)

Hayagriva was probably a totemic figure defeated by Vishnu.

❖ Hayas

The demon king of the horses who lived in the forests along the Yamuna, and was killed by Krishna. (*Harivamsha*)

❖ Hidamba

A yellow-eyed and frightening demon, a forest-dwelling cannibal. Hidamba sent his sister **Hidambaa** to bring the Pandavas to him. But she fell in love with Bhima, one of the Pandavas, and offered to take him away to safety. When the demon came upon the two of them, a terrible battle took place, resulting in the death of Hidamba. Hidamba is described as a cannibal who lived in a śāla tree, had eight fangs, pointed ears and red hair, was very strong and enjoyed the smell of men, which roused him to eat them. (*Mahabharata*) (See Part I, Chapter 3: Demonized Enemies).

❖ Hidambaa

Sister of **Hidamba**, she took on human form and could look into the past and the future. Hidambaa claimed and married Bhima after the death of her brother Hidamba, to fulfil Kunti's wish. She gave birth to a powerful—but good—demon **Ghatotkacha**, who took part in the Mahabharata war and killed several Kaurava warriors. (*Mahabharata*) (See Part I, Chapter 3: Demonized Enemies).

❖ **Hiranyaksha**

His name means 'golden-eyed' and he was a cruel and evil demon, son of **Diti** and **Kashyapa** and twin brother of **Hiranyakashipu**. In a former birth the brothers were **Jaya** and **Vijaya**, doorkeepers of Vishnu's heaven Vaikuntha. But they were arrogant, resulting in some sages cursing them to be born as demons.

Hiranyaksha caused great suffering to the people and even harassed the gods. Finally, he rolled mother earth in a mat and threw her into the ocean. She let out a terrible cry that was heard by Vishnu. Immediately Vishnu took the form of a gigantic boar Varaha and plunged into the water. A terrible

HIRANYAKSHA

fight ensued, in which Vishnu, as the incarnation Varaha, killed Hiranyaksha and saved the earth. (*Mahabharata, Harivamsha*)

Hiranyaksha was a 'fallen angel' who became a demon. The *Shiva Purana* calls him Hiranyanetra or 'golden eyed'. (See Part I, Chapter 3: Demonized Enemies).

❖ Hiranyakashipu

Like his twin **Hiranyaksha**, Hiranyakashipu was a cruel and evil demon. Son of **Diti** and **Kashyapa**, he and his brother were originally **Jaya** and **Vijaya**, the doorkeepers of Vishnu's palace in a former birth. But their arrogance resulted in some sages cursing them to be born as demons.

Hiranyakashipu swore to avenge his brother's death. He performed severe penances till he obtained a unique boon from Brahma: he could not be killed by either man or animal, neither at night nor in the day, neither inside nor outside, not on earth nor in the sky nor under water, with neither a weapon nor fire nor water. The result was to make him invincible and, consequently, evil and cruel. But Hiranyakashipu had an Achilles heel: his son **Prahlada**, who was an ardent devotee of Lord Vishnu. In spite of Hiranyakashipu's admonishments and threats, and even attempts to kill his son, Prahlada would not swerve from his devotion. Finally, Hiranyakashipu asked his son to show him Vishnu and kicked a pillar, asking him whether his god lived in there. From the pillar came the terrible man-lion Narasimha, neither human nor animal. The two fought a long and deadly war, all the while moving towards the front door. Then, at sunset, when it was neither night nor day, on the doorway that was neither inside nor outside, in the firmament that was neither earth nor sky nor water,

Narasimha tore the demon to death with his claws, using neither weapon nor fire nor water. (*Mahabharata, Harivamsha*)

The story of Hiranyakashipu is located in parts of Andhra Pradesh: Ahobalam, where he was killed by Narasimha and Simhachalam, where his son Prahlada reigned. It is likely that these were two different communities who fought till one defeated the other. The victor was a devotee of the solar deity Vishnu. (See Part I, Chapter 3: Demonized Enemies).

❖ Hiranyanetra
A childless demon who lived on Mount Mandara and adopted **Andhaka**, who was later destroyed by Shiva.

❖ Hlada
One of the sons of **Hiranyakashipu**.

❖ Hrada
The name of some **Daityas** who defeated the Devas. The Devas approached Vishnu who created a māyāmoha, an illusionary figure, out of his own body. When the Asuras were meditating on the banks of the Narmada River, Māyāmoha appeared before them dressed in leaves and with shaven head. He told them to follow his preaching, which was to leave the path of the Vedas. Those who followed Māyāmoha's teachings were known as arhats and were critical of sacrifices and Brahmanas. The Asuras were thus dislodged from the true path and were attacked and defeated by the Devas since they (the **Asuras**) had lost the power of the Vedic religion (*Vishnu Purana*).

This is a story created to explain the defeat of the Jainas. Māyāmoha was either Mahavira or one of the arhats.

❖ **Hriyashva**
Father of **Nikumbha**. (*Bhagavata Purana*)

❖ **Hunda**
An **Asura** who lived in a nandanakānana, or sacred garden, of flowers. He abducted Ashokasundari, created by Parvati, and was cursed by Ashokasundari to be killed by her husband Nahusha. Hunda was killed by King Nahusha, son of King Ayus and Queen Indumati and father of Yayati, progenitor of the Yadavas. (*Mahabharata*, *Padma Purana*)

Nandanakānana (also nandavana) is a garden of sacred flowers used for worship. The demon could have been a Yaksha of sorts, since such beings lived in forests and gardens.

❖ **Ilvala**
1. Son of **Simhika** and **Viprachitti** and brother of **Vatapi**, **Namuchi** and **Maricha** he was a **Rakshasa** who who lived in the Dandaka forest. He and his brother revelled in killing Brahmanas till his brother was devoured and digested by sage Agastya. Vatapi would assume the form of a ram, which was offered in sacrifice and eaten by Brahmanas. Then his brother Ilvala would call him and he would tear his way out of the stomachs of the Brahmanas, injuring and killing them. He tried the same trick with Agastya who ate and digested him, so that he could no longer come out. Ilvala attacked Agastya, but was burnt up by the fire from the sage's eyes. (*Ramayana*)
2. Son of **Hrada** and **Dhamani**, he cooked Vatapi for his guest Agastya. He was a follower of Vritra in his battle with Indra (*Brahmanda Purana*). He took part in the war between the Gods and the demons and fought with the sons of Brahma. He was the father of Balvala. (*Bhagavata Purana*)

❖ **Indrajit**

Son of **Ravana**, he was also known as Meghanaada or 'sound of the clouds'. He fought valiantly when his father Ravana attacked Indra's army in heaven. Indrajit also capitalizes on the weakness of the Devas to confer boons on all and sundry. Meghanaada had received the boon of invisibility from Shiva, so when Indra took part in the war, he used his magical powers to become invisible, bound Indra and carried him away to Lanka. The gods led by Brahma went to release Indra, but Meghanaada refused to give him up till he received the boon of immortality. Brahma refused, and named him Indrajit ('conqueror of Indra'), but Meghanaada did not release Indra till he was granted his boon.

The story of Meghanaada probably descibes a single natural phenomenon: the clouds releasing rain (Indra). This may be the reason for Indrajit's black and red-eyed appearance, a description used for Yakshas rather than human beings.

Indrajit is a great warrior who also employs magic against his opponents. In fact, he is famed for his sorcery. First, he creates a phantom Sita, places her in his chariot and kills her before the monkey army, to demoralize them. Hanuman is persuaded that with Sita's death the war need not continue, but Rama believes that as long as Ravana and the **Rakshasa** *adharma* remain, he is duty-bound to kill them. Finally, it is left to Vibhishana to point out that Ravana would never permit the killing of Sita, whom he desired, and that this was a form of Indrajit's sorcery. Vibhishana then informs them that Indrajit was performing a ritual that, if completed, would make him invincible. He has to be prevented from completing the ritual. So Lakshmana and Hanuman go off, raring for a kill. On Vibhishana's advice, they break the Rakshasa formation and shower Indrajit with arrows, trees and rocks. He fights Hanuman

INDRAJIT

but the latter says he is the son of Vayu the wind and dares the cloud (Meghanaada) to fight him. Then Lakshmana sits on Hanuman's shoulders and takes on Indrajit in single combat. The epic describes the variety of arrows and spears the two use against each other. The gods and other celestial beings line up to watch the battle. Finally, choosing an arrow covered with gold, Lakshmana severs Indrajit's head, thereby killing one of the greatest warriors of the Rakshasas. (*Ramayana*)

Indrajit in the *Ramayana* is a contradictory figure. As Meghanaada, his actions are those of the cloud fighting the sky god Indra, who is holding back the rain, and the wind in the form of Hanuman. As Indrajit, he is a much loved prince and an erudite scholar. He counsels his father—unsuccessfully—to send Sita back to her husband. Finally he has to pay the price of his father's greed and immorality with his head and life.

❖ Ishtipashas

A name meaning 'those who steal the offerings' given to demons. The word suggests a non-Vedic people who did not respect but stole the sacred offerings made during the sacrifice.

❖ Jaladhaara/Jalandhara

When Shiva's fire scorched the seas, a demon arose from the steam. He was Jaladhaara, who became the leader of the **Asuras**.

According to another origin story, Indra and the other gods paid Shiva a visit on Mount Kailasa, to amuse him with music and dance. Pleased, Shiva offered Indra a boon. Defiantly, Indra asked for and received a boon to be as great a warrior as Shiva himself. After his departure, Shiva asked his attendants whether they had observed Indra's haughty tone. Immediately, Krodha (Anger) came before Shiva and asked what he could do. Shiva ordered him to form a union with Ganga and conquer Indra. Ganga came down from the skies, united with the ocean and gave birth to a son, at whose birth the three worlds trembled. Brahma came to see the cause of the noise and held the child on his lap. But the child would not let go until his father loosened its hand. Admiringly, Brahma named the child Jaladhaara and said he would be unconquered by the gods.

Jaladhaara led the demons to victory in a war against the Devas, and captured heaven itself. Indra, defeated, went to Brahma for help. He caught Brahma by the throat and shook him till the latter said that Jaladhaara could be defeated by Shiva alone. Jaladhaara's father, the ocean, arranged for his marriage with Vrinda, daughter of the demon **Kalanemi**. The next time Jaladhaara said he was the greatest warrior, Indra said he was not the greatest until he had defeated Shiva, a hermit who lived on Mount Kailasa. Narada praised Shiva's wealth, fortune and his beautiful wife. The lustful Jaladhaara rushed to Kailasa to fight Shiva. Shiva marked out a circle of earth with his big toe and offered to fight Jaladhaara if he could carry the piece of earth. Jaladhaara ripped out the ground and placed it on his head. Suddenly, the circular piece of earth grew in size and began to whirl like a discus. It grew so large and whirled so violently that it decapitated him. As Jaladhaara lay dying, he heard Shiva's voice say that one who could not even carry a piece of earth on his head was certainly not the strongest person in the cosmos. (*Padma Purana*)

❖ **Jalodbhava**

Long ago, the Kashmir Valley was a lake called Sati Saras, named after Parvati, the consort of Shiva. It was a habitat of demons and cannibals who were a threat to human beings. Rishi Kashyapa, the sage, destroyed all the demons, including their king Jalodbhava, and converted the valley into land. (*Mahabharata*)

❖ **Jambha**

1. Leader of the demons who snatched the pot of amrita (immortal nectar) from sage Dhanvantari when he emerged from the ocean carrying the pot during the churning of the ocean. He, along with the other demons was tricked into giving up the nectar by Vishnu in the form of Mohini. He fought the gods till he was killed by Indra who was therefore named Jambhabhedin (*Harivamsha*). Later, this achievement of Indra's was transferred to Arjuna, when Jambha fought the Pandava, but was killed by Krishna.

2.   The name of a demon who led **Taraka's** army in a chariot of one hundred lions. He fought Yama, Kubera, Janardana and others but was finally killed. He fought Arjuna and was killed by Krishna. (*Bhagavata Purana*)

3.   A leader of the demons, who tried to kidnap Lakshmi. The demons carried her off on their shoulders, so her consort Dattātreya, an incarnation of Vishnu, told the gods to attack. They did so. Lakshmi abandoned the demons and the demons were killed. (*Markandeya Purana*)

❖ **Jambumali**

Son of **Prahasta**, he was a great archer and a general of **Ravana's** army. Hanuman clubbed him to death when he went in search of Sita in Lanka. (*Ramayana*)

❖ **Jara**

A **Rakshasi**. The two queens of Brihadratha, king of Magadha, delivered two halves of a male baby. Horrified, the king had them thrown away. They were discovered by the cannibal demoness Jara who put the two halves together to make a whole boy. The child cried so loudly that the king and his two wives came out to see what had happened. The Rakshasi explained what had happened, gave them the baby and went her way. As he had been put together by Jara, the king gave the child the name **Jarasandha**. Jarasandha became a devotee of Shiva and a famous king of Magadha. He attacked Krishna eighteen times, but was defeated every time. He was finally killed by Balarama, elder brother of Krishna, who came to Magadha from Dwarka for that purpose. (*Mahabharata*)

There is a suggestion that Jara was an indigenous medicine woman, a 'witch' in Western terms, who saved either a Siamese twin or a stillborn child. Although a Rakshasi by

JARA

origin, she was given due respect as the child was named after her. The *Mahabharata* even calls her a household goddess.

❖ Jarasandha

He was the child who was made of the two joined halves in the above story (of **Jara**). His name means 'joined together by Jara'.

Jarasandha was a very wicked king who gave his two daughters in marriage to **Kamsa**. When Kamsa was killed by

Krishna, the daughters went back to their father who attacked
Krishna. He fought eighteen battles with Krishna till he was
finally killed. (*Mahabharata, Bhagavata Purana*)

❖ **Jata**
A demon who, disguised as a Brahmana, carried off the
Pandava princes Yudhishthira, Nakula and Sahadeva and the
princess Draupadi. Bhima defeated and killed the demon and

JATASURA

rescued the Pandavas. Several demons trace their origins to Jata. (*Mahabharata*)

❖ Jataharini
A female demon (*Markandeya Purana*). The word jatahāra means a necklace of matted hair, suggesting an unkempt woman.

❖ Jaya
Jaya and **Vijaya** were the doorkeepers of Vaikuntha, Vishnu's heaven. Once, when some rishis led by Sanaka came to see Vishnu, the two did not let them in, thereby incurring the wrath of the sage who cursed them to be born thrice as demons. In the first birth they were born as **Hiranyaksha** and **Hiranyakashipu**, in the next as **Ravana** and **Kumbhakarna** and as **Shishupala** and **Dantavaktra** in the last. Finally they returned to Vaikuntha to serve Vishnu. (*Harivamsha*)

❖ Kabandha
A headless **Rakshasa**, whose mouth was on his belly, who had one huge yellow eye with a red eyelid on his forehead which was on his chest. He caught hold of Rama and Lakshmana in his enormous arms in the southern forests as they went searching for Sita after her abduction by **Ravana**. The brothers cut off his arms and introduced themselves. Then Kabandha explained that he was once a beautiful Gandharva called Vishvavasu who used to take on hideous forms to harass the rishis. On one occasion he angered sage Sthulashiras who cursed him to live with this form till Rama cut off his arms and cremated him, after which his original beauty would be restored. After the cremation and the restoration of his original form, he advises Rama to cross Lake Pampa and reach

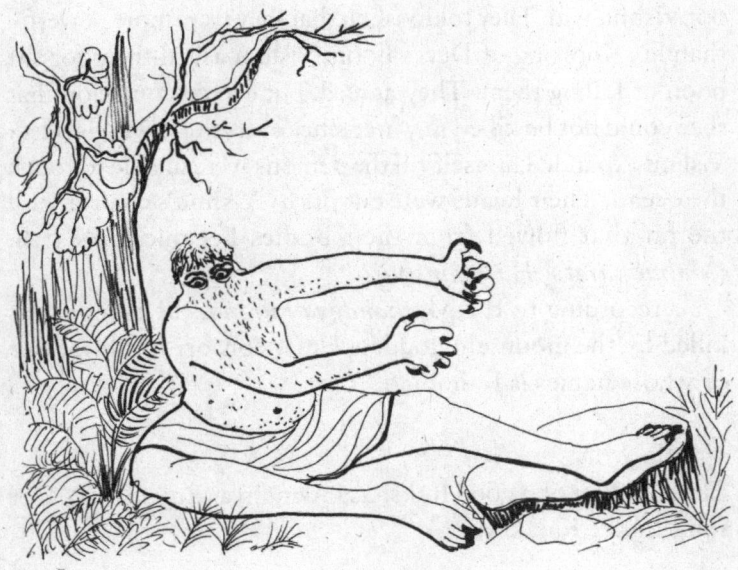

KABANDHA

mount Rishyamukha till he finds Sugriva, who could help him find Sita. (*Ramayana*)

❖ **Kaitabha**
Along with **Madhu,** he came out of Narayana's ear at the end of a kalpa, and the two tried to attack and kill Brahma, seated on a lotus issuing out of Narayana's navel. Narayana woke up and killed the two demons, hence his name Kaitabhajit or Kaitabhahara.

According to another version, Madhu and Kaitabha chanted mantras of praise to Devi for a thousand years till she gave them the boon of dying only when they wished. Thereafter, the two demons stole the Vedas and reached Patala, the netherworld. They fought Vishnu, but neither could the demons nor Vishnu win. They told Vishnu that they were more powerful than he. Knowing of Devi's boon, Vishnu asked them for the boon of killing them. They agreed, but on the condition that they could not be killed in water since everything was flooded. Vishnu expanded himself till the demons were unable to touch the ocean. Their heads were cut off by Vishnu's chakra, and the fat that flowed from their bodies became the earth. (*Mahabharata, Harivamsha*)

According to the *Markandeya Purana*, the demon was killed by the mountain goddess Uma, consort of Shiva, one of whose names is Kaitabha.

❖ Kala
The daughter of a good Rakshasa **Avindhya** (*Ramayana*). Her sons are the **Kalakeyas**.

❖ Kalaka
While the *Mahabharata* says she is the daughter of Daksha, father of Uma, Shiva's consort, the later *Vishnu Purana* says that she was the daughter of the Danava **Vaishvanara**. Kalaka and her sister **Pauloma** gave birth to 60,000 powerful, ferocious and evil giants or Danavas called **Kalakanjas** and **Paulomas**.

❖ Kalakanjas
Sons of **Kashyapa** and **Kalaka**, they were powerful, ferocious and cruel demons. (*Harivamsha*)

❖ Kalakeya, Kaleya
1. Sons of **Kala**. They are the personifications of anger and destruction. (*Mahabharata, Matsya Purana*)
2. Sons of the **Danava Marichi** who was vanquished by **Ravana**

and Durga (*Brahmanda Purana*). They are described by the *Vayu Purana* as **Asuras** who lived in the Devakuṭā hill.

❖ **Kalanemi**

1. The uncle of **Ravana**, he was promised half the kingdom if he killed Hanuman. He took the form of a hermit and waited on the hill of Gandhamadana, where Hanuman went in search of medicinal herbs. He invited Hanuman to eat with him, but the latter refused and went to bathe in a pool. A crocodile seized his foot, but he killed the animal, which turned out to be an apsaras who had been cursed to live as a crocodile till Hanuman released her. She warned Hanuman about Kalanemi, so Hanuman went back, caught Kalanemi by the foot and whirled him through the air till Kalanemi went flying through the air and fell before Ravana's throne in Lanka. Kalanemi is described as having four heads and eight eyes. (*Ramayana*)

2. He was the son of **Virochana** and descendant of **Hiranyakashipu**. He was reborn as **Kamsa** and **Kaliya** during the incarnation of Krishna. (*Mahabharata*, *Harivamsha*)

❖ **Kalika**

Mother of the **Danava Vaishnavara** and wife of **Puloma**.

❖ **Kaliya**

The five-headed king of the serpents, an **Asura** who lived in the river Yamuna with his numerous wives and attendants, Kaliya breathed out fire and smoke and laid waste the surrounding countryside. Because of the poison that he emitted, the entire area was surrounded by a poisonous vapour that killed even passing birds.

The child-god Krishna, who lived with the cowherds at Vrindavan near Mathura, was playing with his friends on the banks of the river when Kaliya came out once again. Krishna jumped into the water and was immediately enveloped in the demon's coils. His friends were horrified, but Krishna remembered his divine power and loosened himself easily. He jumped on Kaliya's head and danced till the serpent's power was broken and Kaliya and his companions begged for mercy. Krishna banished Kaliya and his followers to the ocean. (*Bhagavata Purana*)

The identity of Kaliya can be linked to the Nagas, a well-known tribe of ancient India who were gradually absorbed by the main Vedic people. It is likely that Kaliya belonged to one such fringe tribe, which was defeated by the Yadavas and had to move out of the region.

The icon of Krishna dancing on the defeated Kaliya, known as *Kaliya mardana Krishna*, is very popular in South India

❖ **Kama**
He is the god of love and desire, an Indian version of Cupid. However, the *Mudgala Purana* describes him as the demon of lust, who stole the hearts of men and overpowered their minds. To defeat him, Ganesha was born as Vikata, riding a peacock as his vehicle, and the demon was destroyed. In this story, Kama, or love, is personified and regarded as a vice, an impediment to human evolution, and Ganesha, as the dispeller of obstacles, conquers him. (*Mudgala Purana*)

❖ **Kamalaksha**
Asura son of **Taraka**.

❖ **Kambalavarhisha**
One of the sons of **Andhaka**.

❖ **Kamsa**

He was the wicked king of Mathura and maternal uncle of Krishna who imprisoned his sister Devaki and her husband Vasudeva when he heard the prophecy that their eighth child would kill him. But the baby Krishna was taken away to the home of Nanda in Gokul where he was brought up by Nanda and his wife Yashoda. Kamsa ordered the death of all male babies, but Krishna escaped. He tried several times to have Krishna killed, but was unsuccessful. Finally he was killed by Krishna. Although he was not born a demon, he is referred to as an **Asura**, as it was the demon **Kalanemi** who was reborn as Kamsa. He is also called **Kalankura**, or crane. (*Mahabharata, Harivamsha*) (See Part I, Chapter 3: Demonized Enemies).

❖ **Kapisha**

She was the daughter of **Krodhavasha**, wife of **Pulaha** and mother of the **Pishachas**, who were therefore also called Kapisheya. (*Brahmanda Purana*)

   She is also called the mother of the **Kushmandas**. (*Vayu Purana*)

❖ **Karala**

One of **Mahisha**'s warriors who was killed by Durga. (*Devi Mahatmya, Markandeya Purana*)

❖ **Karanja**

A Rig Vedic **Asura**.

❖ **Karkati**

A **Rakshasi** who lived on the Sahydari hills. First she was married to **Viradha** who was killed by Rama. Then she married **Kumbhakarna** with whom she had a son called Bhima, but Kumbhakarna too was killed. Her son Bhima was later killed by Shiva. (*Shiva Purana*)

❖ **Kashyapa**

A Vedic sage who was the progenitor of the **Rakshasas**. Several Vedic hymns are attributed to him, besides much of creation, including the demons. He married thirteen of Daksha's daughters. With his wife Aditi he produced the Adityas (Devas), while his wife **Diti**'s children were the **Daityas**, particularly **Hiranyaksha** and **Hiranyakashipu**. The sons of his wife **Danu** were the **Danavas**, including the **Paulomas** and **Kalakeyas**. His wife Arishta's sons were the Gandharvas; his wife Surasa was the mother of the snakes (sarpa), his wife Khasha's children were the Yakshas. Surabhi was the mother of cows and buffaloes, Vinata the mother of Aruna and Garuda, the vehicle of Vishnu, while Tamra had six daughters from whom were born owls, eagles, vultures, crows, water-fowl, horses, camels and donkeys. Krodhavasha was the mother of the fourteen thousand Nagas, Ila gave birth to trees and plants, Kadru's sons were also Nagas, particularly Ananta, Takshaka, Vasuki and Nahusha and Muni was the mother of the apsaras (*Brahma Purana*). This long list has resulted in Kashyapa's identification with Prajapati, father of all creation.

❖ **Keshi, Keshin**

1. He was the leader of the **Asuras** who wielded a mace, which he hurled at Indra, but Indra cut it up with his thunderbolt (vajra). Then a furious Keshin hurled a huge mass of rock at Indra, which Indra split with his thunderbolt. The rock fell to the ground, wounding Keshin who fled the scene. Then Indra rescued a beautiful woman who had been seized by the demon, and she informed Indra that her sister had been the previous victim of the demon. (*Mahabharata*)

2. A horse-demon, he was sent by Kamsa to kill Krishna. He adopted the form of a horse and went to Vrindavana. He

KESHIN

tore up the earth with his hooves, shook the clouds with his mane and attacked the sun and the moon. But Krishna killed Keshi, hence his name Keshava. (*Vishnu Purana*, *Bhagavata Purana, Harivamsha*)

❖ **Ketu**

The ninth 'planet' (lunar node) and creator of comets and meteors, with a chariot drawn by eight green horses, a malevolent symbol in astrology, holding a sword and a lamp and having the head of a snake. He is hairless and armless, the demon son of **Viprachitti** and **Sinhika**. He is also described as one of the thirty-three children of **Kashyapa** and **Danu**, and as the tail of **Rahu**, the monster of the eclipse. (*Mahabharata*)

❖ Khara

He was the younger brother of **Ravana**, king of Lanka, who lived in Jasthana and was the first to meet Rama in battle. After his initial dispatch of fourteen **Rakshasas** to kill Rama, who killed them instead, he was fed up. His sister had to taunt and force him to anger, till he decided to take on the brothers himself. Khara watched his companions **Dushana** and **Trishiras** killed by Rama. He attacked Rama with his arrows, mace and even a sal tree, to no avail. Finally, Rama killed and burnt him to death with a blazing arrow. (*Ramayana*)

According to local mythology in Kerala, Khara was a great devotee of Shiva who was entrusted with the administration of the forest of Dandaka by Ravana. Because of his ardent devotion, Shiva gave him three huge lingas. To take them home, Khara took one in each hand and the third in his mouth. Tired, he stopped at Ettamanur, took out the linga from his mouth and placed it on the ground. After a while he tried to lift it and continue his journey, but he was unable to do so. He found Rishi Vyaghrapada and requested him to install the linga at the Vaikatappan ambalam (temple) of Shiva at Ettamanur. He installed the second linga at the Anandaprabhu ambalam at Vaikom and the third at the Shiva ambalam at Kaduthuruthi.

❖ Kichaka

He was the brother-in-law of the king of Virata where the Pandavas had gone to live incognito during the last year of their exile. He tried to make love to Draupadi, for which he was

killed by her husband Bhima, who rolled Kichaka's flesh and
bones into a ball so that nobody could make out how he was
killed. (*Mahabharata*) While Kichaka is not specifically
identified as a demon, the **Kichakas** are a branch of **Daityas**.

❖ **Kichakas**
They are **Kaleya Daityas**. (*Mahabharata*)

❖ **Kilata**
An **Asura** priest, along with **Akuli,** who had a special influence
on Manu. (*Shatapatha Brahmana*)

❖ **Kinkara**
A hideous, strong and violent type of demon. Hanuman
killed all the Kinkaras when he visited Lanka in search of
Sita. (*Ramayana*)

❖ **Kirata**
Forest tribes who lived in the eastern Himalayas, ate raw fish
and lived in the waters. They are described as demons, half-
men, half-tigers, with 'gold-coloured' women and wearing
'sharp-pointed hair knots'. (*Ramayana*)

  The Kiratas could have been tribals from eastern India,
although they have also been identified with the Cirrhadæ,
who lived on the Coromandel Coast according to classical
Greek writers.

❖ **Kirmira**
A demon who prevented the Pandavas from entering the
Kamyaka forest and threatened to eat Bhima. Bhima fought
and killed the demon by strangling him and breaking all his
bones. Kirmira was the brother of **Baka**. (*Harivamsha*)

❖ Kotavi, Kotari, Kottavi

She was the goddess of the **Daityas** and mother of **Bana**. (*Harivamsha*)

Goddess Durga is known as Kottavai in Tamil. It is interesting that the popular Tamil name for Durga is the name of a Daitya goddess. This is an instance where the dividing line between a deity and a demon is practically non-existent.

❖ Kratudvisha

'Enemy of the sacrifice', a Vedic epithet for **Asuras**.

❖ Krauncha

An associate of the demon **Taraka**, against whom Karttikeya led an army of the gods. He was killed by Karttikeya. (*Bhagavata Purana*, *Brahmanda Purana*, *Vayu Purana*)

Also, a hill in the Himalayas split by Karttikeya. The Krauncha hill and island were named after the demon

❖ Kravi

A **Rakshasa** who got heaven and earth into his power and emptied them out. (*Sama Veda*)

❖ Kravyad

Meaning 'flesh eater', it is derived from **Kravi** and is an epithet of **Rakshasas** and other demons. It is also a description of Agni, or fire.

❖ Krodha

1. The demon of anger, whose sons are the **Pishachas**.
2. The demon of vicious and unjust anger. Ganesha was born as Lambodara to destroy him. (*Mudgala Purana*)

❖ **Krodhavasha**
Asura king of Kalinga.

❖ **Kshanadachara**
A night walker or spirit of ill who walks in woods at night, but can assume various shapes, and is therefore an object of dread.

❖ **Kshemaka**
A **Rakshasa** who occupied the city of Kashi (Varanasi) after it was abandoned by Divodasa. He was killed by King Alaka.

❖ **Kujrimbha**
A **Danava** who had acquired the invincible club Sunanda, built by Vishwakarma. He was killed by Vatsapri who rescued the women captured by the demon. (*Devi Mahatmya, Markandeya Purana*)

❖ **Kumbha**
Son of **Kumbhakarna**, he was killed by the Vanara king Sugriva in the Ramayana war. (*Ramayana*)

❖ **Kumbhanda**
A class of demons; also, a minister of **Bana**. (*Harivamsha*)

❖ **Kumbhakarna**
A brother of **Ravana**, he is also described as the son of **Vishravas** by his **Rakshasa** wife **Keshini**. As soon as he was born he started eating everything within his reach. He seized five hundred apsarases, the wives of a hundred sages, cows, and Brahmanas, devouring a thousand people in all. Fearing death, he led a life of austerity for ten thousand years. But the gods were afraid

KUMBHAKARNA

that he would obtain immortality and swallow up both gods and men, so they asked Sarasvati to enter his mind and delude him into asking for sleep. Their plan succeeded, and Kumbhakarna received a boon (or curse) from Brahma to sleep continuously for six months at a time. The Rakshasas were unhappy and asked Brahma to allow him to wake up once in six months for one day only, in order to eat as much as he wished. The wish was granted.

Kumbhakarna was a huge giant whose frame covered the skies; he ate thousands of boars, deer, goats and buffalo, and drank blood and a thousand pots of liquor at a time. Waking

Kumbakarna up was impossible, till a thousand elephants walked over his body. In the Ramayana war, he killed several monkeys and carried away Sugriva, but the monkey king tore off his ears and his nose. Rama then took him on directly. With Vayu's weapon he severed the demon's right arm, which wielded a club, with Indra's weapon the left. Finally, Rama killed him with his most formidable arrow, powered by Indra himself.

Unlike Ravana, who is described as a Brahmana and was always very respectful to the Brahmanas, Kumbhakarna is described as an enemy of the gods and Brahmanas. He and his brother Ravana were **Jaya** and **Vijaya**, doorkeepers of Vishnu's heaven cursed by some sages to take the form of demons for three lives. (*Ramayana*)

Kumbhakarna appears to be a personification of a natural phenomenon, such as the darkness at the poles. Many demons are personifications of natural phenomena. One description of Kumbhakarna seems to justify this: that he sleeps for six months and wakes for the next six months, like the sun at the poles. He is a huge giant, whose frame covers the skies. Although the epic says that he fights several vanars, he does not play an active role either in Ravana's court or in the epic. Like his brother Ravana, he is destroyed by Rama, an incarnation of the solar Vishnu, unlike the other Rakshasas who are killed by Hanuman or the other vanars.

❖ **Kumbhinasi**
Wife of **Madhu** and mother of **Lavana**.

❖ **Kuvalyapida**
An elephant demon used by **Kamsa** to trample Krishna and Balarama to death. However, Kuvalyapida was killed by the brothers. (*Mahabharata, Harivamsha*)

❖ **Lavana**
A man-eating understudy of **Ravana**, he has to be killed by Lakshmana 'at the time when the summer is withdrawn and the night of the rainy season has arrived'. He was the son of **Madhu**, king of Madhuvana (later Mathura) by **Kumbhinasi**, and the nephew of Ravana. He inherited an invincible trident from his father, who had received it from Shiva, but he was caught unawares without it and killed by Shatrughna. He is utilized by Indra to kill Mandhatri. (*Mahabharata*)

❖ **Lobha**
The demon of avarice and greed. Ganesha was born as Gajanana to subdue him. (*Ganesha Purana*)

❖ **Mada**
1. The personification of the vice of intoxication. Created by Rishi **Chyavana**, he was destroyed by Indra and dispersed among liquor, women, dice and hunting. Later, he became a **Pramatha**. (*Mahabharata*, *Harivamsha*)
2. The demon of vanity vanquished by Ganesha in the form of Ekadanta. (*Mudgala Purana*)

❖ **Madanika**
Wife of **Vidyut**, the **Rakshasa** servant of Kubera. She married his killer Kandhara. (*Markandeya Purana*)

❖ **Madhu**
Along with **Kaitabha**, he came out of Narayana's ear at the end of a *kalpa*, and the two tried to attack and kill Brahma who was seated on a lotus issuing out of Narayana's navel. Narayana woke up and killed the demon, hence Narayana was given the name Madhusudana (see **Kaitabha**). (*Mahabharata*, *Harivamsha*)

Madhu is also described as a **Danava** who was forced by **Ravana** to marry the latter's sister.

Madhu was the great founder-king of Mathura, in northern India, the ancestor of Kamsa and Krishna. Apart from the town of **Mathura** in northern India, Madurai in South India was also named after Madhu and Mathura. Thus the demon has been immortalized in the whole country.

❖ **Mahaparshva**
Ravana's minister, who is killed by Angada in the Ramayana war. (*Ramayana*)

❖ **Mahisha**
Rambha (not to be confused with Rambhā, the apsaras), demon son of **Kashyapa** and **Danu** married a Mahishi (female buffalo). They had a son, Mahisha. Rambha and his wife were killed by a giant buffalo, but the son grew up to become the king of the Mahishas.

The demon lived in the Vindhya mountains and, by the practice of severe austerities, gained the strength to drive the gods out of the heavens. So Brahma, Vishnu and Shiva issued energy (Shakti) from their mouths. The energy united and from it emanated Durga as a beautiful woman with ten arms, riding a lion (sometimes she is depicted riding a tiger). She held each god's special weapons in each of her ten hands: discus, conch, club, trident, spear, flame, bow, arrow and quiver, snake and the thunderbolt. She had a terrible laugh and roar that shook the earth.

Several of Mahisha's warriors came forward to fight Devi: **Chiksura** with his army; **Udagra, Mahahanu, Siloma, Vaskala** and **Viralaksha** on their chariots; **Parivarita** with elephants; and **Mahisha** on his elephants and horses. She killed each one

MAHISHA

of them with a different weapon. As Durga approached the Vindhya mountains, the demon tried to capture her. Unable to do so, the demon attacked her, taking several forms, each of which was destroyed by Durga. Finally, he took the form of a buffalo, which she caught with a noose and tied up, before transfixing him with a trident, after which she killed him with her sword. (*Devi Mahatmya, Markandeya Purana*)

Some versions have her tiger mount attacking and killing the demon.

According to the *Mahabharata*, the demon was killed by Karttikeya. But this is not the popular perception. (See Part I, Chapter 3: Demonized Enemies)

❖ **Mahodara**

Described first as **Ravana**'s minister and later as his son, he is killed by Sugriva in the Ramayana war. (*Ramayana*)

❖ **Maidanava**

He was the demon chief during Krishna's childhood at Vrindavan. He was also the father of **Vyoma**. (*Bhagavata Purana*)

❖ **Makaraksha**

Son of **Ravana**'s brother **Khara**, he is a skilled and brave warrior who takes on Rama to avenge his father's death. But he is no match for Rama who kills him with a fire-powered arrow in the Ramayana war. (*Ramayana*)

❖ **Malayavan**

Ravana's maternal grandfather, who predicts doom for his grandson because of Ravana's adharma. He sees portents predicting the destruction of the Rakshasas and recognizes that Vishnu has been born as Rama. He advises his grandson to return Sita to Rama and to make an alliance with Rama. (*Ramayana*)

The name Malayavan is of Tamil origin and means a mountain-dweller of the Malabar region (malai = Malabar / the mountains bordering Malabar), (*Dowson, op. cit.*), (avan = he). The name is an indication of Ravana's origin. (See Part I, Chapter 3: Demonized Enemies)

❖ **Mallina mukha**

Black-faced, a term used to describe **Rakshasas** and other demons.

❖ **Mama**

The demon of attachment and desire, destroyed by Ganesha, who assumed the form of Vighnaraja and rode the celestial serpent Shesha. (*Mudgala Purana*)

❖ **Mandeha**
Demons who try every night to swallow the sun. They were cursed by Brahma to die every morning and revive every night, and a fierce contest occurs daily between them and the sun. (*Vishnu Purana*)

❖ **Mandodari**
1. **Ravana**'s favourite and chief queen and daughter of **Maya**, architect of the **Danavas** who was killed by Indra, and Hema, an apsaras. Ravana carried off Mandodari while she was meditating. However, Mandodari fell in love with Ravana and Maya was happy to accept the handsome and erudite king of Lanka as his son-in-law. Her son was the great warrior **Indrajit**. (*Ramayana*) Mandodari was a pious and good woman who tried, unsuccessfully, to persuade her husband Ravana to return Sita to Rama, and warned that his actions would be fatal to himself and to Lanka. She is one of the panchakanyas—the five ideal women—of Hinduism.
2. Wife of **Daruka** and demon of smallpox, she made Bhadrakali her first victim. So Shiva created the demon **Ghantakarna** who licked the smallpox off her body.

❖ **Manibhadra**
A demonic manifestation of Shiva's anger, along with **Virabhadra**.

❖ **Manimat**
A **Rakshasa** friend of Kubera. Also, **Vritra** reborn as a king who was killed by Bhima. (*Mahabharata*)
    The Daitya town Manimati was named after him.

❖ Maricha, Marichi

Son of **Tataka** and **Shunda**. According to the *Ramayana*, Maricha, along with **Subahu**, attacked and destroyed the sacrifices of the sages at Siddhashrama, till the young prince Rama defeated, but did not kill, him.

Siddhashrama was the hermitage of the demon king **Bali** till it was taken over by Vishwamitra who was Bali's devotee. It is likely that Maricha was trying to drive away the sages and reclaim what belonged to the **Rakshasas**. He was not a full Rakshasa, being the son of Tataka, a Yakshini.

Later, he appears as the minister of **Ravana**. When Ravana decided to abduct Sita and destroy Rama, he approached Maricha, now an ascetic, to turn himself into a golden spotted deer. Sita would ask Rama to catch it for her and, in his absence, Ravana could carry her off. Maricha tried to dissuade Ravana, describing his earlier experience. He warned the king that Rama and Sita were protected by the dharma that guided their actions. If Ravana persisted with his plan, he would see Lanka destroyed and the Rakshasas annihilated. On Ravana's insistence, he flew to Dandaka and took on the form of a golden spotted deer, even though he knew Rama would surely kill him.

As Rama chased the deer, Maricha taunted him by disappearing and reappearing. Realizing it was a demon, Rama decided to kill it. When the arrow pierced his body, Maricha called out for Sita and Lakshmana in Rama's voice. This made Sita send Lakshmana to help Rama, leaving the place free for Ravana's abduction of Sita and setting into motion the Ramayana war. (*Ramayana*)

❖ Marka

An **Asura** priest who was overcome by the Gods.

❖ **Mata**
The demon of envy and jealousy subdued by Ganesha as Vakratunda. (*Mudgala Purana*)

❖ **Maya**
Maya‡ was an architect and builder of palaces, combining divine, demonic and human designs; the demonic equivalent of Vishwakarma, architect of the gods. He built the three aerial cities of **Tripura**, made of gold, silver and iron, and a tank of medicinal waters that could bring the dead back to life. He rode on a gold chariot with arms and weapons. (*Bhagavata Purana*)

Maya was the son of **Viprachitti**, brother of **Namuchi** and father of **Mandodari** and **Vajrakama**, who lived in the Devagiri hills (near Delhi). He built palaces for Agni's friends, since he was spared by Agni from certain death. He built a magic cave as the palace of the Danavas, and even a palace for the Pandavas. He was killed by Indra's thunderbolt for falling in love with an apsaras named Hema. (*Mahabharata*) **Ravana** carried away Maya's daughter Mandodari while she was meditating. (*Ramayana*). (See also **Mandodari**)

His descendants were **Dundubhi** and **Maayaavi**.

❖ **Maayaadevi**
The wife of **Asura Shambara**. She rescues the child Pradyumna when Shambara threw him into the sea and he was swallowed by a fish. Later, she married Pradyumna and returned with him to Dwaraka. (*Harivamsha*)

❖ **Maayaavi**
Son of **Dundubhi**. He fought with the monkey king Vali over a woman. He arrived at Kishkindha one night and challenged

‡Maya the demon architect should be distinguished from māyā, which means illusion and is pronounced maayaa.

Vali to a fight. Vali followed Maayaavi into a cave, instructing his brother Sugriva to close the mouth of the cave with a stone and wait outside for him. After waiting for a year, Sugriva returned to Kishkindha where the ministers insisted on crowning him king, presuming that Maayaavi had killed Vali. But Vali killed Maayaavi and came back to reclaim his kingdom, swearing eternal enmity towards Sugriva. (*Ramayana*)

Maayaavi's role is important in that the necessity to kill him was the cause of the enmity between Vali and Sugriva, necessitating Sugriva's alliance with Rama and the epic hero's subsequent killing of Vali in dubious circumstances. It also won Rama a strong ally in his war against Ravana.

❖ **Mayura**
An **Asura** in the *Mahabharata*.

❖ **Meghanaada**
See **Indrajit**.

❖ **Moha**
The demon of infatuation and delusion. Ganesha was born as Mahodara to defeat him. (*Mudgala Purana*)

❖ **Mooka**
Son of **Upashunda** who took the form of a boar to kill Arjuna. He was killed by Shiva in the form of Kirata the mountaineer. (*Mahabharata*)

❖ **Munda**
1.   A demon killed by Durga (*Devi Mahatmya, Markandeya Purana*).
2.   Another name for **Ketu**.
3.   Mundas are among the oldest indigenous tribes of India.

❖ **Mura/Muru**

A demon who was the builder of Pragjyotisha, with its many protective layers, and an ally of **Naraka**, ruler of Pragjyotisha. He defended Pragjyotisha by surrounding it with nooses as sharp as razors. Krishna beheaded him with his chakra, after which his seven sons—Tamra, Antariksha, Shravana, Vibhavasu, Vasu, Nabhasvan and Aruna—attacked Krishna, who burnt the sons to death. (*Vishnu Purana, Bhagavata Purana*) (See Part I, Chapter 7: Demonic Lands)

❖ **Mushtika**

A famous demon wrestler who was killed by Balarama at the games organized by **Kamsa** to kill Krishna. (*Mahabharata*)

❖ **Nabha**

The son of **Viprachitti** by **Sinhika**, sister of **Hiranyakashipu**.

❖ **Nahusha**

An ancient king, he was the son of Ayus and father of Yayati who was once king of the gods but was later cursed by Agastya to be born as a serpent (ajagara) when his foot touched the sage. (*Mahabharata*)

❖ **Naidunda(ka)**

A **Pishacha** clan. (*Vayu Purana*)

❖ **Naikashatmaja**

They were flesh-eating imps, the sons of **Nikasha**, mother of **Ravana**. They were also called **Naikasheya** or **Pishitashana**. (*Ramayana*)

❖ **Naikasheya**

See **Naikashatmaja**.

❖ **Nairrita**

1. One of the four **Rakshasa** clans, they move about at night and follow Trayambaka. Their king was **Alakhadipa**. (*Bhagavata Purana, Brahmanda Purana*)
2. **Rakshasas** who trouble babies. (*Brahmanda Purana, Vayu Purana*)

❖ **Namuchi**

A demon of drought killed by Indra in the *Rig Veda*.

In the *Mahabharata*, he held off Indra in combat and undertook a promise that Indra would not kill him by day or by night, wet or dry. Indra promised Namuchi and was released, but later killed him at sunset with froth, which was neither wet nor dry. (*Mahabharata*)

❖ **Naraka**

1. Also Naraka Bhauma, literally, son of the earth. He was a very rich and powerful demon king, the son of Mother Earth (Bhumidevi) and the boar Varaha, whose paternity was hidden from Vishnu by his mother. His kingdom was the impregnable fortress of the demons, Pragjyotisha. Naraka stole Aditi's earrings and brought them to Pragjyotisha, so the gods approached Krishna who killed Naraka and returned the earrings to Aditi. (*Bhagavata Purana*)

    Naraka was an implacable enemy of the Devas. He took the form of an elephant and abducted and violated the daughters of Vishwakarma, the daughters of the gandharvas, apsarases, gods and men—16,000 in all— and built a magnificent palace for them. Finally Krishna cut off Naraka's head with his discus and released the women by marrying them. (*Harivamsha*)

    Naraka was a non-Aryan god who was associated

with the Earth, like most non-Aryan deities. The boar represents agriculture, so, as the son of Varaha and Earth, he was associated with agriculture. His kingdom—Naraka or hell—is under the earth, impregnable, yet rich and prosperous, a prosperity bestowed and represented by the earrings of Aditi, the solar mother of the Devas or Shining Ones. He represents the prosperity of food sufficiency and wealth derived from agriculture.

2.   A son of **Viprachitti**.

3.   Another name for hell, where tortured souls go and where the demons dwell. There are twenty-seven hells where unrighteous people go depending on their sins. After a certain period spent in hell, they are reborn as lower beings depending on their actions. (*Manu Samhita*, *Brahmanda Purana*) (See Chapter 7: Demonic Lands).

The killing of Naraka is celebrated annually in southern India during the festival of lights or Deepavali, also known as Naraka Chaturdashi, the fourteenth day after the full moon in the Tamil month of Aippasi. According to popular belief, Krishna and Naraka fought all through the night till the hour before dawn, when the demon's life slowly ebbed away. Before he died, Naraka took a promise from Krishna that he would be remembered forever and his death celebrated, and that people everywhere would be rid of their sins if they bathed with oil and water an hour before dawn, when the water becomes equivalent to Ganga water. Accordingly, it is the custom to wake up before dawn, have an oil bath, wear new clothes and burst crackers before the sun rises. In Goa, Deepavali or Naraka Chaturdashi is celebrated by burning the image of Naraka, in the Ramlila tradition of North India.

❖ **Narantaka**
1.   **Ravana**'s son, killed by Angada, crown prince of the Vanars. (*Ramayana*)
2.   A demon who was harassing the three worlds and was destroyed by Mahotkata, an earlier incarnation of Ganesha in the krita yuga, who was born as the son of sage Kashyapa and his wife Aditi for the purpose. (*Ganesha Purana*)

❖ **Nikasha**
A demoness, mother of **Ravana**, she was also the mother of the **Naikasheya** (also **Naikashatmaja** or **Pishitashana**). (*Ramayana*)

❖ **Nikumbha**
1.   Son of **Kumbhakarna**, he was killed by Hanuman in the Ramayana war. (*Ramayana*)
2.   The **Asura** king of Satpura who, with his magical powers, could assume several forms. His austerities won him a boon from Brahma, that only Vishnu would kill him. He abducted Bhanumati, daughter of the Yadava chief Bhanu (or Brahmadatta), a friend of Krishna. Krishna killed the demon and gave the Yadava chief Nikumbha's kingdom. (*Bhagavata Purana*)
3.   He is also described as the son of **Hriyashva** and father of **Barhanashva**. (*Bhagavata Purana*)

❖ **Niruta**
The giant-guardian of the south-west (direction). Green in colour, he rides a crocodile and holds a fish flag, ring and wine jug in three of his four hands. He is a devotee of Shiva.

❖ **Nishumbha**

Along with his brother **Shumbha**, Nishumbha performed penances for eleven thousand years and obtained a boon from Shiva that he would exceed the gods in riches and strength. So the gods propitiated Durga, who agreed to help them.

Durga took the form of a beautiful woman and went to the Himalayas where she was seen by **Chanda** and **Munda**, demon spies of Shumbha and Nishumbha, who went back to tell their master about the beautiful woman. Shumbha sent a proposal of marriage, to which Durga replied that she would only marry a person who could defeat her in single combat. Shumbha sent his general Dhumralochana to capture her, but Durga destroyed him with a roar. Then the demons sent an army led by Chanda and Munda, but Durga cut off their heads, and devoured the demon army. Shumbha and Nishumbha set out to fight her with their demon army. Durga then produced seven goddesses from her hair—the Sapta Matrikas or seven mothers—who killed the demon army. Finally, she took on the two demons one at a time, and killed them off. (*Shiva Purana, Devi Mahatmyam, Markandeya Purana*)

❖ **Nishunda**

The **Daitya** son of **Hlada**.

❖ **Nirriti**

Destruction, a deity in the Vedas who is a minor goddess. Later, she is described as the wife of Adharma and the mother of Fear, Terror and Death.

❖ **Nivata kavacha**

Demon descendants of **Prahlada**, who lived beneath the sea and were killed by Arjuna. (*Mahabharata*)

❖ **Paka**
A fierce demon killed by Indra.

❖ **Panchajana**
He was a demon who lived under the sea, in the form of a conch shell. He captured and abducted the son of Krishna's guru Shandipani. Krishna killed the demon and rescued the boy, taking the demon's conch shell for his battle horn. The conch shell was named after the demon, hence Krishna's conch is known as the Paanchajanya. (*Mahabharata*)

PANCHAJANA

❖ Pani
Aerial demons who inspire foolish actions, slander and disbelief, and encourage men to neglect their worship of the gods. They are described as Dasyus in the *Rig Veda*, but are described as demons in later literature.

❖ Paramayogin
One of Shiva's three demon devotees, along with **Sheelapara** and **Viraktayogin**, who refused to be persuaded by Vishnu as the Buddha to give up their devotion. When Shiva destroyed Tripura, all the demons, except the three steadfast devotees who hid in the sea and meditated on Shiva, died. The three realized what would have happened to them if they had also been deluded by the Buddha. Shiva made them his doorkeepers on Kailasa. The lesson is that that one must not associate with heretics. (*Shivarahasyakhanda* of the *Skanda Purana*)

❖ Parnaya
A Rig Vedic **Asura**.

❖ Patala
See Part I, Chapter 7: Demon Lands.

❖ Patalaketu
An **Asura** who had kidnapped Madalasa who was in love with prince Kuvalyashva. Along with his demons, he was killed by Kuvalyashva. (*Markandeya Purana*)

❖ Paulastya
Sons of **Pulastya** and another name for **Rakshasas**.

❖ Pauloma
Danava sons of **Puloma**.

❖ **Pipru**
A Rig Vedic demon of drought, probably another name of
Vritra. Accompanied by Vishnu and the Maruts, Indra fights
and defeats the demon.

❖ **Pishacha**
See Part I, Chapter 3: Demonized Enemies.

❖ **Pishitashana**
See **Naikashatmaja**.

❖ **Pithara**
An **Asura** in the court of **Hiranyakashipu**.

❖ **Prabhavati**
Wife of the **Asura Bala**, who defeated Indra in battle. Cleverly,
the god sang the Asura's praises till Bala offered Indra a boon.
Indra asked for Bala's body, which the Asura gave, and which
Indra cut into pieces and threw about. Gold (or diamond)
mines appeared wherever the body fell, as a result of Bala's
merit of keeping his promise to Indra. After his death, Bala's
wife Prabhavati asked **Shukra** to bring him back to life, which
Shukra said he could not do. He suggested that Prabhavati
should leave her body and join her husband. Prabhavati did
so, and became a river of the same name. (*Mahabharata*)

❖ **Praghasa**
A **Rakshasa** deputed by **Ravana** to guard Sita and persuade her
to marry Ravana. Hanuman killed him when he went to Lanka
in search of Sita by hurling a mountain peak at him. (*Ramayana*)

❖ **Prahasta**
Father of **Jambumali**, Ravana's general, he was killed by the
great monkey warrior Nila in the Ramayana war.

❖ **Praheti**
Father of **Sumali**, a **Rakshasa**. (*Brahmanda Purana*)

❖ **Prahlada** (also **Prahrada**)
Prahlada, son of **Hiranyakashipu**, was a 'good demon' and a great devotee of Vishnu who insisted on worshipping the gods despite his father's orders to the contrary. Prahlada would have been killed if Vishnu had not incarnated himself as the man-lion Narasimha. After his father's death, Prahlada became the emperor of the demons in Patala. Finally, he gave up his kingdom to his son **Virochana** and spent his final years in meditation and worshipping Vishnu. (*Vishnu Purana*)

Prahlada was known as the just ruler of ancient Simhachala, near Visakhapatnam. His grandson was **Bali**, whose devotion to Vishnu could not prevent his removal from his throne and kingdom. However, in spite of his obvious Rakshasa origins, he is never called a demon.

❖ **Prajangha**
A **Rakshasa** who was killed by Angada in the Ramayana war.

❖ **Pralamba**
A demon who was sent by **Kamsa** to kill Krishna, but was killed, instead, by Krishna. (*Mahabharata*, *Bhagavata Purana*) He joined the boys in their game in order to devour them, but was defeated by Balarama whom he had to carry on his shoulders. He began expanding and running away, but Balarama squeezed the demon between his knees, beat his head and killed him. (*Vishnu Purana*)

❖ **Pramatha**
Demon attendants of Shiva.

❖ **Preta**
See Part I, Chapter 3: Demonized Enemies.

❖ **Pulastya**
A Prajapati, or mind-born son of Brahma, who was the progenitor of all the **Rakshasas**. He received the *Vishnu Purana* from Brahma and communicated it to Parashara, who communicated it in turn to mankind. He was the father of **Vishravas**, father of Kuvera and **Ravana**.

❖ **Puloma**
1. **Asura** son of **Danu,** he was a follower of **Vritra** in the battle against Indra. He fought against Agni in the war between the Devas and Asuras. (*Bhagavata Purana*)
2. Son of the **Rakshasa Prahati**. (*Brahmanda Purana*)
3. A class of **Danavas** born to **Kashyapa** and his wife **Puloma**. They were powerful, ferocious and cruel, but were killed by Arjuna. (*Harivamsha*)
4. An Andhra king.

❖ **Pulomaa**
The *Mahabharata* says she is the daughter of Daksha, father of Uma, Shiva's consort. The later *Vishnu Purana* says that she was the daughter of the Danava Vaishvanara. Married to **Kashyapa**, Pulomaa and her sister **Kalaka** gave birth to 60,000 powerful, ferocious and evil giants or Danavas called **Paulomas**.

❖ **Puloman**
He was the **Danava** father of Shachi, wife of Indra. Puloman was killed by Indra when the Danava wanted to curse him for ravishing his daughter.

❖ **Pushpotkata**
She was a **Rakshasi**, wife of **Vishravas** and mother of **Ravana**
and **Kumbhakarna**. (*Mahabharata*)

❖ **Putana**
A female demon who was sent by **Kamsa** to kill Krishna. She
tried to suckle him to death with poisoned breasts, but Krishna
killed her by sucking out her life, even as he drank the milk
from her breast. Putana is also described as the daughter of
Bali. (*Bhagavata Purana*)

❖ **Rachana**
The **Daitya** wife of Tvashta and mother of Vishvaroopa who
became the priest of the gods. But Indra was never too sure
of Vishvaroopa and chopped off the latter's three heads. So
Tvashta created the giant demon **Vritra** to fight Indra.
(*Bhagavata Purana*)

❖ **Rahu**
The eldest of the fourteen sons of **Viprachitti** and **Sinhika**,
from whom he also gets the name Sainhikeya, he was a servant
of **Hiranyakashipu**. He had four arms and a tail. When the
ocean was churned for amrita, the nectar of immortality, **Rahu**
managed to take a few sips of the nectar, but Surya (sun) and
Chandra (moon) learned of this and informed Vishnu, who
beheaded Rahu with his chakra. But Rahu did not die, since
he had tasted the nectar of immortality. He became an enemy
of the sun and the moon, both of whom he attacks on new
moon and full moon days although Sudarshana, the discus
of Vishnu, makes Rahu withdraw finally (*Bhagavata Purana*).
When Rahu leaves the moon, it is comparable to getting rid

of all one's sins by having a bath in Prayaga (*Matsya Purana*), so a bath after an eclipse becomes a must.

Rahu is identified with the eclipse, which chases the sun and the moon and even swallows them from time to time, as it was the sun and the moon who had informed Vishnu about Rahu's theft of amrita. He resembles the Chinese dragon, the wolf Managarm of Teutonic mythology, and the Grecian demons who devour Helena, the sun-maiden and sister of the twin Dioscuri.

The Vedic **Svarbhanu** became the epic Rahu. He is also considered to be a planet in astrology, as well as the ascending node, represented by the dragon's head, while Ketu is also the descending node, represented by the dragon's tail. Rahu's other names are Abhra Pishacha (demon of the sky), Bharani bhu (born of the asterism Bharani) and **Kabandha** (headless).

❖ Raka
The **Rakshasi** wife of **Vishravas** and mother of **Khara**. (*Mahabharata*)

❖ Rakshas
Son of **Khasha** and father of the **Rakshasas**.

❖ Rakshasa
See Part I, Chapter 3: Demonized Enemies.

❖ Raktavija
He was a demon whose austerities had won him a boon from Brahma by which every drop of blood that fell from his body would produce thousand more demon clones. He was killed by Kali (or Chamunda) who held him, pierced him with a spear

and drank up all the blood as it gushed out. (*Devi Mahatmya*, *Markandeya Purana*)

❖ **Ravana**
The demon king of the **Rakshasas** and of Lanka. **Vishravas**, son of Prajapati **Pulastya**, had two wives: a Brahmana woman named **Ilavida** who gave birth to **Kuvera**, the god of wealth and the leader of the Yakshas, and a **Rakshasi** (demon) woman named **Nikasha** or **Kaikesi** who gave birth to three sons—Ravana, **Kumbhakarna** and **Vibhishana**—and a daughter named **Shoorpanakha**. Pulastya is said to be the progenitor of the whole race of Rakshasas, of whom Ravana became king and expelled his half-brother Kuvera from Lanka. He is a Brahmana and a **Yatudhana** dauhitrah (grandson of a Yatudhana on the maternal side). He is also described as a nairṛta Rakshasa or nairṛta rāja, a demon from the north living in the south. He and his brother **Kumbhakarna** were **Jaya** and **Vijaya**, doorkeepers of Vishnu's heaven cursed by some sages to take the form of demons for three lives.

Ravana was an ardent devotee of Shiva and several myths describe his devotion. One important legend is the story of Ravana and Mount Kailasa. Ravana used to travel every day from his home in Lanka to Kailasa, to worship Shiva. But increasingly, he found these daily trips inconvenient and decided to take Kailasa to his kingdom. He tried to shift the mountain when Shiva and Parvati were seated on it, but Shiva suppressed his pretensions with a pressing down of his toe. Unable to stand the pain, Ravana began to sing in praise of Shiva—the Shiva stotra is credited to him—till he was pardoned by Shiva. He was a great musician who, in the Puranas, is credited with the composition of the *Sama Veda*, and the design and construction of the Rudra veena, a musical instrument.

Another version of this story is that Ravana, as he entered Kailasa, was stopped by a monkey-faced dwarf called Nandishvara. The demon laughed derisively, to which Nandishvara replied that Ravana would be destroyed by the monkey race. The Rakshasa threw his arms around the mountain and tried to lift Kailasa, but Shiva pressed the mountain down with his toe and crushed the demon. Ravana sang Shiva's glory for a thousand years till he was finally released.

Ravana performed a severe penance and obtained the gift of invincibility from Brahma, but was too proud to ask for protection from people and animals. He had ten heads and twenty arms, and looked like Mount Mainaka, situated in the ocean. He had the strength to agitate the seas, split the mountains and stop the course of the sun and the moon, and the ability to change his form and appearance at will. His chief wife was **Mandodari**, daughter of **Maya** and mother of **Indrajit**. He defeated the Naga king Vasuki and abducted another Naga king Takshaka's wife; he conquered Kuvera and took away his flying chariot Pushpaka, created by Vishwakarma. He terrorized the world, breaking all laws and ravishing other men's wives, till Vishnu decided that he would incarnate himself on earth as Rama, son of Dasharatha, to destroy Ravana.

The story of Rama's banishment from his royal abode at Ayodhya to the forest is the story of the epic Ramayana. In the course of Rama's confrontations with the Rakshasas, Ravana carried off Sita and asked her to marry him, which the virtuous Sita refused to do. With the help of Hanuman and the armies of monkeys, bears and squirrels, Rama attacked Lanka. Gradually, all the demons were killed till Ravana alone was left. Initially, Lakshmana and Ravana fought a bitter war in which Lakshmana was nearly killed. The physician Sushena sent Hanuman to the Himalayas in search of the life-restoring herb Sanjivani described by Jambavat the bear king, who was the sage counsellor of Rama's army. Unable to identify them, Hanuman brought the mountain itself, thereby creating the popular icon of Hanuman flying in the air carrying a mountain of herbs.

Rama returned to fight Ravana. It was a terrible battle in which Ravana slowly lost his confidence and clarity. His charioteer tried to steer him away, but Ravana was so crazed with anger that he demanded to be taken back. Then Rama's arrows cut off his head, but no sooner did a head of the demon fall than another sprang up in its place. The epic says that hundred such heads were cut off, although Ravana had only ten heads. Finally, Rama picked up Brahma's bow (Brahmastra) and released it. It shot off at full speed, pierced Ravana's chest and heart, came out of his back, dipped into the earth and returned to Rama's quiver. Ravana was finally dead. (*Ramayana*)

During his sojourn in the forests Rama had killed several Rakshasas, and this angered Ravana. The insult to Shoorpanakha was a good occasion and reason to fight Rama. Unfortunately, he permitted his passion to get the better of him and he abducted Sita, putting himself in the wrong.

As Ravana was a Brahmana, Vedic rites were performed over his dead body by his brother Vibhishana.

Although Ravana is generally described as having ten heads and twenty arms, he often had but two arms and was described as beautiful. In fact Hanuman, on seeing him, exclaims: 'O, the beauty, firmness, goodness, glory and union of all marks of distinction in this king of Rakshasas'. He is also described as a thick cloud or mountain, with the marks of wounds inflicted on him through so many wars. He was so strong that he could move the seas and split mountains. He stopped the sun and moon and prevented them from rising. He had a weakness for women and other men's wives.

RAVANA

Ravana's piety earned him approval and a boon from Brahma of immunity from all spirits, yet not from men because he despised men. Ravana drove a chariot driven by asses. He was cursed by many women, including Rambhā, Sita and Uma. He conquered the gods and overran Bhogavati, he forced **Madhu** the **Danava** to marry his (Ravana's) sister and **Maya** to give his daughter in marriage to him.

Ravana, son of a Brahmana father and a Rakshasa mother, was accepted as a Brahmana and a great Sanskrit scholar. But his constituency was undoubtedly primitive: the crude **Shoorpanakha**, **Khara** and **Kumbhakarna** and the Rakshasas of Lanka. The grandson of **Pulastya** apparently inherited the kingdom of Lanka from his Rakshasa mother. In popular view, the Lanka of Ravana was the present Sri Lanka. Primitive tribes populated the island before the advent of the Tamils and Sinhalas. Obviously these tribes—non-Aryan, primitive and with alien customs and practices—were designated as 'demons' to differentiate them from the devas or 'shining ones'. (See Part I, Chapter 3: Demonized Enemies)

❖ Rudhira

A **Rakshasa** who entered the body of Kalmashapada and ate up sage Vashishtha's son (*Linga Purana*).

❖ Ruru

He was a demon who wanted to marry Parvati, and performed such terrible austerities on the Malaya mountain that Shiva asked Parvati to do something about it. Parvati went to him looking terrible, wearing a lion's pelt with its blood smeared in her hair. Ruru refused to recognize the goddess who, furious, created several Shaktis from her body. She killed the demon, skinned him and drank his blood. (*Shiva Purana*)

❖ Saharaksha

The fire of the **Asuras**.

❖ Sainhikeya

1. The sons of **Viprachitti** and **Sinhika**.
2. A sect of **Danavas**.

❖ Shakata

When he was three months old, Krishna was placed by his mother under a handcart for safety, since his mother was welcoming guests. She was not aware that the cart was a demon called Shakata, or that her baby was a divine child. However, the baby Krishna, being divine, was aware and began kicking at the cart. The brass and metal utensils piled in the cart fell down, the wheel separated from the axle, the spokes of the wheel broke and scattered everywhere, and the cart collapsed, completely destroyed. Thus Shakata was killed. (*Bhagavata Purana*)

❖ **Shakini**
Female demon attendants of Durga.

❖ **Shakuni**
A female demon, daughter of **Bali** and sister of **Putana**.

❖ **Shalavrika**
Demonic animal.

❖ **Salya**
The **Danava** son of **Viprachitti**.

❖ **Shambara**
1. An **Asura** who was defeated by king Divodasa and whose castles were destroyed by Indra (*Rig Veda*). He was a personification of the drought, similar to **Vritra**.
2. A demon employed by **Hiranyakashipu** to kill Prahlada.
3. A demon who knew that Pradyumna was destined to kill him. He kidnapped the baby and threw it into the sea where it was swallowed by a fish. The fish was caught by some fishermen who sold it to Shambara's kitchen. When the fish was cut, the baby was found inside by Shambara's

housekeeper Mayavati. She went to Narada who told her the story and asked her to bring up the baby Pradyumna well. She taught him māyā or magic and, when he grew up told him the story of Shambara. Pradyumna challenged Shambara to a duel and killed him, replying to magic with magic. Then he returned to Krishna and Rukmini, and married Mayavati. (*Vishnu Purana*)

❖ **Samvara**
The **Daitya** son of **Kashyapa** and **Danu,** he was requested by **Hiranyakashipu** to destroy his son **Prahlada.** He tried hard, but he was unsuccessful. (*Mahabharata, Harivamsha*)

❖ **Shanda**
An **Asura** priest who was overcome by the gods.

❖ **Sanhalada**
The youngest son of **Hiranyakashipu.**

❖ **Shankhachuda**
1. A demon assistant of Kuvera who wore a valuable conch-shaped jewel on his head, he abducted all the gopīs of Vrindavan. Hearing their cries, Krishna and Balarama pursued the demon. Krishna broke his head into two, and a jewel came out of the demon's forehead, which Krishna gave away to his brother Balarama. (*Bhagavata Purana*)
2. The demon husband of Tulasi, a devotee of Narayana who wanted to marry the god. The demon was torturing the gods and destroying their cities. Shankhachuda owned a talisman given to him by Krishna which made him invincible. Brahma had also given him a boon to the effect that Shankhachuda would die only if his wife took

another man as husband and lived with him. Finally, Krishna came in the form of a Brahmana and asked for and received the jewel. Then, when the demon was in battle, Krishna took his form and visited Tulasi, and the demon was killed. Tulasi was given immortality as the river Gandaki and the sacred basil (tulasi) plant.

❖ **Shankushiras**
The **Danava** son of **Kashyapa** and **Danu**.

❖ **Sharabha**
A **Danava** monster with eight feet who killed the lions found on mount Kraunca and on Gandhamadana. (*Mahabharata*) As the destroyer of the demon, Shiva is called Sharabheshvara.

❖ **Sarama**
The **Rakshasi** wife of **Vibhishana** who had been deputed by **Ravana** to guard Sita. She was kind and loving to Sita and kept her informed of Ravana's plans. (*Ramayana*)

❖ **Sarana**
Ravana's minister. Along with **Shuka,** he was instructed by Ravana to take the form of a monkey to assess the strength of Rama's army. **Vibhishana** recognized the two demons, who were then taken to Rama. Rama spared their lives and sent them back to their master, warning him of the impending destruction of Lanka and the Rakshasas. (*Ramayana*)

❖ **Sharmishtha**
The daughter of **Vrishaparvan** the Daitya king, she married Yayati and gave birth to Puru, ancestor of the Kauravas and Pandavas. (*Mahabharata*)

❖ **Saubha**
See Part I, Chapter 7: Demonic Lands.

❖ **Saudasa**
Son of King Sudasa and descendant of King Bhagiratha, he was cursed by Vasishtha to become a **Rakshasa**. But he returned to his human form after he touched the holy water of the Ganga river. (*Narada Purana*)

    This story is used to emphasize the sanctity and mystical powers of the river.

❖ **Saushkala**
Ravana's messenger sent to the court of Janaka to ask for the latter's daughter Sita's hand in marriage for his king. He refused to participate in the test of bending the bow and left after Rama won the contest. (*Ramayana*)

❖ **Sheelapara**
One of three demon devotees of Shiva, along with **Paramayogin** and **Viraktayogin**, who refused to be persuaded by Vishnu as the Buddha to give up their devotion. See **Paramayogin**. (*Shivarahasyakhanda* of the *Skandamaha Purana*)

❖ **Sindhu**
A demon killed by Ganesha as Mayuresa in treta yuga. (*Ganesha Purana*)

❖ **Sindhur**
A demon killed by Ganesha as Gajanana in dvapara yuga, after which the god taught the world the *Ganesha Gita*. (*Ganesha Purana*)

❖ **Sinhika**

A massive **Rakshasi** who tried to swallow and eat Hanuman on his first journey to Lanka. The monkey-god ripped her mouth from inside and killed her. She is the mother of **Rahu**, who is also regarded as an **Asura**. She is also described as the sister of **Hiranyakashipu**. (*Ramayana*)

SINHIKA

❖ **Shishupala**

This was the final birth of **Jaya,** one of the doorkeepers of Vishnu's heaven Vaikuntha who, along with his brother **Vijaya,** was cursed by some sages to take three lives as a demon. He was born to King Damaghosha of Chedi. At birth, he had three eyes and four hands, and brayed like an ass. A voice predicted that his third eye and extra hands would fall off when he sat on the lap of his killer, and that warrior turned out to be Krishna. He joined **Jarasandha** and attacked the northern gate of Mathura. He was promised to Rukmini by her brother Rukmin, but the princess appealed to Krishna, who carried off and married Rukmini. He vilified Krishna as a cowherd and hurled several insults at him. But Krishna had promised King Damaghosha that he would let Shishupala curse him ninety-nine times and would kill him only on the hundredth occasion. Krishna kept his word and swallowed ninety-nine insults. On the hundredth, he let loose his chakra, and the prince lost his head. As he died remembering Narayana, Shishupala attained moksha or salvation, and was reabsorbed into Vishnu's heaven as doorkeeper. (*Vishnu Purana, Bhagavata Purana*)

❖ **Shonitaksha**
A **Rakshasa** who was killed by Mainda, the monkey general, in the Ramayana war. (*Ramayana*)

❖ **Subahu**
Along with **Maricha**, he attacked and destroyed the sacrifices of the sages at Siddhashrama, till the young prince Rama killed him. (*Ramayana*)

❖ **Shuka**
Ravana's minister. See **Sarana**. (*Ramayana*)

❖ **Suketu**
Mother of **Tataka**. (*Ramayana*)

❖ **Shukra/Shukracharya**

The son of Kavi and Divya, grandson of **Hiranyakashipu** and father of **Devyani,** he was a powerful magician, who used his powers to help the **Asuras**. He taught the demons to free themselves from the false teachings of Vishnu as the Buddha, because of which he lost one eye. He was the one-eyed adviser and teacher of the demons, who advised them to beware of the gods, who taught them ways and means of defeating the gods and who knew a magical incantation that would bring them back to life every time they were killed.

Shukra was known for his sexual escapades. The first was as a boy, when he fell in love with Vishvachi, an apsaras in Indra's heaven. He used up all his virtues and fell from heaven. In his next birth as a Brahmana's son he fell in love with a doe who was a cursed apsaras. He forgot his austerities and was bitten by a snake and died. This went on through several births, till his father decided to bring him back to life. By worshipping Shiva he learned the mystical chant for restoring life, the mritasanjivani. He heard the Purana from Vayu and narrated it to Brihaspati. (*Matsya Purana*) He brought **Bali** back to life with the mritasanjivani and warned him that Vamana was Hari, although Bali did not listen. (*Bhagavata Purana*)

The gods asked their teacher and adviser Brihaspati to recite a mantra that would bring them back to life every time they were killed, as Shukra did the demons, but Brihaspati did not know such a mantra. The gods then threatened to banish him till he found a way. So Brihaspati's son Kacha decided to go to Shukra as a disciple, but did not reveal his identity. Shukra's daughter Devyani fell madly in love with the handsome Kacha, but the demons did not trust him. One evening, when Kacha was tending his teacher's cattle in the forest, the demons killed him. But Devyani forced her father to bring him back to life, albeit reluctantly. They killed him twice, but Devyani made her father bring him back to life again. The third time they ground his body to ashes and mixed it with wine and gave it to the liquor-loving Shukra. Again Devyani made her father recite his magical incantation. This time Kacha's voice came from inside Shukra's body, and he told his teacher what had happened. Shukra and Devyani were in a dilemma. If Kacha came out, Shukra would die, and if Kacha stayed inside, he would die. Then Devyani had an idea. Shukra would teach Kacha the magical incantation. Then he would come out, Shukra would die, then Kacha would recite the incantation and Shukra would come back to life too. Thus it happened. As Kacha prepared to leave, Devyani declared her love for him, but Kacha refused, saying a student was like a son to his teacher and, as he had come out of the teacher's body, he was even more of a son. So Devyani could only be a sister to him. Kacha then sped away to heaven, with the knowledge of Shukra's magical incantation, which was used to bring the gods back to life and fight the demons. (*Bhagavata Purana, Harivamsha*)

❖ **Shumbha**

He, along with his brother **Nishumbha**, had performed penances for eleven thousand years and had obtained the boon of immunity from Shiva. So the gods propitiated Durga, who agreed to help them. See Nishumbha. (*Shiva Purana*)

❖ **Sumali**

1. A son of **Praheti** the **Rakshasa**. (*Brahmanda Purana*)
2. A follower of **Vritra** who was killed by Hari. (*Bhagavata Purana*)

❖ Shunda

Son of **Jambha** and father of **Maricha**. He belonged to the family of **Hiranyakashipu**. (*Mahabharata*) He enslaved the Nagas and killed several *rishis* till the Devas used the apsaras Tilottama to enslave and thereby kill him. (*Vayu Purana*)

❖ Sundagara

Husband of **Tataka**. (*Ramayana*)

❖ Surasa

Mother of the Nagas and a **Rakshasi** who appears in the *Ramayana*. She lived in the sea and wanted to test Hanuman's strength and grit, as well as save her relative **Ravana**. So she told Hanuman that anyone who crossed the sea had to enter her mouth first. To avoid being swallowed by her, Hanuman grew larger and larger, while Surasa's mouth grew equally large. Suddenly, Hanuman shrank till he was the size of a thumb, darted in through her mouth and out of her ear, and sped off on his way. (*Ramayana*)

In popular belief, Surasa personifies the dangers that are faced when crossing the ocean.

❖ Shoorpanakha

Sister of **Ravana**, and a **Rakshasi**, Shoorpanakha fell in love with Rama and made advances to him. Rama referred to his married state and suggested Lakshmana instead, but the latter refused and sent her back to Rama. Furious at their rejection, she attacked Sita, so Lakshmana chopped off her ears and nose with his sword. She went sobbing to her brothers Khara and Ravana, raving about Rama's wife and demanding revenge. This led to Ravana's abduction of Sita, the war between Rama

SHOORPANAKHA

and Ravana and, ultimately, Ravana's defeat and death at Rama's hands. She is the catalyst for Ravana's actions and destruction, which the epic acknowledges when it calls her an 'ill-omened creature'. Even the Rakshasas blame her overtures to Rama in the forest for Ravana's downfall and **Indrajit**'s death. (*Ramayana*)

   (See Part I, Chapter 3: Demonized Enemies).

❖ **Sushna**
A Vedic demon of drought, also known as **Vritra**, who was killed by Indra. (*Rig Veda*)

❖ **Svarbhanu**

The Vedic predecessor to **Rahu,** he is a demon who eclipses the sun with darkness. He appears very rarely. (*Rig Veda*)

❖ **Tamra**

An Asura of **Mahisha**'s army, killed by Durga who uses her arrows to slay him. (*Devi Mahatmya, Markandeya Purana*)

❖ **Tara**

Demon father of **Taraka.** (*Matsya Purana, Brahmanda Purana*)

❖ **Taraka**

Performing powerful penances, the demon **Taraka,** son of **Vajranga** and **Varangi,** had obtained two boons from Brahma, one was of invincibility and another of death at the hands of Shiva's son. Thereafter, he became a terror to people and gods alike, the Amritalinga that he wore around his neck protecting him from the wrath of the gods. The gods then retreated to the city of Amaravati or Dhanyakataka on the banks of the river Krishna. They asked Shiva for help, but the latter declined, since his blessings were too powerful to be reversed. But he sent his son Skanda to fight the demon. Skanda was unsuccessful, so Shiva told him to destroy the Amritalinga around the demon's neck. Skanda's spear destroyed the Linga, which fell at five places in Amaravati. Taraka died at once. Then Shiva installed and consecrated the five places where the linga fell. Called Pancharama, they are Ksheerarama, Amararama, Somarama, Draksharama and Bhimarama. (*Matsya Purana, Brahmanda Purana*)

❖ **Tarakaksha**

Asura son of **Taraka.** (*Matsya Purana, Brahmanda Purana*)

❖ **Tataka**

She was the wife of **Shunda** and mother of **Maricha**, who haunted the forests on the banks of the river Sarayu, destroyed the sacrifices of the sages and the cities of Malada and Karusha, built by the gods. The young princes Rama and Lakshmana were taken by sage Vishwamitra to kill her. As Lakshmana cut off her nose and ears, Tataka tried to confuse the brothers with her magic, raining stones and rocks and clouds of dust. Finally, Rama killed her with his skilled archery. (*Ramayana*)

❖ **Trijata**

An old **Rakshasi** deputed by **Ravana** to guard Sita and persuade her to marry **Ravana**. She had a dream that Ravana would be killed and Lanka destroyed. She advised the Rakshasis who were guarding Sita to make their peace with Sita and to run away and hide from certain death at Rama's hands. (*Ramayana*)

❖ **Trinavarta**

A servant of Kamsa, he appeared in the form of a whirlwind and picked up the child-god Krishna. He raised such a duststorm over Vrindavan that the whole town became dark and nobody could see anything. Trinavarta went high into the sky, but the baby became so heavy that the demon was brought to earth with great force by Krishna, who caught him by the neck till Trinavarta's eyes popped out. The demon fell down, hit the stone, smashed his limbs and died. (*Bhagavata Purana*)

❖ **Tripura**

1. **Vidyunmalin, Tarakaksha** and **Kamalaksha,** the three Asura sons of **Taraka,** won three impregnable flying cities

of iron, silver and gold on earth, heaven and the middle region between the two, the three cities called Tripura. They were beautifully built and equipped by **Maya**, architect of the demons. They were also granted a wish from Brahma that they could only be killed by a single arrow. The demons flew everywhere in their cities, but could not be killed because they were devotees of Shiva. The gods visited Shiva, but were denied access. Then Vishnu became Buddha and, with Narada as his disciple, deceived the demons with a māyāśāstra and sweet words and destroyed the chastity of their wives by gifting them jewels. Vishnu persuaded them to give up worshipping Shiva and worship him as the Buddha, creating clothes, ornaments, money and women to entice the demons. However, three demons—**Paramayogin**, **Shilapara** and **Viraktayogin**—refused to be swayed from their devotion to Shiva. Then, leaving a part of himself behind as Buddha, Vishnu went to Mount Kailasa, but was denied access as he had led away Shiva's devotees. So he performed tapas at Lake Manasa. The Devas took up Shiva's Pashupata bow in a bid to flatter the god, and a pleased Shiva agreed to battle the demons. From his third eye appeared fire which burnt up the three cities. Then from his bow which was Mount Meru, whose string was Vasuki, Shiva sent forth an arrow made up of the gods, with Vishnu as the arrowhead. All the demons, except the three steadfast devotees who hid in the sea and meditated on Shiva, died. The three realized what would have happened to them if they had also been deluded by the Buddha. Shiva made them his doorkeepers on Kailasa. The Devas then understood that one must not associate with heretics (*Shivarahasyakhanda* of the *Skandamaha Purana*).

2. Another version of the legend makes Tripura the owner of the three cities. Tripura represented a challenge to the gods themselves, for its subjects were god-fearing followers of Shiva and its women chaste wives and mothers. To corrupt its citizens, Vishnu generated Māyāmoha Purusha to obstruct their holy rites. Meanwhile Narada made them question the Vedas and forget Shiva, and misled the women from the path of chastity. In later art, Tripura was represented as the demon.

The gods wanted to destroy Tripura, but it seemed impossible. Then Brahma said that a single arrow shot by an expert archer had to pierce all three cities at one time, when they were aligned in a single line. Only Shiva, also known as Sharva the cosmic archer, could do it. So the gods built a war chariot out of the Earth. The Sun and the Moon were its wheels, the Vedas were its horses and Brahma the charioteer. Meru the mountain was the shaft of the bow and Vasuki, king of the serpents, its string. Finally Vishnu turned himself into an arrow. Taking his ugra or angry form, Shiva chased Tripura across the firmament and the galaxies, into the waters and through the netherworld. He waited till the three cities were aligned in a straight line and then shot his Vishnu śastra (weapon). Tripura burst into flames. All the Asuras who lived within were destroyed and the remains became the meteors, comets and asteroids of the cosmos. Shiva came to be known as Tripurantaka, or destroyer of the three cities. The gods celebrated, but Shiva was unsmiling, for he could not rejoice in the death of any person, animal or place, however evil. Then, predicting that the entire cosmos would, one day, become so evil that he would have to destroy it, he dipped three fingers into the charred remains of Tripura and drew three horizontal lines across his forehead. Thus the three lines on the forehead of Shiva and his followers are a reminder of how the evil demon city of Tripura was destroyed and how the rest of the earth will also go the same way one day. (*Shiva Purana*)

The story of the destruction of Tripura is an allegory for a cosmic event, an explanation for the death of stars, cosmic debris, meteors and unexplained heavenly bodies shooting around space.

3. According to a variation of the story, the three sons of Taraka obtained boons from Brahma and built three forts made of gold, silver and iron, one for each. They ruled atrociously, making Mother Earth pray to Shiva for redemption. Shiva immediately burnt the forts to ashes. He would have killed them too, but the three begged Shiva for mercy. Moved by their tears, Shiva made two of the sons his gatekeepers or dvarapalas and the third his damaru, which he held in his right hand.

The destruction of Tripura is believed to have taken place at Thiruvathigai on the banks of the river Gadilam in Tamil Nadu.

❖ **Trishiras**
'The three-headed', he was the son and one of the generals of **Ravana**. A companion of **Khara**, Ravana's brother, the epic says that he was killed by Rama in the Dandaka forest, when Khara attacked Rama in retaliation for the disfigurement of **Shoorpanakha**. Rama let loose three arrows which severed Trishiras's three heads. He appears again in Lanka when he is described as Ravana's son and was killed by Hanuman in the Ramayana war. (*Ramayana*)

TRISHIRAS

❖ **Tunda**
A demon destroyed by Nahusha, son of Ayus. (*Padma Purana*)

❖ **Tvashta**
One of the four sons of **Shukra**, married to Yashodhara-Vairochini, daughter of **Vairochana** and father of **Trishiras**, Vishvaroopa and Vishwakarma. His daughter Samjna was given in marriage to Surya, the sun. (*Brahmanda Purana*)

❖ **Udagra**
An **Asura** of **Mahisha**'s army, killed by Durga with stones and trees. (*Devi Mahatmya, Markandeya Purana*)

❖ **Uddhata**
An **Asura** of **Mahisha**'s army, killed by Durga with a mace. (*Devi Mahatmya, Markandeya Purana*)

❖ **Ugrasya**
An **Asura** of **Mahisha**'s army, killed by Durga with her arrows. (*Devi Mahatmya, Markandeya Purana*)

❖ **Ugravira**
An **Asura** of **Mahisha**'s army, killed by Durga with her arrows. (*Devi Mahatmya, Markandeya Purana*)

❖ **Upashunda**
The son of **Nishunda**, brother of **Sunda** and father of **Muka** (*Mahabharata*), he belonged to the family of **Hiranyakashipu**. He enslaved the Nagas and killed several rishis till the Devas used the apsaras Tilottama to enslave and thereafter kill him. (*Vayu Purana*)

❖ **Urnavabha**
A Rig Vedic demon of drought; another name for **Vritra**.

❖ **Usha**
A Daitya princess and the daughter of Bana, son of **Bali**. See **Bana**. (*Vishnu Purana*)

❖ **Vairochana**
Another name for **Bali**.

❖ **Vaishvanara**
The **Danava** father of **Puloma** and **Kalika**.

❖ **Vajrakama**

Son of **Maya**, the demon architect, and brother of **Mandodari**.

❖ **Vajranga**

Father of the demon **Taraka**.

❖ **Valaka**

A **Rakshasa** who kidnapped a Brahmana's wife because the Brahmana was performing yajñas and reciting mantras that could drive off the Rakshasas. The lesson is that a man can never perform a sacrifice satisfactorily without his wife. (*Markandeya Purana*)

❖ **Vangrida**

A Rig Vedic **Asura**.

❖ **Varangi**

Mother of the demon **Taraka**.

❖ **Vashkala**

An **Asura** of **Mahisha**'s army, killed by Durga with an axe. (*Devi Mahatmya, Markandeya Purana*)

❖ **Vatapi**

Son of **Hrada** or **Viprachitti** and brother of **Ilvala**, he was a **Rakshasa** who lived in the Dandaka forest. (*Ramayana*) See **Ilvala**.

The ancient town of Vatapi (modern Badami and the capital of the early Chalukyas) in Karnataka is named after the demon who lived and ruled in this region when he encountered Agastya and was killed by the sage.

❖ **Vatsa**

A demon sent by **Kamsa,** he took the form of a calf and mingled with Krishna's cows in Vrindavan. But Krishna recognized the demon, caught him by the two hind legs and tail and dashed him against a tree, thereby killing him. (*Bhagavata Purana*)

❖ **Vetala**

Leader of the spirits or **Bhutas,** he is generally a dissatisfied person whose spirit enters a corpse. He is an important figure in Tantric worship.

The Vetala appears in the *Mahabharata*, where Yudhishthira, to regain the lives of his brothers, has to answer ten questions posed by the spirit. He reappears in the stories of Vikramaditya of Ujjain. In both, he is a wise and erudite spirit whose soul is released by the encounter.

❖ **Vetra**

The son of **Vritra** and Vetravati River, he was the ruler of Pragjyotisha (in Assam), and was killed by the goddess Gayatri. (*Varaha Purana*)

❖ **Vibhishana**

His name means 'the terrible'. Although he was a brother of **Ravana,** he is an example of a good demon. He too propitiated Brahma and obtained a boon that he would never do anything unworthy or immoral, even in the face of extreme provocation. He was opposed to the actions and behaviour of the Rakshasas, and remonstrated with his brother Ravana to return Sita to her husband. Finally, Ravana lost patience and kicked him out of Lanka. Vibhishana flew to Kailasa and met Shiva who advised him to join Rama. Vibhishana did so, and was received by Rama as a friend and brother. After Ravana's death he was crowned king of Lanka. (*Ramayana*)

Vibhishana is an example of how men can rise above the limitations of birth to become superior beings. He is also an example of those who allied with the conquering victors and survived.

❖ **Viduratha**
Brother of **Dantavakra**, he attacked Krishna after the death of his brother, but was killed by Krishna instead. (*Bhagavata Purana*)

❖ **Vidyudhvijja**
Ravana's sorcerer. (*Ramayana*)

❖ **Vidyunmalin**
The **Asura** son of **Taraka**.

❖ **Vidyut**
Kubera's servant who killed Garuda's descendant Kanka. In revenge, he was killed by Kanka's brother Kandhara. (*Markandeya Purana*)

❖ **Vihunda**
Son of **Hunda**, he picked the flowers born of Kamoda's tears and offered them to Shiva. This act so angered Parvati that she killed him. (*Padma Purana*)

❖ **Vijaya**
Brother of Jaya. See **Jaya**.

❖ **Vikata**
Rakshasi deputed by **Ravana** to guard Sita and persuade her to marry Ravana. (*Ramayana*)

❖ **Vinata**
Rakshasi deputed by **Ravana** to guard Sita and persuade her to marry Ravana. (*Ramayana*) She is not to be confused with Vinata, wife of sage Kashyapa and mother of the Nagas.

❖ **Viprachitti**
The king of the Danavas, he was born of **Danu**, and father of several demons, including **Rahu**. He led the **Asura** army in the war between the Devas and Asuras that followed the churning of the ocean. (*Mahabharata*)

❖ **Virabhadra**
Along with **Manibhadra**, Virabhadra is a demonic manifestation of Shiva's anger, not an **Asura** or **Rakshasa** or any other form of demon.

When Shiva's wife Sati, unable to stand her father Daksha's taunts and insults, immolated herself in the fire of her father's sacrifice, Shiva, in grief and anger, pulled out a strand of hair from his matted locks and dropped it on the ground. Volcanoes leaped up from the spot and, from the fire, came Virabhadra, the demonic creation of Shiva. And, from every spark of fire, came a demon of anger, smaller than Virabhadra and yet resembling him in face and figure. They sang and danced of hatred, death and vengeance, and killed and destroyed Daksha's priests, guests, palace and possessions. Meanwhile Virabhadra found Daksha and cut off his head. But Daksha's wife Prasuti begged for his life, which Shiva granted. The demons cut off a goat's head, placed it on Daksha's body and stoned and tormented it, till Prasuti took him away. Then Shiva lifted Sati's body and walked away, and his heart was so heavy that the rains vanished, plants died and animals and children wasted away. Seeing the universe consumed in the fire of Shiva's grief, the gods prayed to Vishnu, who shot arrows at Sati's body.

Wherever a piece of her body fell, people built a temple in her honour. When the last piece had fallen, the weight of his anger left Shiva, and he found himself back on Kailasa. The demon of anger had left him. (*Shiva Purana*, *Vayu Purana*)

❖ **Viradha**
Born as the son of **Jaya** and Shatahrida, his austerities earned a boon from Brahma by which no weapon could maim, cut or pierce him. He is described as huge, fat and deformed, besides being a cannibal. He wandered around with three lions, four tigers, two wolves, ten deer and an elephant's head impaled on the head of his spear. As Rama, Lakshmana and Sita entered the Dandaka forest, he objected to their ascetic appearance belied by the presence of a woman and their bows and arrows. He grabbed Sita and declared his intention of making her his wife. For this the brothers chopped off his arms. Then Viradha revealed that he was actually the gandharva Tumburu who was cursed by Kubera to be born as a demon till he was freed by Rama. Before dying, he told the brothers how to survive in the forest and asked them to throw his body in a pit, the primordial ritual for dying **Rakshasas**. (*Ramayana*)

❖ **Viraktayogin**
One of three demon devotees of Shiva, along with Paramayogin and **Shilapara**, who refused to be persuaded by Vishnu as the Buddha to give up their devotion. See **Paramayogin**. (*Shivarahasyakhanda* of the *Skandamaha Purana*)

❖ **Virala**
An **Asura** of **Mahisha**'s army, he was beheaded by Durga with her sword. (*Devi Mahatmya*, *Markandeya Purana*)

❖ **Vira Martandam**

He was one of the demon sons of **Diti,** wife of the sage **Kashyapa** and co-wife of Aditi, mother of the Devas. Seeing the Devas constantly successful over their **Daitya** step-brothers, Vira Martandam, on the advice of **Shukracharya,** guru of the demons, did penance and obtained several boons from Brahma, the Creator. Then he created hell on earth. His victims prayed to Shiva to rid them of the demon, so Shiva took the form of Aghoramurti Virabhadra and killed him ('Shivarahasyakhanda' of the *Skandamaha Purana*).

This is a local legend about events believed to have taken place in Tiruvengadu, near the ancient port town of Poompuhar.

❖ **Virochana**

He was the son of **Prahlada** and father of **Bali.** He was also known as Drishana. (*Vishnu Purana*)

❖ **Virupaksha**

Ravana's general and a mighty warrior. Hanuman defeats him with a sal tree when he goes to Lanka for the first time, in search of Sita. He is killed in the Ramayana war.

Virupaksha is a good demon, the rakshasadhipati of Meruvraja. He is devout and gives gifts lavishly to Brahmanas. (*Ramayana*)

❖ **Vishravas**

Son of **Pulastya,** he fathered Kubera through his Brahmana wife Ilavida and the **Rakshasas Ravana, Kumbhakarna, Vibhishana** and **Shoorpanakha** through his Rakshasi wife **Nikasha** or **Kaikesi,** daughter of **Sumali.** (*Ramayana*)

The *Mahabharata* has a variation of the story in that

Kubera gave him three Rakshasa women: **Pushpotkata**, mother of Ravana and Kumbhakarna, **Malini**, mother of Vibhishana, and **Raka**, mother of **Khara** and Shoorpanakha. (*Mahabharata*)

❖ **Vitunda**
Son of **Tunda**, he was destroyed by Bhagavati. (*Padma Purana*)

❖ **Vivindhaya**
A demon killed in battle by Charudeshna, son of Krishna. (*Mahabharata*)

❖ **Vrika**
A demon who received a boon from Shiva by which anyone he touched would die immediately. Vrika wanted to try it out on Shiva himself, so Shiva fled to Vishnu, who told the demon that Shiva's boons did not work and, if he did not believe it, Vrika should put his hand on his own head and see what happened. The **Asura** did so and died. (*Bhagavata Purana*)

    This story also indicates sectarian rivalry, with Shiva making a mistake and Vishnu coming forward to right the wrong.

❖ **Vrishaparvan**
Son of **Kashyapa** and **Danu**.

❖ **Vritra**
Also known as **Ahi** and **Sushna**, he is the demon of drought in the *Rig Veda*, the very first demon mentioned in Sanskrit literature. The word Vritra means foe and comes from the root *vri* meaning to enclose. He is the son of **Danu** and is described as

'. . . *footless and handless* . . . (R.V., 1.32.7).

'*The serpent concealed in the depths, mysterious* . . .
Dwelling enveloped, deep within the waters,
Who checked heaven and stayed the floods from flowing
. . . *The magician who lay beleaguering the mighty river* . . .'
(R.V., 11.11.5)

Vritra was '. . . *enveloped in a cloud* . . .' (R.V., 11.31.3), thus
identifying him with water vapour.

Indra '. . . *slew the demon, then disclosed the waters,*
And cleft the channels of the mountain torrents,
He slew the dragon lying on the mountain . . .
. . . *Like lowing kine in rapid flow descending,*
The waters glided downward to the ocean
When Indra had slain the demons . . .
And overcome the magic of the magicians (demons)
. . . *Indra with his own great and deadly thunder smote into*
pieces Vritra, worst of the Vritras . . .
He like a mad weak warrior challenged Indra,
The great impetuous many-slaying hero
Who, brooking not the clashing of weapons,
Crushed his foe, the shattered forts in falling.' (R.V.,
1.32.2–6)

Indra sets free '. . . *the many waters that were encompassed*
by the demon
Down rolled the rivers, as if on chariots borne . . .
. . . *The god* [Indra] *terrific, with his weapons,*
Mastered these opponents,
Indra in rapturous joy shook down their castles:
He slew them in his might, the thunder-wielder' (R.V., 7.21.3–4)

Indra then '. . . *forced the clouds, slaying Vritra, stayer of
their flow . . .
. . . Struck off with might the head of Vritra,
Tyrant of the earth and heaven.*' (R.V., 1.53. 2–10)

The Veda says that Indra killed Vritra
'. . . *Who besieged the waters,
And dug out the all-supporting channels.
The insatiate one [Vritra], extended, hard to waken,
Who slumbered in perpetual sleep . . .
The demon stretched against the seven prone rivers . . .*'* (R.V.,
4.20.2–3)

　　Indra, the god of thunder and rain and the hero of the
Rig Veda, is constantly at war with Vritra, overpowering him
and releasing the rain. Indra is helped in his endeavours by
Vishnu, the sun god of the *Rig Veda*. While Indra does the actual
killing, Vishnu takes his mighty strides to come to his aid, an
allegory to illustrate the power of the sun coming to the aid
of the rain god as he is about to destroy the demon who encircles
(chokes) and prevents the rain. As the slayer of Vritra, Indra is
also called Vritrahān. The battle is described frequently and at
length, with graphic details of the commencement of the rainy
season and the severe thunderstorms that accompany this
change of season. Finally, the war is over. As a result of Vritra's
defeat, the rains descend and the earth is made green and
fertile with crops.**

---

　　*The seven rivers are the Sindhu (Indus), the five rivers of the Punjab
(Vitastā, Asiknī, Parushnī, Vipāsi, Śutudni) and Sarasvati
　　**According to Wilson, in the *Rig* Vedic suktas, 'we have an ample
elucidation of the original purport of the legend of Indra's slaying Vritra,
converted by the Pauranik writers into a literal contest between Indra and
an Asura, or chief of the Asuras, from what in the Vedas is merely an

VRITRA

Vritra is also an anthropomorphic representation of drought, and the ending of drought by rainfall is illustrated in the Vritra–Indra war. Under the leadership of Vritra, the demons are able to upset the eternal balance between prosperity and famine. In the conflict and the victory are portrayed the power of Indra and the blessings he is able to grant.

Vritra and his slayer Indra, also known as Vritrahān, have their parallels in the ancient Persian Verethra and his slayer Verethraghna, born of the water and having ten incarnations,

allegorical narrative of the production of rain. Vritra, sometimes also named Ahi, is nothing more than the accumulation of vapour, condensed or figuratively shut up in, or obstructed by, a cloud. Indra, with his thunderbolt, or atmospheric or electrical influence, divides the aggregated mass, and vent is given to the rain which then literally descends upon the earth.' (Cf. Griffith, Vol.I, p. 43).

whose name means victory over an adverse attack. Indra uses both magic and his strength to defeat Vritra.

With Indra's gradual loss of popularity, Vritra was also forgotten. Yet he is the first demon to be mentioned in Hindu mythology. In later mythology Vritra is sometimes described as a Brahmana, and Indra's ineffectiveness is attributed to his crime of killing a Brahmana. His crime sometimes pursues him in the form of a Chandala (outcaste), and Indra has to perform several sacrifices to free himself.

Later Puranic literature has a story that explains the origin of Vritra. King Chitraketu and his wife became Gandharvas and received as a boon the ability to fly. They flew over Mount Kailasa where they saw Shiva and Parvati at play. Chitraketu laughed in amusement. He was cursed by Parvati to be born as the demon Vritra.

❖ **Vyansa**
A Rig Vedic demon of drought.

❖ **Vyoma**
Son of **Maidanava**, chief of the demons, **Kamsa** sent him to Vrindavan to kill the child Krishna. However, he was killed by Krishna (*Bhagavata Purana*).

❖ **Yatu, Yatudhana**
See Part I, Chapter 3: Demonized Enemies.

❖ **Yupaksha, Yupakhya**
Ravana's general. Hanuman defeated him with a sal tree when he went to Lanka in search of Sita. He is killed by the monkey general Dvivida in the Ramayana war. (*Ramayana*)

Bibliography

PRIMARY SOURCES

Agni Purana, Anandasrama Sanskrit Series, Poona, 1900.

Aitareya Brahmana, (ed. and tr. M. Haug), The Sacred Books of the Hindus, Allahabad, 1922.

Atharva Veda, Vishveshvaranand Indological Series, Hoshiarpur, 1960–64.

Bhagavat Gītī, Central Chinmaya Mission Trust.

Bhagavata Purana, T.R. Krishnacharya, Kumbakonam, 1916.

Brahmanda Purana, Sri Venkateswara Steam Press, Bombay, 1912.

Mahabharata, Asiatic Society of Bengal, 1837.

Manusamhita, Education Press, Calcutta, 1830.

Markandeya Purana, (ed. M.N. Dutt, H.C. Dutt), Elysium Press, Calcutta, 1896.

Matsya Purana, Anandashrama Sanskrit Series, Poona, 1907.

Ramayana, (tr.) R.T.H. Griffith, Chowkhamba Sanskrit Studies, Varanasi, 1963.

Rig Veda, The Chowkhamba Sanskrit Series Office, Varanasi, 1965.

Shatapatha Brahmana, (tr.) J. Eggeling, Sacred Books of the East, Motilal Banarsidass, Delhi, 1963, 1966.

Skanda Purana, Sri Venkateswara Steam Press, Bombay, 1965.

Taittirīya Brahmana, Anandasrama Sanskrit Series, Poona, 1898.

Taittirīya Samhitā, (ed.) Vasant Sripad Satavalekar, Oundh, Satara.

Vayu Purana, Anandasrama Sanskrit Series, Poona, 1905.

Vishnu Purana, Sri Venkateswara Steam Press, Bombay, 1910.

SECONDARY SOURCES

Bhaktivedanta Swami Prabhupada, A.C., *Krsna—The Supreme Personality of Godhead*, London, 1974.

Bhandarkar, R.G., 'The Aryans in the Land of the Asuras', *Journal of the Bombay Branch of the Royal Asiatic Society,* 25 (1918).

Bhattacharji, S., *The Indian Theogony*, Penguin Books India, New Delhi, 2000.

Blake, William, *Book of Job*, William Blake, London, 1825.

Brown, W. Norman, 'The Creation Myth of the *Rig Veda*', *Journal of the American Oriental Society* (1942).

Crooke, W., *Folklore of India*, Aryan Books International, New Delhi, 1993.

Dowson, J., *A Classical Dictionary of Hindu Mythology and Religion*, Rupa & Co., New Delhi, 1982.

Elmore, W.T., *Dravidian Gods in Modern Hinduism*, Asian Educational Services, New Delhi, 1984.

Frazer, J.G., *The Illustrated Golden Bough*, George Rainbird Limited, New York, 1978.

Funk and Wagnalls, *The Standard Dictionary of Folklore, Mythology and Legend*, New York, 1949.

Griffith, R.T.H., *The Hymns of the Rig Veda*, E.J. Lazarus & Co., Benares, 1920.

Hale, W.E., *Asura in Early Vedic Religion*, Motilal Banarsidass Publishers, 1999.

Harness, D.M., *The Nakshatras*, Motilal Banarsidass, Delhi, 2000.

Hopkins, E.W. *Epic Mythology*, Indological Book House, Delhi, 1968.

Jagannathan, S., and Krishna, N., *Ganesha*, Vakils, Feffer & Simons Ltd., Bombay, 1992.

Kenoyer, Jonathan Mark, *Ancient Cities of the Indus Valley Civilization*, Oxford University Press and American Institute of Pakistan Studies, Karachi and Islamabad, 1998.

Khanam, R. (ed.), *Demonology*, Global Vision Publishing House, Delhi, 2003.

Kinsley, D., *Hindu Goddesses*, Motilal Banarsidass Publishers Pvt. Ltd., Delhi, 1998.

Krishna, N., *The Book of Vishnu*, Viking, New Delhi, 2001.

Krishna, N., *The Art and Iconography of Vishnu Narayana*, D.B. Taraporevala Sons & Co. Pvt. Ltd., Bombay, 1980.

Kriwaczek, Paul, *In Search of Zarathustra*, Phoenix, London, 2003.

Macdonell, A.A., *A History of Sanskrit Literature*, Delhi, 1958.

Mackenzie, D.A., *Indian Myth and Legend*, Smriti Books, New Delhi, 2000.

Misra, R.N. *Yaksha Cult and Iconography*, Munshiram Manoharlal Publishers Pvt. Ltd., 1981.

Norman, D., *The Heroic Encounter*, U.S.A., 1958.

O'Flaherty, W. D., *The Origins of Evil in Hindu Mythology*, Motilal Banarsidas, Delhi, 1988.

O'Flaherty, W.D., *The Rig Veda*, Penguin Books India, New Delhi, 2000.

Oppert, G., *The Original Inhabitants of India*, Oriental Publishers, Delhi, 1972.

Pargiter, F.E., *Ancient Indian Historical Tradition*, Motilal Banarsidass Publishers Pvt. Ltd., Delhi, 1997.

Parker, H., *Ancient Ceylon*, Asian Educational Services, New Delhi, 1981.

Radhakrishnan, B.P. and Merh, S.S., *Vedic Sarasvati*, Geological Society of India, Bangalaore, 1999,

Raja, K., 'Rig Veda, Asura Māyā', *Journal of the Royal Asiaic Society of Great Britain and Ireland*, January 1917.

Renu, L.N., *Vedic Record on Early Aryas*', Bharatiya Vidya Bhavan, Mumbai, 2004.

Sethna, K.D., *The Problem of Aryan Origins*, Calcutta, 1980.

Shendge, M. J., *The Civilized Demons: The Harappans in Ṛgveda*, Abhinav Publications, New Delhi, 1977.

Shulman, D.D., *Tamil Temple Myths*, Princeton University Press, New Jersey, U.S.A., 1980.

Shulman, D.D., *The King and the Clown in South Indian Myth and Poetry*, Princeton University Press, New Jersey, U.S.A., 1985.

Tod, J., *Annals and Antiquities of Rajasthan*, Vol. I & II, Calcutta, 1884.

Valmiki, *Ramayana,* Penguin Books, New Delhi, 1996.

Wheeler, R.E.M., *The Indus Civilization*, Cambridge University Press, 1968.

Wilkins, W.J., *Hindu Mythology*, Rupa & Co., New Delhi, 1982.

Williams, G.M., *Handbook of Hindu Mythology*, ABC-CLIO Inc., U.S.A., 2003.

Zimmer, H., *Myths and Symbols in Indian Art and Civilization*, Bollingen Foundation, New York, 1963.